A Perfect Harmony

A Perfect Harmony

The Intertwining Lives of Animals and Humans throughout History

Roger A. Caras

NotaBell Books
A imprint of Purdue University Press
West Lafayette, Indiana

First NotaBell edition, 2002

Library of Congress Cataloging-in-Publication Data
Caras, Roger A.
A perfect harmony : the intertwining lives of animals and humans throughout
history / Roger A. Caras
p. cm.
Includes bibliographical references (p.   ) and index.
1. Animals and civilization. 2. Domestication—History. I. Title
QL85.C37
306.3'49—dc20   96-9220

ISBN 1-55753-241-9

To the one person who has shared it all—Jill—and to the two who have shared some of the best parts, Pamela and Clay, and their other halves, Sheila and Joe. And to the succeeding four who are now on the team, Sarah, Joshua, Abaigeal and Hannah. It is a wonderful team and I am so very grateful.

Contents

Roger Caras—An Appreciation

On Sunday, February 18, 2001, Roger Caras died at age 72.

Roger Caras was an author, broadcast journalist, and champion of both wild and companion animals. His last career post was president of the American Society for Prevention of Cruelty to Animals in New York City and the longtime announcer at the Westminster Kennel Club's annual dog show. He missed the last show in February at Madison Square Garden because of his illness. Roger wrote more than 60 books about animals. Three are particularly good resource books: *Venomous Animals of the World* (1974), *Dangerous to Man* (1964), *The Dog Owner's Bible* (1978). One is an amazing concise summary of human's relationship with animals: *A Perfect Harmony*, first published in 1996.

No one doubts that two of the most important adaptations of human beings are their intelligence and social behavior. Primarily we survive because we are a social species, that is, live in groups that help us find food and shelter and address the world's adversity. We have also learned not only to understand our world—nature—but incorporate it into our own personal world. We live with animals, using them for food, transportation, fiber, research about our own bodies, and companionship. We even domesticate them to be a part of our world. The survival of all domestic animals and human beings is a shared journey.

A Perfect Harmony is a history of that journey; how people and their animals influence each other and all that we call culture, civilization, and natural history. It documents how the survival of each was a direct result of the other. It is a carefully thought out book that is insightful and enjoyable. From insects to the family pet, there are new insights for us all.

ALAN M. BECK
· Dorothy N. McAllister Professor of Animal Ecology
Purdue University School of Veterinary Medicine

Foreword

You may well wonder why an armchair astronaut like myself got involved with a natural history buff like Roger Caras, so I feel a few words of explanation are in order.

I first met Roger—as well as Commander Jacques Cousteau, whose pioneering movie *Silent World* Roger was promoting—at a meeting of underwater explorers in Boston in 1959. Neither of us could have guessed that, just five years later, we would be jointly involved in the most demanding enterprise of our careers: the movie *2001: A Space Odyssey.* Roger's original background was in the public relations side of the movie business, and when *2001* started shooting in England, the director, Stanley Kubrick, persuaded him to leave Columbia Pictures and join his operation to run the PR side. This was an exhilarating but often frustrating business, because Stanley wouldn't let anyone look at the footage until it was almost due for release. It's hard to think of a more exasperating situation for a PR man—attempting to build public interest in a film that he's not allowed to show. However, Roger survived, and the rest is movie history.

It was while writing the screenplay of *2001* that I first became fully aware of Roger's interest in the animal kingdom. The "Dawn of Man" sequence, involving our man-ape ancestors of some four million years ago, required a great deal of research and a visit to a small private zoo in the north of England which housed all the great apes among its resident guests. (That was the first—and only—time I ever met a gorilla socially; a particularly engaging little infant made me rather nervous, however, when it explored my shoes with its impressive teeth). During this period, I also had the privilege of meeting the famous anthropologist Dr. Louis Leakey and his now equally famous son Richard, to discuss the African background for the opening sequence of the movie. In different ways, Leakey and Caras have worked on parallel tracks—tracing the intertwining lives of animals and man.

For more than a decade, Roger has spearheaded a campaign to interest the public in the creatures who share our planet—and, as it turns out, who have also helped us to build our civilization. During the years following the completion of *2001,* Roger made several visits to Sri Lanka in connection with his TV and radio programs. On one memorable occasion, we had the opportunity to take a ride on adjacent elephants—an impressive experience, to say the least. Roger seems to have a way with large and dangerous animals (especially wolves and tigers), and I have enjoyed *The Custer Wolf* and *Sarang,* his books on these subjects. I hope that one day someone films the latter—a moving tale of a little Indian boy and his pet tiger (or was it the other way around?).

One of the unfortunate outcomes—and great defects—of modern urban life is our resulting estrangement from the natural world. I was lucky enough to be brought up on a farm, and I am sorry for any child who knows nothing but the concrete jungle of the city. All my life I have been surrounded by animals (my killer Chihuahua, Pepsi, is sleeping at my feet at the moment) and my garden contains the graves of a Rhodesian ridgeback, four beloved German shepherds, and two little monkeys—all badly missed. But until I read *A Perfect Harmony,* I did not understand the enormous impact and influence of domesticated animals—particularly of goats, sheep, reindeer, oxen, and horses.

During the next millennium, with the development of robots and even more highly advanced forms of artificial intelligence, we will find ourselves sharing this planet with a new class of sentient beings. It will be an interesting challenge to see if we can coexist with them as successfully as we have done with their animal counterparts.

Assuming, of course, that this time we have any say in the matter.

ARTHUR C. CLARKE
21 May, 1996
Colombo, Sri Lanka

Time Line
100,000 Years of Human History

BP (YEARS BEFORE PRESENT)

100,000–15,000
- Paleolithic—Old Stone Age
- Man is in caves

15,000–14,000
- Beginnings of domestication
- Goat and dog, sheep and reindeer
- Still in Old Stone Age

13,000–12,000
- Possible first stages of horse domestication

11,000
- Jericho, first walled city, built

10,000–9,000
- End of last Ice Age
- Beginnings of agriculture
- Chicken domesticated in what is now Vietnam

10,000–6,000
- Beginning of pig domestication
- Possible beginning of turkey domestication
- Neolithic—New Stone Age

7,000	• Pigeons kept in Mesopotamia
6,000–4,000	• Serious domestication of the horse
	• Domestication of the cat in Egypt
	• Sumerian civilization flourishes
	• First use of Bactrian camel
	• Water buffalo domesticated in India
5,000–3,000	• Silkworms cultivated in China
	• Carp cultivated in China
	• Humped cattle kept in India and Mesopotamia
	• Dromedary used in Arabia
	• Guanaco descendants, llama and alpaca, domesticated in South America
	• Dynastic period in Egypt begins
	• Mesopotamian empire established
	• Trojan War
	• Construction of Babylon begun
	• Stonehenge completed
	• First known use of papyrus
	• Cheops begins Great Pyramid
3,000–2,000	• Wild Ass domesticated in Nile Valley, perhaps in what is now Libya
	• Distinct cattle breeds in Europe
	• Minoan Culture on Crete—first "rodeos"
	• David and Solomon establish Israelite kingdoms
	• Aesop, Confucius, Buddha, Croesus, Pythagoras and Cyrus the Great flourish
	• Ptolemy Philadelphus establishes camps in Sudan and Ethiopia to train elephants
	• Hannibal takes elephants across Alps (2218 BP)
	• Chicken reaches British Isles
	• Chicken reaches China
	• Chicken in Greece and Rome and their colonies
2,000–1,000	• Ferrets kept in Europe
	• Yak domesticated in Tibet and China
	• Sleds and wagons established technology
1,000–500	• Camel saddle invented

AD

1000	• Goldfish cultivated in China
	• Monks domesticate rabbit in Europe
1494	• Horse-breeding farms established on Hispaniola
1500	• Cortez brings chickens to New World
1524	• Turkeys introduced to Europe
1600	• Tarpan becomes extinct in Europe
1627	• Last known aurochs dies in Polish park
1880–1890	• First mink farms established

Preface: What If?

This book is about two subjects that are inextricably joined, the animal kingdom and our own history. And, of course, it is about how these two children of Earth came together in a series of incredible relationships. Each of the chapters that follow will examine our increasing dependence on animals as the facilitators of our own cultural evolution. The premise? We could not have done it alone. We arrived at the human state incomplete, willing but unable to take giant steps. At each turn in our evolution as culture-makers, animals enabled us to move on to the next level.

We are here to examine what might have happened to man had one really rather simple idea *not* occurred to him, or at least if he had *not* explored its originally invisible potential. Then we will see what really did happen and what wonders—and problems—have occurred as a result. And finally we will speculate, insofar as we can, on where all this may lead in the future.

Why play "What if?" Why imagine that what did happen never had? Because, very simply, the blessings would not be apparent unless we first examine how our lives might have been without them. A naked man in the Arctic shows more clearly the need for clothing than a man wrapped in furs and wool. It is a game, in a way, but one justified if we are to understand how we came to be who and what we are.

One of the best ways to evaluate the human condition is to stand well apart from the consuming reality of ourselves as we are now and look at our manipulated world, seeing it as a stranger might. Where did our cultures come from, and what might have happened to us had their evolution been other than the historical reality we believe we know? And then look at what actually did happen and how very different those two scenarios are. That is our quest.

We slumbered in the loins of apish creatures and then distinct pre-hominids unsettlingly like ourselves for several millions of years. The actual length of our species' gestation will be argued perhaps forever, although forever is admittedly a long time. And before that, what would one day become the genes with which we now replicate ourselves lay ripening in even lesser creatures. They say a tree shrew, no more exciting a creature than that, probably started us on our way. At least it pointed us in the direction we eventually took before it dropped out of our history forever. As it scrambled away toward the mist along a branch in an ancient tree whose species is now extinct, we moved off, too, in search of ourselves and our own destiny. But whatever happened and however long it took, we are the proof of it all and, ready or not, world, here we are. But what might we be like "if?" What might our history have been and what of our planet's condition with just one idea missing: the domestication of animals?

On the Matter of Definitions

In this book, the words *domestic* and *domesticated* are used to identify animals that have not only been held captive by human beings, or have been tamed by us to be manageable or even affectionate and responsive, but also animals that have been *genetically altered* as a direct result of their involvement with us. They are now almost always distinguishable as animals different in some significant way from their wild ancestors, whether those predecessors are now extant or extinct. We have replaced natural selection with selective breeding and thereby made these animals our own. My definition of these words, although not uniquely my own by any means, does not necessarily match that of other writers, nor does it take into account the other meanings they undeniably have. However, they are used here in this one sense only.

The word *feral* refers to animals that were once truly domesticated in terms of the above definition but are now living in a wild state. Either they escaped, or were lost or abandoned, and they frequently have managed to breed into a more or less viable population. They commonly breed with their ancestral species, creating hybrids, and may eventually eliminate their ancestors as a pure species. (The word applies as well to plants of this condition.)

Wild is taken here to mean an animal that was *never domesticated.*

Tame refers to an animal still a member of a wild species that has *as an individual* been behaviorally adapted to tolerate the proximity of man.

On the Matter of Time

The study of the domestication of animals is properly the study of the history of mankind, as I hope will become obvious in the pages that follow. Historians generally are obsessed with time, an obsession that is far more intense in the contemplation of recent events than it is for events that occurred in the distant past.

On November 22, 1963, President John F. Kennedy was tragically murdered in Dallas, Texas. Historians writing about that world-shaking event still ponder whether Lee Harvey Oswald, the man blamed for the shooting, could have fired the fatal shots in 6.3 seconds or whether he would have required 11.4 seconds. They want to know where all the key figures in this drama were thirty seconds, one minute, ten minutes, one hour, one day, one week, one month and one year before the shots were fired. Of equal interest, of course, is where they were after the event, minute by minute, hour by hour. Time, always time, the element by which all other elements can be ordered, assigned, related, understood and evaluated. Time is one of the most revealing keys to our understanding of *recent* history.

Compare the Kennedy assassination with other historical events, however, episodes that are within the scope of this book. The domestication of the goat, or at least the decision to hold goats and selectively slaughter them, or the first attempt to milk a cow or a goat to save an infant whose mother had died in childbirth, these were all events of far more long-term significance to mankind than World War I and World War II combined, as difficult as that may be to accept for those who have lived between and through them. But when historians, bolstered by the findings of archaeologists, paleontologists, dendrochronologists, stratigraphers and a veritable platoon of other specialists, ponder man-and-goat and man-and-cow, they are satisfied with dates that span thousands of years. (Perhaps not really *satisfied* but resigned.) There is no November 22 for events that occurred millennia ago. We should keep that fact in mind in our explorations here. It would be interesting, certainly, but not really essential to know time sequences in exquisite detail.

Everything has to happen for a first time no matter how often or in how many places it ultimately occurs. The time of that first occurrence of any past domestication of animals is something we probably will never be able to identify. We will also find the who and the precise where of it equally elusive. The people who first did these marvelous things and thereby forever changed the course of human history have no names and no faces. But they were essential threads in that incredibly complex fabric we call mankind. For the actions of these nameless, faceless men and women not only changed the course of our history, they defined it as well. They offered us the key to our destiny. If ever the stars reached down and touched a human being, it was the unknown man or woman who first conceived of capturing and keeping a goat instead of hunting one. We should not weep, then, for the want of details unknowable but rather ponder the consequences of those events in their grander aspect, appreciate their historical magic, their absolute necessity and thus their inevitability.

On the Matter of Gender

Without arguing the case and without begging the question, I believe that phrases like "him or her," "he or she," "his or hers" appearing again and again in virtually every paragraph of a book is not only poor writing but also downright tedious for both the writer and the reader. In the vast majority of cases, we simply do not know what might have been done by men and what by women in strange, exotic and long-ago cultures. *Man,* as used here, refers to mankind, human beings of both sexes, species *Homo sapiens,* us, we, altogether combined. In no way is it a reference to gender unless that is so stated. It is a short way of saying that it was mankind who did such-and-such a thing. It has no other implication or connotation here.

ONE

The Other Scenario

The Stage

If we are to have a context for ourselves, and our relationships with animals wild and domestic, we should first examine just what kind of planet we live on. We are, after all, its children, and however wondrous we are, we are as beholden to the realities of our "place" in the cosmos as the earthworm and the bladderwort.

Everything we are to consider in this book happened because of the nature of this nurturing bit of cosmic debris. All living things we know of are never free for so much as an instant from our planet and the opportunities it offers and, in turn, their own limitations. Even as we move off into space for the next stage of our evolution, we can do no more than carry a bit of our planet's stuff with us to sustain us while we are away from home. We will probably have to brown-bag it all the way to the edge of the universe.

The planet Earth has an excellent water supply, and there is plenty of oxygen, nitrogen and carbon dioxide, the gases needed in varying degrees by all of the life forms they engulf. Water passes through its several phases here with ease—gas to liquid to colloid to solid—without requiring exotic temperature extremes or pressurized containment systems. Small temperature shifts occur and the physical state of that combination of two molecules of hydrogen attached to a single molecule of oxygen changes. As a mist, it can rise into the sky and then turn again into liquid and fall back to Earth somewhere else. In that way, water can run uphill, even the steepest mountains on our planet. It simply changes its form in response to ambient temperature and moves on its way, governing all life that it touches, or fails to touch. All living tissue is dependent on water in one way or another. That link is absolute.

The full, naturally occurring temperature range on Earth's surface is perhaps 340 degrees Fahrenheit, excepting only those geothermal and volcanic disruptions that reach the surface. That has been a gentle and tolerable spread. Almost all plants and animals spend their entire lives well within a stress-free range of 110 degrees on the Fahrenheit scale, most by far in a narrower thermal zone yet. Compare that to ranges of thousands of degrees or more in just a single location in a single day, however long or short that day may be, on other planets and their moons. Our ocean basins, in one place at least up to seven miles deep, offer an incredible range in pressure but only a small range in temperature. Life has been able to flourish everywhere on Earth, perfectly adapted to the circumstances of place and its own evolutionary potential.

Tectonic plate movements on our planet are minimal or at least extremely slow. There is some seismic activity, some uplift and subsidence, of course, some stress and shift and heave, some thrusting, slippage and abrasion along fault lines. But in relation to surface area and the potential for real destruction, what activity there is creates only minor disturbances. The major adjustments that do occur are generally so slow that we are unaware of them. What we think of as a horrific earthquake is in reality an Earth-shrug, a minor modification in response to stress.

Our mountains grow slowly and die more slowly yet. Active volcanoes have steadily decreased in number and generally in violence over tens of millions of years. Ecuador, for example, has the largest number of volcanoes of any nation on Earth. Two hundred and sixty-five, although presently quiet, are listed as active. However, in that same area, uncounted thousands of volcanoes have settled back down and died. No, Earth is reckoned a quiet planet despite occasional upset within its mantle and even a rare loud "pop" like Krakatoa or the nagging petulance of Vesuvius. It was not always so, but it is now, and that is one reason we are here. First, the volcanoes had their history, now we have ours.

We are not the only debris in this cosmic neighborhood, and some of it has collided with our planet. We assign all manner of catastrophes to these collisions including the extinction of the dinosaur. Perhaps, but no more than that intensity of likelihood. At any rate, other space debris has not been significantly disruptive recently. And if the big collisions come every fifty to a hundred million years or so, we can take comfort in the thought that when the next one occurs, we will probably have evolved into something beyond *Homo sapiens* and may not even live here anymore. *(Homo electronicus* or, perhaps, *Homo exodus?)* The relative serenity of our planet is another reason we live here now.

Life

The evolutionary course life took on Earth once it appeared was breathtakingly swift, barely more than three billion years. The living forms we see around us now have probably all been inevitable. Those that were not inevitable are probably extinct. (Perhaps that was inevitable, too.) Some dead-ended, while others gave rise to better forms and faded in the ensuing competition with what they had begotten.

The network of life-forms that has survived an enormous amount of trial and error constitutes about as good a biological matrix as any evolving intelligence could ask for. Its diversity is absolutely astounding, and it has been supportive of us in ways we can now, finally, scientifically oriented as we have become, begin to comprehend. Of particular concern here are those animals that, over the millennia, have played a vital role in man's evolutionary course. Was that also inevitable?

What If?

That, then, is our world, but imagine what it would be like if we had chosen to remain apart from other animals except insofar as we hunted them, turned them into carrion and fed on it. Imagine our life if we had not engaged in domestication. Let's examine our planet and ourselves a region at a time and see how different things might have been.

Far North/Far South

Without domestication, the two polar regions, above 66 degrees north and south latitudes, would be uninhabited. Attempts to explore them, much less settle in the North (no one we know of has tried in the South), would have been abortive without domestic dogs that were brought to these regions. Yet, in the North or Arctic polar and subpolar zones, sixty- to one-hundred-pound wolves still roam free despite their proven potential for domestication. The same is true of much of Greenland. Uninhabitable by man on his own, without dogs it would be a blank.

Siberia? Virtually blank. A vast land incredibly rich in fish, game, timber, oil and mineral resources, it would have remained largely unexplored and uninhabited. Winters are long and fierce there and prolonged journeys without sled-pullers would have been all but impossible. Even in summer, the vast distances would have prevented human bands from carrying their young and old and all their material possessions themselves. Generally, they would not have been able to reach safety before the snow and ice came again. Still, a few small bands apparently did make it across Siberia when winters were both mild and late in onset, and a few did actually reach the western rim of the Pacific Ocean. But the great land mass itself would have remained virtually uninhabited if people had tried to go it there alone. (Surely, they tried again and again and failed, again and again.)

Australia

One whole continent, Australia, when it was discovered by Europeans, was inhabited by bands of hunting-gathering people, but the so-called Aborigines were, in terms of their physical culture, among the most primitive humans on Earth. They were not living in the New Stone Age—the Neolithic—or even the Middle Stone Age—the Mesolithic—but actually in the Paleolithic—the Old Stone Age. They hadn't invented the bow and arrow even as other people, members of their own species, sailed out to them from Europe carrying guns and printed books.

The genius was there, however, the sparks of intelligence, creativity and ingenuity that characterized their culture. The Aborigines' concept of Dreamtime, their belief in their relationship with the land, their wonderfully sophisticated sense of a vast unity, and their extraordinarily complex family and clan relationships and their sense and system of social responsibility were stunning cultural achievements. They had fascinating plastic art and a rich store of imagery and tradition. But theirs was genius unable to lift them out of the cave. Perhaps it was more than coincidence that no native animal was ever domesticated in all of vast, diverse, fauna-rich Australia. The animals surrounding the people there remained prey and never became partners. As we will see in other parts of the world, man has first had to have a relationship with a species before he could domesticate it. Perhaps the nature of the primitive marsupials and monotremes available to the original peoples of Australia precluded this essential first step.

Europe

In the northern reaches of Europe, without domestication there would have been a cutoff of significant human activity by mid-Scandinavia. Reindeer do abound there, but they would have remained wild. And life without sled-pullers and a manageable source of meat and hides would have been too difficult. Exploratory attempts would have been made to expand in that direction, north, but nothing would have come of them. Alone, even that far north, the societies of man would have been doomed. Toeholds might have been gained, but a couple of bad winters in a row and man would have been dislodged.

In Other Places

At another extreme on our planet, in areas like Indonesia, the Caribbean and Africa south of the Sahara, very few cultures ever really expanded before the benefits of domestication were made available to them from outside, although thousands evolved and some of them were remarkable in their splendid isolation. In what is now Zaire, at a site called Katanga, an astounding fact appears to have been revealed. Elaborate fishing spears were being used fully seventy-six thousand years before their equal appeared in Europe. If the findings are being interpreted properly at the National Science Foundation and at Rutgers University, men were making elaborate notched fishing equipment ninety thousand years ago in Stone Age Africa, and only fourteen thousand years ago in Stone Age Europe, not just coincidentally around the time that domestication began.

Some Stone Age cultures without domestication did blossom, but they were quick and lonely affairs, like unseen fireworks displays. The world and all history but their own were untouched by them. Trapped into compact areas, they could neither get nor give the genius that inevitably evolves periodically in cultures but which shrivels up and dies when it cannot be cross-fertilized. A culture can never be maximized when it is forced to stand alone. Genius does not come to full realization at the village level. In those Stone Age cultures, coincidentally, no native animal species were ever domesticated, with the possible exception of the dog. And the dog, as we will see, is a profound mystery.

In the Middle East, the awesome religious concept of monotheism evolved, but it would have died there had it not been able to travel. It appeared at the edge of vast and fearsome deserts that swallowed whole bands of people who attempted to cross them on foot, burying their rags and bones in shifting mountains of sand. But the concept was able to travel because of domestic animals, and it, with its several refinements, altered the entire world. Only the domestication of those animals was to have a greater impact.

Not until there were camels, oxen, horses and asses under human control could there be caravans. And without caravans, there would have been no way for the concept of monotheism and its refinements to travel. No prophets would have been heard much beyond their own villages, no apostles could have set forth except by sea, and sea travel would have remained essentially coastal. Some primitive travelers did get to Australia, and the evidence suggests some reached the New World, but their numbers were small, their visits few and probably extremely far between. They were certainly accidental and most were probably one-way journeys. We know little about them, and their influence is a mystery.

The New World

North America was once much like large areas of sub-Saharan Africa in that there were vast herds of wild animals on which small bands of Stone Age hunters preyed. But since the animals were wild and nomadic, the people had to be, too. No native species of food or burden-bearing mammal was ever domesticated, although there would have always been likely candidates. It is probable that dogs were, in fact, domesticated in North America at least ten to twelve thousand years ago. But dogs, as we shall see, are anomalies, confounding creatures with a history not easily decipherable.

There were agricultural Indians in North America, descendants of the small bands of early hunters and gatherers who reached the Pacific by crossing Siberia. Eventually, they crossed the Bering Sea on a temporary land bridge, then moved down from northwestern Canada into the eastern forests of the continent, the American Southwest and the Great Plains in between. (That is the accepted scenario, now.)

The southwestern tribes were, at least in part, of the Athabascan linguistic stock, and as Navajo and Hopi, Zuni and some earlier designations, they did build a number of isolated civilizations. But they could not spread. When the wildlife near them was decimated, and during periods of recurring drought, the concentrations of people broke up, and they abandoned their agriculture and, in some cases, their remarkable cliff-front architecture. Many of the earlier subgroups simply vanished. It was as if they had their fifteen minutes of glory and then simply walked off the face of the Earth. They had no domestic animals except, again, dogs and the turkey.

The Anasazis were among those early Southwest builders. Their structures in Chaco Canyon were remarkable. At Pueblo Bonito, there were nearly six hundred rooms, and the area must have been home to as many as a thousand people at its peak. It was in places five stories tall. The Anasazis traded in turquoise with people from Mexico. Yet, in less than a century, it was all over. They couldn't go it alone. Sheep and goats would have been far more valuable to them than turquoise, but there was no domestication of food animals except, again, the turkey. They had no burden-bearers except dogs, and these were not very large ones at that. The world went forward and the Anasazis went into oblivion, their apparent genius in construction as well as social organization along with them. They could not take the next step alone, and so it wasn't until centuries later that the rest of the world even discovered they had been here at all.

To the north, the Indians on the plains hunted in a sea of bison, deer and pronghorn, alongside the buffalo, wolf and grizzly bear. But the bands could never stay still long enough to develop an agriculture. They didn't even invent pottery. They were slaves to the herds along whose edges they scurried, hunting and eating as they went. Their cultures were rich and complex and their pride and temperaments fierce. They had dogs but no really efficient beasts of burden. Their great flowering as warriors, coupled with their destruction, awaited the Europeans who would bring them the horse. Plains Indians on foot were far less impressive than they would become historical moments before they were killed or conquered. The remnants that remain remember and take pride in their last moments as a people of power and independence. The horse had given them their destiny, but it was too late to matter. The horse had served their conquerors far longer and had given them much more.

To the east, in the woodlands and along the coast, there were complex tribal factions and clever but fierce politicians among the Indians, but the people there, too, had to hunt and gather. Their simple agriculture was rarely enough to sustain anything but small villages and sometimes no more than families and clans.

In time, the number of distinctive cultures on the continent of

North America is believed to have exceeded two thousand, but alone or collectively, they had no effect whatever on the rest of the world. In the centuries before Columbus and the Spanish invasions, and for millennia before the earlier and, we assume (but only that), brief visits of the Norsemen, no one knew those cultures were here. Most were not even known to each other. There was no tradition acknowledging them in Europe or the Middle East before Columbus, which is why that Johnny-come-lately gets so much credit. He was one of the greatest rediscoverers in history. Again, the dwellers in the entire northern half of the New World were without domestic animals with that mysterious exception, the dog, and one pretty big bird, the turkey.

In Mexico, a cluster of brilliant, innovative cultures arose, but they did not appear to have anywhere to go. They did, in fact, have many places to go but no way of getting there. They did not develop marine technology to a significant degree. And so they lingered and then imploded—the Aztec, Toltec and Quantopec, among others. There was genius then, incredible sophistication in design and decoration, architecture, symbology, religion, astronomy and politics. Clearly, there was mathematics—their artifacts today reveal extremely complex imaging—but those singular minds were alone in the wilderness. They conquered everyone within reach, but that is not saying much, really. They were pitted against simple, unadorned Stone Age cultures. The crushing effect on these brilliant cultures of the European invasions from the early 1500s on was just a part of the story behind their collapse. For all their genius, they were not destined to ignite the world. Like the Anasazis, they were waiting for oblivion. They had no tradition of domestication except the dog and the turkey.

South and east, another remarkable cultural explosion occurred among a people known as the Mayans. Genius was there, but it, too, struggled against cultural isolation without success. It moved into some areas in Central America, but it did not develop the technology that would have permitted it really to expand. There was little exchange with other cultures. Once again, genius died aborning, albeit at the feet of magnificent temples. They had no domestic animals except the dog.

On a recent visit to an as yet unstudied archaeological Mayan site in the deep forest of Quintana Roo Territory on Mexico's Yucatán Peninsula, I walked along paved avenues not yet completely hidden by jungle debris. Crumbling temples covered with extremely complex stonework towered on either side, draped with vines and trees growing from each plateau and crevice. It was a place from another world. Butterflies and wild orchids were everywhere. There were scattered dwellings of surviving Mayans through-out the area. In one, I found what had apparently been an altar stone for human sacrifice lying outside a simple native hut. It had a large indentation in it, presumably to hold the sacrificial victim, and was now being used as a trough for hogs. They were feeding at it when I came upon them. The hogs were descendants of European pigs brought to the New World a long time ago but too late to make a difference. The combination of elements—the strange discrepancy between brilliant architecture, bewildering color, fabulous religious imagery and an impoverished people, and European domestic swine—seemed somehow to suggest that if those same elements had come together in another sequence, the Mayan culture might have survived the European intrusion and gone on to enrich the world.

Far to the south, on a connected but separate continent, on the west coast, the Inca appeared in the highlands. Other fascinating cultures like the Chimu blossomed on the coastal lowlands—with a flare for pottery of explicit sexual design that bordered on the obsessive. The Lamayeque people built their culture here, too. The shards we know as the pyramids of Tùcume remind us of another vanished moment of glory. Yet, again, genius flourished only briefly. Agriculture was practiced at a low technical level before the dissolution of the cultures themselves. To their north, in modern Ecuador, on the west coast of the Andes, there was a variety of interesting cultures that did not spread far or seduce many neighboring peoples. Sophisticated pottery figures found there date back at least six thousand years, but there are no domestic animals among them.

In the fertile valleys of Peru's otherwise arid coastal plains, the Moche flourished shortly after the time of Christ and built amazing pyramids, one of which was the largest known structure in South America before the European invasions. It was 135 feet tall and its base covered over twelve acres. These people worked gold into wonderful figures and designs, but they did not domesticate animals and their influence did not spread far afield. There, too, genius was alone. No one fed on it. And so it vanished like so many before and after.

The two huge land masses, North and South America, and the giant isthmus that joins them, Central America, demonstrate the problem—isolation, no cross-fertilization. There were brief, brilliant and very localized cultural flashes, but 99 percent of the inhabitable land masses on the two continents and their bridge remained home only to scattered Stone Age cultures, some of which briefly did remarkable things. A few of those cultures have lingered into our own times as ragged shards overwhelmed by time and other cultures with domestic animals always in the forefront.

There were, for example, vast earthworks in Ohio and adjacent areas, but the genius that produced them had no lasting effect on the history of the world. Again, no one came to see the pyrotechnics. The Mound

Builders, remarkable though they assuredly were, did not number domestication among their accomplishments. They never moved beyond the Stone Age. Had their laboriously created mounds achieved the status of mountain ranges, had their refinement of stone blade technology gone beyond the seemingly possible, they would still have gathered berries, nuts and roots, fished with spears and hunted woods bison, rabbit, squirrel, raccoon and porcupine, bear and deer with weapons of wood and stone.

Particularly in what we now call Latin America, the incredible art and architecture, the ceramics and fabrics, and the concepts behind them attest to the genius, individual and collective, of these cultures. There was sophistication, there were flashes of insight into astronomy and mathematics, but it was all imprisoned by the Stone Age. The genius came and went, the Stone Age persisted. These cultures peaked and their implosions were completed in the 1500s A.D. All of the world's major domestications had already been accomplished thousands of years earlier. Time and the freedom to evolve beyond their Stone Age culture and connect with genius elsewhere had passed the people of the New World by.

And what of domestication? Except for the dog, there were only four other domestic animals in the entire hemisphere, three in South America. There were two New World camelids, the llama and the alpaca (descended from wild species, the vicuña and the guanaco). But they were savanna (pampas) and mountain animals and were held in check by the jungles of the Amazon Basin. They and the genius they could have helped spread northward were blocked.

And in all of North, Central and South America combined, an area of 16,648,935 square miles, in towering mountains, steaming lowlands, lush rain forests, huge deserts, vast savannas, along enormous rivers, in productive forests, amid thousands of bird and mammal species, and along tens of thousands of miles of coastline, only one mammal was domesticated for food—a rodent, the one- to three-pound guinea pig. It is astounding that this single success didn't trigger an avalanche of domestications, for the raw materials, vast stores of wildlife, were at hand. But it never happened. If the "discovery" of the New World had waited another thousand years, perhaps it would have. And what wonders might have unfolded had the cultures of the Western Hemisphere found their own way out of the Stone Age.

Nutrition

Everything we do on Earth centers on the single matter of nutrition. All over the world, agriculture has always leaned heavily toward a few highly specialized crops—maize, millet, barley, rice and legumes—favoring species and varieties high in protein. (Among these crops, however, rice would not have been able to achieve the role it has come to play because it is so labor-intensive for people without animal power.) The people's own natural selection, their survival rate, guided their agricultures. But without food animals and working animals nothing could be taken for granted. Everything else that has happened in our history occurred only after the people had fed themselves. And that remained a full-time job, and an *iffy* one at best, where domestic animals were not available.

There are fishing cultures on our planet, but they have been traditionally among the most rigidly fixed of all. They might have evolved a primitive maritime technology, but nothing like the offshoots of the technologies we have developed—things like metallurgy, meteorology, electronics, computerized navigation, portable refrigeration, the ability to fast-freeze for longer storage, communications, aircraft and a global marketing strategy waiting to distribute a highly perishable sea harvest.

The problem all along has been that large urban centers cannot feed themselves, and without controlled animal populations, they break apart even as they begin to grow. Protein has always had to come in from the outside, first driven in on the hoof for slaughter, now processed outside the city and transported toward urban areas in refrigerated trains and trucks. With only wild animals to draw upon, anything remotely like that would be impossible. Wildlife near centers that have started to grow is quickly used up. Those species that might survive hunting pressure have traditionally had their habitat usurped and turned to agriculture. And soon after coming together, it is necessary for city dwellers or their suppliers to go so far afield to hunt that the concentration of humanity itself becomes a bad idea and protein-poor populations unravel and shred.

Without beasts of burden, even agricultural produce could not reach people who were unable to grow their own food. And without the technology that evolved from their use, there would be no wheeled vehicles, no roads and certainly no tunnels or bridges.

Gossip and Culture

Without large population centers (cities born of crossroads and markets and supported by the domestication of animals), there would be no cultural institutions into which genius could flow for pollination and growth. None of the technology that we enjoy in our time would have come to be: metallurgy, anything but rudimentary mechanics, electronics and therefore communications, flight, astronautics, printing, medicine, computer technology. None of these things can evolve as cottage industries. They are all built on layer after layer of technical accomplishments that are, in turn, the products of interaction, cross-pollination and the resulting growth, i.e., cultural evolution. We would not have glass, plastics, synthetic fibers and metals had we not been able to build and maintain the cities and industries that caravans of domestic animals seeded for us. (Unless, of course, one wishes to assume that had the domestic versions of the horse, wild cattle, camels and asses not been "invented," man would still have gone on to invent the railroad, the turnpike, and the airplane. That is a very doubtful assumption, I believe.)

The word *trivia* in our language derives from two Latin words—*tri* and *via:* three roads. And in the ancient world, wherever three roads met, there would be a market, which was why the roads converged there in the first place, for the market and water. So trivia was the "gossip" one heard where the three roads met. But there was far more than gossip at that hive-busy place of convergence. Universities were the outgrowth of traveled men and women meeting at crossroads. They met at first in small groups, sitting on the ground in the shade and by fires at night, speaking of the wonderful things they had seen and heard. The libraries, classrooms and laboratories would come much later.

So "gossip" is a species of wisdom exchanged at crossroads. But people could not reach (or create or even learn of) crossroads without the transport that domestic animals and their mechanical descendants were able to provide. Without the exchange, without specific places for genius to thrive, cultures are doomed to stagnate. A genius in a village of hunter-gatherers, or even of rudimentary agriculturists, is like the apocryphal tree falling in a remote, undiscovered forest during a wind storm. With no one to hear it, is there a sound? Is there genius?

A Critical By-product

An unknown number of cultures have had their agricultural enterprises collapse because their soil resources gave out. Manure, one natural resource that could have saved their soil and renewed it endlessly, was too hard to come by without closely held domestic herds and flocks to produce it. Ultimately, a society must fail if it expends more energy in producing or collecting food than the food provides. That is the inescapable fact of our energetics. And so, without domestication, tribes and clans would have moved on or stayed and deteriorated, suffering from a myriad of diseases and deficiencies common to perpetually undernourished people who are at the same time inbred more intensely with each generation. One of the most vital gifts domestic animals have facilitated in us, our own gene dispersal, would not have come to pass with anywhere near the speed or expansiveness we have experienced.

The peoples of Earth, without the cultural exchange first market-places and then universities have given them, would not have been perpetually challenged by new ideas. Therefore, there would not have been the endless searching for answers. Without the questions being asked or the answers being pursued, little that was new would have occurred, things like the wheel and the alphabet. There would have been no need to look for coal or petroleum, and the natural energy contained within Earth would have been largely unexploited and its hundreds of by-products would have remained for the most part undiscovered. (From the point of view of the environment, that would not have been all bad.)

The Human Equation

The physical condition of man in areas where the soil has not been exhausted and where hunting is still profitable is generally quite robust. Without companion animals to relieve stress and lower blood pressure (the critical "cuddle-factor"), individuals prone to those conditions tend to die off early in their lives and not pass along their troubled genes to many offspring.

An ironic set of circumstances has thus evolved. Domestic animals, by acting as beasts of burden and by providing a reliable protein source, have given us large concentrations of people, which has created an ever-growing sense of competition, personal isolation and alienation. Cities are brilliant cultural displays, but they are not always psychologically nurturing. The cuddle-factor of a high-rise is low. But animals have surrendered themselves up to us as companions and have helped us reduce the loneliness of the crowd. Psychologically, animals have been self-fulfilling prophecies. They have come forward to help us solve the troubles into whose midst they have transported us. We would not have come to have these urban stresses without them, but neither, in all probability, would many of us be able to cope with them as well as we do.

There is another irony that is linked to human health. When beasts of burden and meat animals in combination gave us population centers where trivia could be heard, they also gave us mammoth problems. Caravans moving between cities, markets and cultures changed forever the ecology of disease organisms. Isolation for microbes, too, came to an end. Bacterial diseases like plague spread and laid the ground for future pandemics. Bacteria and viruses of all kinds were spread and then they mutated in response to the new opportunities available to them and the new challenges. Densely populated centers facilitated the spread of sexually linked diseases and viral respiratory ailments that then sat waiting for the next caravan to help move them around. When growing rice and other agricultural crops requiring large, ready water supplies was made possible by plow animals, parasitic diseases caused by water-borne organisms came to dominate human health.

The great facilitators made great demands: global ecological warfare —man against his planet, the need to conquer animalcules in order to survive and peace of mind torn away by the madding crowd. Our destiny as provided to us by the animals we domesticated was not to come cheaply. In total, it has proven to be the greatest single trade-off we have ever had to make.

Man's languages would be thin, without great beauty and wanting art in isolation. Languages evolve driven first by need. Without new sciences, new intellectual pursuits, new social problems, linguistic needs can be minimal. The space age and computer technology, rudimentary as they may be, are just two recent cultural blips that have given us more language, more new words each than are contained in the total linguistic inheritance of some nontechnical cultures still extant.

Cross-pollination is vital to the growth of language, and that could never have occurred without caravans. The natural aging that languages are prone to would have occurred, of course, but it would not have been able to work off a sophisticated base because animals were not available to help us export and import ideas and enrichments. A beast of burden moving from one culture to another carries far more than trade goods. Its most precious cargo has no physical substance. It consists of ideas.

Slavery

Once agriculture was born, there would have been profound social pressures placed on man if he had been forced to survive with the power of people alone to work the fields and carry the produce to where he needed it. Without domestic animals and all that naturally followed—roads, wheels and vehicles—slavery would have had to have been common to all cultures.

Anyone who could be taken alive in warfare would be indentured for life. Everyone would be a prospective slave-owner, everybody a potential slave.

Of course, unevolved cultures tend to produce their own slaves, even though they are not called by that name. They are women, the people who work the fields while the men hunt and perform the mystic manhood rights universally associated with that pursuit. Someone has to hunt and someone has to take up a stick and scratch the earth. She who does the latter has slavery built into her condition.

Women would have had to carry, too, when slaves were few. As beasts of burden, they would not have participated as intellectual equals, and so half the genius of the people would have been lost, sorely depleting our species' potential. Domestic animals freed slaves in a ripple effect that moved around the world, and they freed women, too, to be culture-building partners and not property. We are in the middle of that revolution today. No culture now extant will be able to survive the intellectual dawn that is rising if it continues to cripple itself by ignoring 50 percent of its own potential held prisoner by the tyranny of ancient reality and blind to the light of today.

The fact that the slavery and servitude of women still do exist in cultures that have domestic animals is a devastating anomaly in cultural evolution. Such repression is based on factors far beyond our scope here. The domestication of animals has made it possible for cultures to evolve otherwise. That they have not in so many instances is human aberration. Parallel situations are war, crime and famine. There is more than enough food produced on Earth now to feed the people already here, yet people starve and struggle and kill as if responding to facts that do not exist. What will happen in the next century if populations actually do outstrip food supplies is anyone's guess.

Warfare

People steal and kill each other for any number of reasons. But warfare would exist in a world without domestic animals primarily as a means of obtaining slaves, and it would be endless, because the spoils of conquest would always be in demand. Breeding slaves would not be worthwhile, not when the life span of the slave-owner probably would not exceed thirty-five to forty years. A slave-owner could not rear and train a slave, breed him or her and profit from the labor of the child in his own lifetime. Slaves would, of course, be bred, but replenishment of the supply would require constant raids on other populations and the cultural disruption that such warfare always entails.

Weapons would be primitive without the technology that evolved through animal-facilitated cultural exchange (an undeniable plus). They would be striking devices, largely—daggers, clubs, swords and axes—and simple projection devices like bows and arrows (the example of the Australian Aborigines notwithstanding), throwing-sticks, boomerangs, shaped throwing-stones, spears and spear-throwers. Weapon systems requiring metals, chemistry and complex machines would not have come into being, again, a plus, although the societal principles involved in both the primitive and advanced weapons of war are identical. Domestic animals neither created nor eliminated warfare, again a human aberration. They did, however, change its style.

Since men would have to carry everything they needed themselves, warfare would have remained pretty much a localized affair. Coastal peoples could travel by boat, but they would have no protein on the hoof. Sea travel would be slow because they would have to stop and fish or put ashore to hunt and gather. Really long voyages would be accomplished the way future protracted space journeys are envisioned now. They would be generational. Those who left would never come back. Eventually, some far-removed descendants might visit out of curiosity or through a kind of reverse exploration. Ties would be tenuous. Homesickness has a short life span, exactly one generation. (Root-seeking is another process and is frequently a romanticized reaction to alienation.)

Building their lives around slave-hunting and warfare would not be acceptable as the sole means to define their self-image. So peoples would have inevitably evolved tribal mystiques to better suit that purpose. They would simply declare themselves superior to everyone else. They would have to be, for that is the ultimate rationale for tribalism and the justification for slavery. And it is a mind-set that has always produced arrogance that, in turn, has guaranteed cruelty. Societies that have domesticated animals have, throughout human history, also engaged in slavery and savage racial, religious and ethnic warfare. But aggression and cruelty have not been, perhaps, proof that we are not *that* far from the cave. That they still exist is a social aberration.

Isolation

In a world without animal transport, mountains, ice fields, deserts, oceans, all natural features, would be formidable barriers contributing to isolation and to the distrust of foreign peoples. Languages with very limited areas of use would have proliferated, but without markets and caravans would have remained as isolated as the people who created them. Ignorant of what really lay beyond natural barriers, people would be openly hostile to other people or ideas that came from unknown areas—i.e., most of the rest of the world. Suspicion would rule all lives and reflect a universal dread of the new and the unknown. In isolation, people feel that only isolation is safe. And to some degree, they might be right, given the export/import patterns of disease organisms.

When wildlife or arable land gave out, people would be forced to migrate, and only then, or in fleeing catastrophe, would they encounter people foreign to them. Travel would be dangerous because at any moment, the travelers might be detected, perceived as enemies and enslaved or killed and perhaps eaten if they resisted. Others would do unto them as they would almost certainly do unto others. The cannibals in our history, where they have existed, except when their practices have been strictly ritualistic, generally have not possessed livestock.

The fact that man as a species probably evolved in only one or two regions and then spread around the world does not contradict the idea of isolation. Evolving man heading upward from *Homo erectus* toward Neanderthal status or its equivalents did not pack his bags and move like an emigrant bound for a distant port and a new life. Groups of people expanded slowly, fairly oozing around at least half of the world, moving precipitously only during periods of glacial advance or other catastrophic events. Generally, however, it was a matter of hunting berries over the next ridge, and the next, always easing into another adjacent area that would provide food, shelter and water. It is thus ironic that so much emotion is invested in racial identity. We speak of the races as if they were discrete. Given the facts of our species' history, we are all of one race. We may be of different "colors," but we sprang from the same roots—and not all that long ago.

Wildlife's Lot

The effect that the lack of domestication had on wildlife would have been seemingly contradictory. The close-in effect would have been devastating because without domestic protein, wild-caught protein would be critical for human survival. Wildlife would be decimated anywhere near human habitations. And the degree to which this happened would be in direct proportion to the density of the human population.

In contrast, outlying wildlife stocks would have learned fear and learned it well. But its slaughter would still have been relentless and the success of the hunt would have determined how large human families and clans could be. No less than with other species, man's ability to reproduce and survive is a function of the availability of food. Near where man lives, food is always on a downward availability curve, and if he relies on hunting and gathering, he would always have to go farther afield to find protein, which could be as dangerous as any other form of travel.

In areas where there were major animal migrations, man would follow, and tribes, clans and families would live in dread of meeting foreigners because that could lead to cultural confrontation. If one side or another needed slaves or women to work as slaves and be wives at the same time, an excuse to wage war would be generated and entire populations wiped out. The victors could go home with plenty of meat and hides because they would have new slaves to act as beasts of burden.

The overall effect of man without domestication on wildlife and the environment would not have been entirely negative. Man's impact on nature is ultimately a function of his own population and technology. And populations have always been and must always be functions of nutrition. Because actual numbers would have remained small, nontechnical man's overall impact would have been slight. Animal species would not have been driven to extinction. No dams would have diverted rivers, forests would not have been clear-cut, there would not have been strip mines and no reason to slash and burn, no pesticides, and no pollution from agricultural chemical runoff. No areas would have been overgrazed by large herds of goats, sheep and cattle. Soil erosion, acid rain, air pollution, eutrophication (lake-silting) would not have occurred. Domestic animals have enabled man to thrive on easy, predictable food and thus increase to obscene numbers. Had that not happened, his impact would have been slight and both habitat and wildlife would have been spared most of today's tragic reality.

Another thing that would not have happened is hybridization. Domestic animals always have the potential of escaping, becoming feral, and even as new species, they often can breed back into their parent species and in effect exterminate them. Once a gene pool is sullied by hybridization, in theory at least, it can never really be cleansed. It is generally believed that domestic horses escaped and bred back to the remnants of their wild ancestors, technically destroying their gene pool. The same thing is presently happening with dogs and coyotes.

There is no serious argument that *Homo sapiens* is the most intelligent species of animal on Earth so far. But without the domestication of other species, we would have missed a vital part of our own evolution, something that was meant to be. That it was also meant to be a part of the evolution of the species we have taken into custody and whose evolution we have in large measure governed is not to be dismissed. It could be said that man's domestication of other species has been by mutual agreement. It has become a new dynamic that dominates the planet, this interdependence of species. Domestic species, it is true, owe their existence to man, but they have repaid the debt ten-million-fold. What we owe them is our ability to achieve our own destiny. We would have been incapable of doing it on our own.

The point I wish to make, I think, is clear. We are the products of cultures, histories and events all made possible because there have been animals for us to eat, some to milk, still others to wear, ride and otherwise burden. They have been the constants in our cultural and intellectual evolution, surpassed in importance only by the potential of our own brain. And if we have profited hugely from their contributions, we surely did not reckon, or care to reckon, the price the animals would pay. It all just happened, drawing man and animal closer and closer together until there was no way to break free. And that is where we are today. We are in a partnership far more important in our lives than even our wonderful minds could have imagined.

PART ONE

BEFORE AGRICULTURE

TWO

The Goat:
The Animal That Changed the History of Man

As the Gods See It

Even gods had surnames back in the times when myths were being created, particularly in ancient Greece. Dionysus was originally Dionysus *Aego*bolus, meaning the goat-killer, a name that probably evolved because goats are notoriously bad for the grape vines Dionysus was bound to protect. Hera was Hera *Aego*phagus, meaning goat-eater, and it was Zeus *Aegi*duchos because he had been suckled by a goat. Some stories say that Zeus later took a goat unto himself and that *Aegi*pan, father of Pan, was the result. Goats were the sacrificial animals of choice in the worship of Aphrodite, Apollo, Artemis, Asclepius, Dionysus, Helios, Hermes, the Nymphs and the great Zeus.

First Domestication?

The animal that figured so prominently in the traditions of the ancients was possibly the first animal man ever domesticated. The goat came into our lives in the preagriculture stage of our development, during the Middle Stone Age, between twelve thousand and fifteen thousand years ago —at the end, then, of the last glacial period. It was to be a momentous event, helping to shape the history of man as perhaps no other single event or accomplishment ever has.

The only other preagriculture domestic animals man was to take in from the cold were the dog, the reindeer and the sheep. But the goat probably did come first, judging from the bones we have found and their demonstrable age. The range of the reindeer and the wild goat nowhere overlapped, and the dog as a carnivore is so distinctly different that confusion is not possible, but it is quite a different matter with sheep. Lacking a skull and horns, it can be difficult or at times impossible to tell sheep bones from goat bones, particularly the long bones, and so the osteological evidence can be inconclusive. Still, most people conclude that the goat was the first species in our keep. At worst, it was second, slightly behind the sheep. However that sequence evolved, the dog was right there running along beside, never far from the center of the action, a position it holds to this day. But the dog has always been an enigma, and the conventional wisdom about its origin may be neither wise nor conventional. It has been, rather, convenient.

Today, there are estimated to be between three and four *billion* goats in the company of man. It is, with the exception of the dog, the most widespread of all domestic animals. Since it was almost certainly the first, is today the most widespread and one of if not *the* most populous food animal on the planet, it has been among the most important in terms of our development.

The goat is often referred to as the poor man's cow, because in areas where no other animal could possibly survive, goats thrive. They eat bitter, aromatic vegetation not palatable to other species. They graze at higher altitudes than most other animals and are adaptable to almost as wide a range of temperatures as man is. All that has enabled man to extend his own range deep into desert and mountainous areas by taking the milk and meat of the goat with him.

Goats are prolific (gestation is 150 days and does are typically bred every year) and are easily managed even by small children, an important point. Their milk is nourishing and so easy to digest it is often prescribed for infants and invalids. It is likely that the goat was the first animal man learned to milk, although that could have been a giant step that did not occur until the domestication of the cow several thousand years later. At any rate, goats have been providing man with milk, meat and fiber for clothing and housing, skins for clothing and lightweight watertight containers (critically important in arid areas), and offerings to the gods since before the birth of what we generally refer to as civilization. In many areas, goats are still currency, providing dowries for young girls, and are basic units of trade. That is true, of course, of just about all domestic animals, at least food and fiber species.

Early Association

For man to have started to keep animals and eventually to breed them selectively depended on a predomestication association of some kind. Man and his eventual possessions had to be familiar with each other and come from the same general habitat. Man is not known ever to have set out for strange places to seek exotic species to domesticate. That would have been a highly unlikely scenario.

Many thousands of years ago, human beings and wild goats were well established as two species living naturally side by side. Add that to the fact that kids are easy for a reasonably agile person to catch until they are three days old, and then consider man's natural tendency to keep pets and the natural mothering instinct of the human female and you have the beginning of an association. But exactly where the domestication of the goat occurred, when and by which tribe, culture or clan are now unknowable.

As for why, one factor *could* have been the relationship of man to totemic animals. A great many cultures have had totem animals that cannot be killed without incurring unimaginable retribution. If the wild goat, for example, were a totem for a tribe (and it seems certain it must have been time and again, given the richness and depth of the mythology surrounding it), it would be safe among those people at least, and lose its fear of them. And that would have led to an association that grew easily and probably without intent on the part of man. It was serendipity at work. (Serendipity would also have a great deal to do with what was to come with other species.) An original relationship would have happened naturally. And perhaps the first step in some domestications was the totemizing of the species.

The Theory of Endearing Characteristics

A mystery in all domestications centers on that idea of selective breeding. Without knowing anything, really, about genetics, how did man know how to breed selectively or even to interfere in the process at all? The answer is not difficult to envision. It is probable that people tended to keep longest and trade for animals with characteristics that they found desirable or ingratiating. Except in times of famine, these animals would not have been killed as readily as other animals. Therefore, they would have tended to produce more young with the same desirable characteristics. And, in time, those attractive traits would have intensified until they were dependable, that is, bred true. Given the probable dates of the earlier domestications and envisioning the level of sophistication man would have exhibited even in the Middle Stone Age, clearly much was left to chance. In the first millennia of the goat association and the other associations that were to follow, refinement would have been slow in coming.

Thus, when we refer to archaeological sites where bones have been found, we should keep in mind how long it must have taken for types or breeds to evolve. If "breeds" or kinds of goats or other domestic animals are identified and assigned a plus/minus date by carbon dating or stratigraphy or some other temporal yardstick, the species itself would have been in the company of man for thousands of years before that.

Livestock must have been allowed to feed off the land in the centuries before agriculture. We can assume that the early domesticators became pastoralists, the way the Maasai are in Kenya and Tanzania today, insofar as they can be. The wanderers had to have been constantly searching for food and water for the animals that were, in turn, feeding them and giving them status. Pastoralists generally do not offer the archaeologist the reference points that town dwellers do. The whole world is their midden. So, again, it is uncertain just how long it may have taken domesticated species to evolve, with or without the interference of man.

The Wild Goats

In Pakistan today, there is a former Indian province called the Sindh. It is an area of 48,136 square miles, with its capital at Karachi. It is bounded by the Arabian Sea in the southwest; in the west and north by Baluchistan and West Punjab; in the south by a great swamp, the Rann of Kutch; and in the east by Rajasthan, much of that state being mountainous and arid. Somewhere in that rugged land of deserts, mountains and lush river valleys lies the eastern anchor of the prehistoric wild goat's range. From there, it extended north and west through Persia, over most of Asia Minor across to Crete and in the west among the approximately 220 islands known as the

Cyclades, which are spread over 996 square miles of the Aegean Sea between the Peloponnesus Peninsula and the Dodecanese Islands.

Somewhere between those east-west points, the goat was domesticated, and from there it spread until today it blankets the inhabitable world except for the polar regions. It is probable that the actual domestication took place on the periphery of the wild goat range. Around the edges of their ideal or core habitat, animals are more prone to develop variations in order to accommodate themselves to different habitats. Biologically, they are more inclined to vary and differ; i.e., to be domesticated and altered through natural selection or selective breeding. Genetic malleability is literally a fringe benefit.

The goat in ever-evolving styles and sizes went almost everywhere that man went in those early days, and the harsher the trials man experienced, the more important the goat was. Goats have become an elegant hobby animal and a pet without economic importance only in the last few moments of our relationship's history, and only in a limited number of almost absurdly affluent societies. All but a tiny fraction of the nearly four billion domestic goats alive today are critically important to the people who herd them, often intermingled with sheep, cattle, horses, donkeys and camels.

Capra hircus is the scientific name for the domestic goat. But to that should be added at least two subspecies, *C.h. girgentana*, the screw-horn goat generally associated with Sicily, and *C.h. mambrica*, the mamber goat, first evolved in Palestine. The most important wild ancestor of the domestic goat is the bezoar goat, *Capra aegagrus*, the hardy animal with that Sindh-to-Aegean range. Many authorities today assign milk breeds and mohair-producing breeds to two domestic species, not one, *C. hircus* and *C. angorensis*. Thus, the genealogy of the goat is complex.

As for the ibex, the name is used loosely. There are actually three species, but none of them figured in the ancestry of the domestic goat. Their ranges overlapped those of both the wild and domestic goat as well as that of man, yet, for some reason, the ibex was ignored in the domestication process.

A single Nubian ibex that I "knew personally" helped reestablish the species in Israel. He was found wound up in a barbed-wire fence and his struggling had done massive damage to his legs. Israeli veterinarians managed to save his life and he was installed in a wildlife sanctuary and breeding facility near the Red Sea called Hai-Bar. Females were captured and brought to him from all over Israel and almost without exception they bore him young. He was a striking animal with mammoth horns and a huge harem when I went to photograph him. His offspring were used to establish wild herds in a number of other reserve areas in the young nation, where the species is strictly protected.

Although this distinctly dominant male was living in a natural setting with a large number of his own kind and was not "handled" after his recovery from surgery, he became a very docile animal, obviously perfectly comfortable near people. He would have been easy to "tame," and using him in a selective breeding program would have been equally easy to do. In fact, he was used that way, but the females made available to him were selected for the best wild characteristics of the species and not for other things that might have benefited man in an economic sense. He did demonstrate, however, how very easily the wild goat that was domesticated could have been brought under human management thousands of years ago.

The story of the splendid wild Nubian ibex had a tragic end. During the Six-Day War, an Egyptian or Israeli jet fighter, it has never been determined which, streaked over Hai-Bar at low altitude to avoid detection and the sonic boom so startled the ibex that he panicked and ran into a pile of huge rocks placed there for his climbing comfort. The impact broke his neck, killing him instantly.

The Evidence We Have

At the end of the Pleistocene era, in postglacial times, Mesolithic hunter-gatherers wandered over Syria and Palestine as they did over most of the Middle East and much of Europe and Asia, too. One distinct cultural group, the Natufian, regularly stopped off at a cave in Palestine known as El-Khiam and left behind clues to their lifestyle. They had domestic goats with them. That was at least ten thousand years ago. Scientists today place those goats somewhere between the wild ancestral goat and a truly domesticated animal. The process was "in the works" and had been for some time.

Not far away, in the world's oldest walled city, Jericho, goat remains were discarded along with pottery shards. (The more debris earlier people created, the more we know about them. One culture's garbage spawns another culture's Ph.D.'s. What cavemen threw over their shoulders eventually landed in our museums.) Not too many hundreds of years separated the bones found at Jericho from those of El-Khiam. Within another thousand years, goat remains were buried at the site known as Belt Cave on the shores of the Caspian Sea and at numerous sites in Iran. The domestic scimitar-horned goat had evolved and was in central Europe by the start of the New Stone or Neolithic Age, approximately ten thousand years ago in that area. Shortly after that, still in the Neolithic Age, it was a common animal in northern Europe.

Not only the domestic goat but domestication itself was on the move. Mankind would never be the same again; it couldn't be. The goat had battered down the walls of isolation, opening the way to an apparently boundless future. Travelers could take food on the trail and even out to sea with them. Mankind could feed ever-growing concentrations of people, allowing towns and later cities to grow. Herders had valuable trade goods with legs of their own. Man no longer had to carry his wealth on his back; it walked on ahead of him. Many times, I have watched Maasai herders in just that position, walking behind huge flocks of goats, controlling their movements by low whistles to which the goats responded almost without hesitation. Often, hundreds of goats were involved and no more than two teenage or even preteen herders were required.

The goat had finally given us our crossroads, and the way was clear for our incredible potential to be realized. The domestication of the goat was the greatest single cultural breakthrough *Homo sapiens* had yet achieved. The evolution of man was free to move forward, and that movement would include a growing diversity in domestication and eventually a slavish dependence on that one cultural accomplishment. It has continued into our time, and we have shown no real signs of evolving beyond that dependence. Thus, the domestication of the goat and other species was a double-edged sword. It set us free of old dependencies, only to create new limits and restrictions on our behavior, many of which remain even to this day.

Fiber

Angora goats, although not as prolific as the milk breeds, provided the fiber for mohair, and that fabric was in use at least as early as the time of the Israelis' flight out of Egypt about 1200 B.C. It became commercially valuable in Turkey, in Ankara Province, very much later. Interestingly enough, mohair is not as fine today as it was in biblical times. In the nineteenth century, the Turks were so anxious to capitalize on the demand for mohair that they foolishly used their finest Angora bucks to breed with cruder, more common does, and those rough and hardy crossbreeds became the ancestors of the Angoras we know today.

In 1881, the sultan of Turkey, jealously guarding a profitable cottage industry, banned the export of Angoras, but it was too late. Herds had already been established in Europe, South Africa, South America and the

United States. (Milk goats had come to the Americas with the early settlers in Virginia.)

In the United States today, the mohair industry is centered in Texas. Oil from mohair washing or "scouring" is shipped out in tank cars and is used largely in the cosmetics industry because of its high lanolin content. Without knowing it, many of us are using goat products today from breeds and varieties that were evolved before Moses parted the Red Sea.

The Real War of the Worlds

Predictably, man, in his enthusiasm for his new and profitable possession, began keeping far more goats than were needed for his own survival. As the symbol of wealth, the goat was hoarded then as it is today, just as other cultures hoard gold and paper wealth. Goats provided status and political power, and they were standard items in a bride's dowry. A man's wealth was measured by the number of goats he kept, just as we measure our wealth today by the size of our bank accounts. There is, however, an enormous difference. Gold and paper fiscal instruments do not require feeding, while goats in large numbers are extremely demanding of the land.

Compared with the havoc wrought by domestic goats over the millennia, strip-mining and oil spills are minor ecological glitches. The goat, while it led man out of the darkness of the cave, became one of his worst ecological insults. By the thousands, then the millions and now the billions, goats have stripped the vegetation off the land and changed the face of continents. The Sahara Desert was probably largely goat-made and so was the climate of the Mediterranean and southern Europe. The tropical storms that arise in the South Atlantic and periodically lash North America are also born in the 3,500,000 square miles of desert in North Africa, and are thus at least in part the products of ancient goat cultures and their excesses. Greece's land was impoverished by goats, and so was much of the Middle East. The mark of the goat is upon our planet perhaps forever.

At remote Wadi Mukateb in the Sinai, there are found petroglyphs of unknown authorship that depict the plains animals and marshland wildlife that lived in the area before it was a harsh desert environment. The petroglyphs, and there are thousands of them, show vast numbers of goats. I have wandered there among the shards of cliffs dislodged in some unremembered seismic event and marveled at the mixture of wildlife and domesticated animals, if such those goats were.

It must have been hazardous to hang from the top of the cliff on ropes and record whatever event it was that was so important to some people that it had to be done. High up on an exposed cliff, almost indecipherable without binoculars, and there on the desert floor in the dry riverbed, the goats march on. Was it a census, a caravan count of some kind? I wondered then; I wonder now.

Something else started with the domestication of the goat. Man now had wealth to protect, and soon the predators around him with which he had lived in comparative peace became implacable enemies. Man could no longer live in harmony with animals that he felt threatened his flocks. Then hoofed animals became foes, too, because they competed with his goats, his wealth and status, for food and water. Man no longer had to hunt for meat and hides, so he could barricade water holes and starve or chase away wild animals. They were not only useless but also competitive, and that became the basis for man's war against them.

The goat didn't ask much of man, only that he go to war with the natural world and begin dismantling the system from which both goat and man had evolved. And we have had to pay an extravagant price for our future. We are still trying to set the balance points for our own lavish demands, the joy and profit of domestic animals and the sanctity of our habitat—Earth. It has proven to be a confounding issue, complex beyond our imagining.

The domestication of the goat was one of the most profound steps man as a species would ever take and, at the same time, the first stage of what he would turn into his own worst ecological blunder. Once he had goats, and goats quickly became power, man had no idea what to do with them except profit. And when profit is the only item on the agenda, loss is inevitable.

The crossroads, the cities and the universities that were to come, were too slow in evolving. The harm was done to our planet long before environmental awareness evolved, and today goats, the "cattle" of the emerging peoples of the world, belong by far in the largest numbers to those who are least able to comprehend ecological considerations. And even if the goat-keepers of the world could understand environmental stress, they would still be the people least likely to respond to a call for moderation.

As cultures, we have placed the goat between ourselves and our planet and must accept the consequences. Most of us are no longer able to hunt and gather for ourselves, so our goats and other domesticates must do it for us. The fruits, vegetables, nuts and berries of the Earth that man must have to feed directly upon the land are elegant and relatively rare when compared with grasses, sedges, barks and buds. Goats convert what man cannot eat into flesh and fiber, milk, hides and currency. The goat today could wander free of the association and survive. Goat-keepers could not, not possibly. In the final analysis, then, who domesticated whom?

A Postscript

It should be noted that the goat emerged as a domestic animal in areas that were and generally still are less than "lush." That has been true of most domestications. People in food-rich places like rain forests did not domesticate the animals at hand. They used their blowguns or bows and arrows to kill them and settled for that.

Domestication has almost always been a response to need. It has rarely if ever been a casual or gratuitous affair. It has also been profoundly disruptive of cultural emphasis and focus, but it was required if man was to get on with things. Domestication was a survival tactic, although man has never been able to envision the environmental threats and the startling changes that were wrought. One suspects that even if man knew what was coming, he still would have been willing to pay the price.

THREE

The Sheep:
From Fiber to Factory

As They Saw It

In the Greek colony of Kyrene in Libya, men and boys worshiped the god Aristaios with faith and passion. He was the consort of the goddess Autonoe, but more importantly, he was the god of herdsmen and beekeepers. He watched over the herdsmen and their flocks, protecting them from weather, wolves and lions and, too, from those malignant forces with names that no one would dare speak.

In Kyrene, herdsmen were important enough to have a special god just for themselves, a god who could understand the fears and concerns of the keepers of sheep. In contrast, during the range wars (and they actually were vicious wars—men, women and children died) between cattlemen and shepherds in nineteenth-century Arizona, the cattlemen insisted that the only things more worthless and stupid than sheep were the men who kept them. And sheep, especially ewes, had barely enough brains to be ornery and nothing more. But the reality of shepherding is quite different from either extreme. And it ran on parallel tracks with the civilizing of man.

The Domestications

The domestications of goats and sheep were historical events, or sequences, not far apart in time. In fact, we cannot be certain which came first. Without a skull and horns, you will recall, it is difficult, at times impossible, to identify the bones we find.

(Note, please, that both sheep and goats, like cattle, have horns, not antlers. Horns grow up from a core on the skull and are not shed. Antlers grow up from a "bud" and are shed every spring, after the breeding season has passed and fighting for females is no longer necessary. The only known exception is the North American pronghorn—it is distinctly *not* an antelope —that has horns but sheds them. The pronghorn, like a number of other species with horns, is a relic, a stubborn bit of paleontological history that fortunately just won't go away. It is apparently not closely related to any other animal still alive. That is true as well of the North American mountain goat, which is not a goat at all.)

The affinity of sheep and goats can be seen in today's surviving wild sheep. There are two so-called "blue sheep." In Mongolia and Tibet, the bharal, *Pseudois nayaur,* still ranges, and it is thought to be about midway between goats and sheep. It is probably closer to goats. The aoudad, or Barbary sheep, is found from Morocco to Egypt and the Sudan. It is so closely related to the goats that, according to reports, it can be bred to one and produce fertile offspring. If that is so, the distinction between sheep and goats is fuzzier than we have so far admitted. One day, science will revisit all of this and we will have new and perhaps surprising definitions.

The genus *Ovis* contains eight species of sheep, one of which, *O. aries,* is today's domestic sheep. In its various forms, and there are a great many of them, it is worldwide in distribution. For the record, the seven surviving wild members of *Ovis* are:

O. vignei, the urial, is found in Iran, Afghanistan, Pakistan and India. It has been suggested that this species may have figured in the creation of the domestic sheep. Probably not.

O. ammon, the argali, is native to Siberia, China and the Himalayan region. This species, too, has been thought by some to have contributed to the ancestry of the domestic sheep. Again, probably not.

O. orientalis, the mouflon, is almost universally thought to be the real and, in all likelihood, the sole ancestor of our domestic sheep. In the wild, its range has been Iran and Asia Minor, Sardinia, Corsica, Cyprus and into Central Europe. Hunting has wiped it out in many parts of its range. That is true of all wild sheep. They are among the most coveted of all big-game trophies. (They actually look much more impressive when they are alive. All of the wild sheep I have seen had a majesty about them that must have somehow affected even the men who hunted them out of necessity and then later brought them into the fold. We cannot, of course, know the level of Stone Age man's aesthetic appreciation of natural wonders. But wild sheep did, after all, play a very important, intense role in his life.)

O. canadensis, the American bighorn or mountain sheep, recently has ranged from Alaska and western Canada down through the western United States into Mexico. It has not figured in the history of the domestic sheep.

O. dalli is the Dall sheep, also known as the white sheep, and is still found in Alaska and northern British Columbia, Canada.

O. nivicola is the Siberian bighorn, found only in northeastern Siberia.

The wild sheep of the world, then, range in a great arc from southern Europe in the west along the coast of the Mediterranean, across Asia Minor and then Asia itself, up through Siberia across to North America and down through Alaska, Canada and the western United States into Mexico. It is a huge range, the Iberian Peninsula to Mexico, the long way around. Presumably, domestication could have occurred with any species along that great arc. However, it happened in that portion of the arc occupied by the mouflon—Asia Minor to Central Europe—and it probably happened on the mainland rather than on an island, judging from how quickly the idea spread across cultural lines. Cultures had to abut and somehow interact for ideas even as good as the domestication of sheep to be adopted. It was an idea that was to bring man material wealth beyond anything he could have imagined at the outset of the newly structured association. And it would cost him far more.

The Scenario

Today, we think of wild sheep as mountain animals, as if that were their only natural range. It is less their range than their retreat. They were driven there by hunting pressure, especially after man began holding some of their kin as livestock. Wild sheep and domestic sheep will exploit the same food and water sources. The wild flocks were originally grassland animals. But once man began holding them, he was able to occupy the grasslands himself, since he could take his food with him wherever he went, and meat ceased to be an important item on his gathering agenda. He no longer had to follow herds of migrating animals or anticipate and intercept their movements. There were new mandates, new imperatives.

People with sheep were immeasurably richer than people without them. Envy had to have been a force in the interaction of cultures from the time of the earliest domestication. There was now actual wealth to be had far beyond the "pickings" hunters and gatherers had always relied upon. More than swapping was possible; there could be marketing. And turf came to be important, not for what men and women could gather there, but for how much food and water at first managed and later domesticated flocks could find. Sheep, like goats, were the great converters. Grass and other vegetation that had not fed man in the past now could do so, only one step removed. Together, sheep and goats redefined our relationship to the soil and plant life. It was a whole new world that had to be understood and intellectually accommodated.

As with the goat and all of the other domestications that were to come, there had to have been some kind of relationship between the bands of technology-poor "cavemen" and targeted species. Surely, bands of Mesolithic hunters didn't happen upon a species of wildlife new to them and decide on the spot to catch and selectively breed it. It is reasonable to believe that was not the scenario with any of history's domestications. Each time, that process had to have been an easing together of two species (one of them us), species already well known to each other over a long period of time. How conscious man was of what he was doing is not possible to know. Perhaps, when he had done it once or twice, it was easier for him with new species. We don't really know that any species was domesticated only once, by one people, at one time, in one place. Many cultures were on parallel tracks, and one culture could well have been as ready as another to take the next step in its evolution.

Wild sheep as open grassland creatures would have been familiar to hunters. Certainly, they were hunted for food and their skins. Everything was. (Weaving had not yet been invented. The use of animals as sources of fiber was a concept still far in the future, although within the last two thousand years, North American aborigines in the Pacific Northwest did learn to weave the hair of wild mountain sheep without ever having domesticated any animals themselves. The designs they created are artistic masterpieces.)

In the process of feeding their bands, the Mesolithic wanderers of the period 8000 to 3000 B.C. were likely to have followed two scenarios that could have contributed in the awesome move from hunting to holding.

In the first, lambs, like the kids of wild goats, would have been easy enough for a teenager or a spry adult to catch in the three or four days after the ewes had dropped them. Ewes can be surprisingly fierce in defense of their newborn lambs, surprising because sheep generally are considered to be the meekest large species we have domesticated. Still, a band of hunters with rocks and sticks could have driven the ewes away and taken their lambs. And since sheep, wild as well as domestic, all drop their lambs at about the same time, there must have been an embarrassment of riches every spring.

The second scenario could have involved the evolution of some primitive form of herding. Driving wild flocks into culs-de-sac, or just surrounding them, could have changed hunting (which must have been difficult on open grasslands with primitive weapons) into selective slaughter. It would have been very much the more sophisticated way to obtain food and hides. And it would have naturally led in time to the process by which *O. aries* was extracted from *O. orientalis*. It is difficult to establish which process, capture or simple wild herd manipulation, would have worked faster toward the evolution of a new, domestic species. They could have worked together. While manipulating a herd of wild sheep, man could have easily taken the lambs he wanted to eat or to raise. And orphaned lambs would have provided another opportunity for man to interact with "his" animals in a new and more personal way.

It is possible that the domestication of the dog had just begun when the first sheep were being held. But even if it had, there probably would not have been time to transform the wolf into a dog capable of accepting enough direction to help in herding. The natural herding instinct in dogs is controlled aggression and today is a characteristic of special breeds, the herding breeds. Those breeds did not yet exist when sheep and goats were first taken under control. They were still hiding, along with the poodle, the Chihuahua and the golden retriever, in the eye of the wolf and just possibly another contributor of genes.

In a sense, wolves do "herd" their prey in order to single out the weak, the young and the old, but in all likelihood, that capability would not have been available at the outset of domestication. True cooperation between our two species would come somewhat later. When man started to evolve his herding breeds, he was almost certainly reawakening an ancient instinct in those dogs. But it took an extended period of time, we believe, to evolve a dog whose aggression toward the likes of sheep was sublimated to duty toward human beings.

So, in the beginning, whatever herding man did, he probably did alone, but, then, his flocks would have been small. Even so, with sheep newly taken into custody, it could have been tricky work. One can suppose there were injuries from well-horned rams. Meekness had to be built into the species. Man would have had to select for easy-keepers.

Man was not yet milking his animals, so dairy and fiber considerations were to come later. And culinary sophistication was probably at a pretty low level in the days of the cave, although surely some things tasted better than others to our distant ancestors. Meat versus fat, trim weights, growth rate, conversion efficiency, fiber length and texture and the other things that are major considerations now could not have mattered then. But behavior would have been important from the beginning.

Animals that are not easy to manage are labor-intensive. All of the megaspecies we have taken into custody down through the millennia were selected in part for that one characteristic—ease of handling. Those that were not proved to be false starts. There have been many of them, including the zebra, some pigs and some relatives of the cattle ancestors finally selected. (The term *megaspecies* is used to exclude animals like silkworms, hamsters, guinea pigs, goldfish and canaries, none of which are known to be particularly dangerous to man.)

In all probability, there could have been the tendency among hunters who lived by their skill to kill only males during the first half of the year unless they were really desperate for meat. Through the end of winter into early spring, females carrying young, and living off poorer fodder than summer offers, cannibalize their own bodies, draining away the fat reserves they built up the previous summer and fall. Meat is much poorer in taste and lower in nutritional value in that condition. It would have been no different with naturally grazed domestic flocks. That fact would keep females safe during the period they were most needed, when their new young were nursing. If early shepherds did kill the females in their flocks, it would have been only in the really early stage of the art. They would have quickly learned to do it after the young were able to survive on their own. It is more likely that they killed surplus male lambs, as is done today. There are certain basic truths of husbandry that time doesn't change. Neither has its aesthetics improved with time.

Impact

Accepting an animal into a pattern of life is a huge step for a culture to take. Language has to be invented, and a way of grading animals and establishing their worth evolved. How many sheep constitute a bride-price? Buying and selling becomes inevitable and perhaps in that lie the roots of coinage. There is a whole new mind-set, dreams to be dreamed, gods to imagine into being, a value system worked out, taboos to inculcate into the very fabric of existence, traditions to create and new legacies to be passed on. The extremely difficult concept of wealth has to be accommodated. And all of this has to be linked directly to the animal and treated with ever-growing respect by the people. In fact, far from being an incidental event in a people's history, domestication is as awesome an upheaval as we can imagine. The impact sheep were to have has been as socially violent as any event in our history as a species. It was to change the way we viewed each other.

Things that were all-important before, like the migration of wild herds, no longer really matter much at all, while things that weren't significant are suddenly all-consuming, like predators and property and class structure. Where a people may live, seasonal moves they have to make to accommodate their flocks and herds, the things that must be feared—all of these become related to the new imperatives of domestic animals. What kind of structures people build for themselves to live in depends on how often they have to move their flocks, and the kinds of clothing they wear will depend on what their flocks provide and what they themselves have learned to use. New crafts have to be developed, an artisan class accommodated. And all of this has to be incorporated into the culture while the culture is being itself molded to it.

Livestock gives man something else, time—time to think, time to worry, time to invent, and new reasons to make war. A whole new subculture automatically grows up, stock-stealing, and with that new laws or, at least, customs of control and punishment. Of course, that requires enforcers, police, and they would also support the new concept of property and wealth. Eventually, new or adapted skills have to arise, butchering, shearing, carding, spinning, weaving, veterinary medicine. None of these skills evolved early on in the process. The work of the butcher would have been the first skill to achieve the status of craft. Men who hunted already had that skill, or the women of the clan did. Both men and women have done that kind of work in different cultures.

There are essentially two forms of evidence that we rely on for our history of what early man did with the animals he had begun enfolding into his life. In the earliest period, the evidence is in the form of bones. In later periods, it is pictorial. From cave paintings and petroglyphs, carved figures, miniature idols perhaps, friezes, ceramics, fabrics, paintings and sculpture, the record of each domestication has been an exercise in aesthetic record-keeping. Whether in supplication or boastful pride, man has always recorded the image of each new animal that became his. It is a gallery without walls that is suspended in time. And, too, a place where stories are told and memories solidified. Interestingly enough, man seems to have had no tribal memories before his relationships with animals. It is not just that it was so long ago when he was without them, but that there probably wasn't all that much to engrave on stone or in his mind. We emerged as human beings hunting and recorded that, and then we became shepherds and beyond. It was at that interface that the world opened up for us.

By five thousand years ago, domestic sheep remains accounted for a high percentage of all the bones present at many sites, insofar as they can be distinguished from goat remains. At one site, Shah Teepee in northern Iran, the remains of over one hundred domestic sheep have been found, and mixed in with them is evidence of three wild sheep. It is interesting to speculate why a band of people who were regularly slaughtering their own sheep for food would expend the energy necessary to hunt down wild sheep, which by then had to be fewer in number and more easily frightened off than they had been before domestication. Possibly wild sheep tried to link up with domestic flocks. Perhaps they tried to come in from the cold and found the butcher's knife waiting. Man would have learned early on that he did not want wild rams servicing his domestic ewes. It tended to make the lambs difficult to manage. It would have set "ease of handling" back when it occurred.

In Mesopotamia, about five thousand years ago, distinctly different breeds of sheep were identifiable, so things were moving along. One hairy breed had a throat ruff that was somewhat like an urial, but its tail had already lengthened and its horns were straight corkscrews, not curved. No wild sheep has horns like that. But in the Uric Period of Mesopotamia (up to six thousand years ago), there are thirty-one different ideograms for sheep. Allowing for two sexes and different ages, we still must speculate on there having been more than the two breeds we have identified in that area by bones alone. Because so much was going on, people were moving with newly discovered ease. The paramount problem of being able to feed themselves away from home base was no longer a difficulty to overcome. Goats and sheep could go anywhere Stone Age man could go. The effect that fact was having on man is not in the least obscure.

At Nasa (in Mesopotamia), a third breed evolved, a sheep with spiral curved horns, later known as the horns of ammon (and hence the fossil known as ammonite). It was clearly a domestic animal. It had fleece, its ears drooped and its nose was convex. Man was picking and choosing and breeding for what he wanted. We can't even guess if it was all done for practical considerations or for aesthetic reasons. Perhaps there were idealized animals earlier than we have suspected. At Ur, a fourth breed appeared, a fat-tailed sheep whose image was fired on a bowl that has been found there. Pottery had been invented by then, and before that, in that area, agriculture. The changes were enormous once domestication had forced the reformation of cultures. A fifth breed also appeared at Ur, a true wool sheep with long sticklike horns.

It is important to note that no wild sheep has ever had a woolly coat that was both heavy and curly. That is the coat of the domestic sheep. Even though wild sheep exposed to harsh winters develop a winter coat to augment their normal hairy covering, it has never been the fleece of the domestic sheep. There is some confusion, because as early as eight thousand years ago at Tepe Sarab in Iran, there were distinctly woolly sheep. We really can't reconstruct the sequence to our satisfaction, but we can draw lines like arrows into a richer future for the people of the cave and the flint chip. By the end of the Bronze Age in Europe (about 4000 B.C.), the transition from leather to woolen clothing was well advanced. Hairy sheep still persisted; perhaps they were dairy animals or preferred by some people for meat, but woolly was definitely "in."

Another change brought on by domestication was color. Wild sheep in the process of domestication became first white and then some white with black or brown faces and legs. No wild sheep ancestral to our domestic flocks has anything like those color conformations. And it is likely that the color white preceded woolliness. Man, purposefully or inadvertently, breeding for some characteristics, released other potentials locked in the genes of his new domestic animals. He got them whether he wanted them or not. That is still the case. Recessive genes crop up in our domestic animals today just as they did thousands of years ago, and some of them are highly undesirable.

Another feature that came before our version of woolly and essentially white animals was hornlessness, a characteristic that goes back ninety-five hundred years at least. It was probably the result of an effort by man to evolve animals that were less difficult to keep. If he was close-penning his sheep at night, hornlessness would have been an advantage. And another twist, this time in Poland: sheep with four horns, also a strictly domestic characteristic. At one and the same time, then, man in a number of locales was breeding selectively for sheep with no horns, two horns curved, two horns straight and four horns. There was a lot of experimentation going on and a lot more serendipity, we can be sure. Fat rumps, fat tails, short tails and tails that dragged on the ground, as well as many different grades of wool, were all being developed from the basic idea of the wild sheep turned white and woolly.

And how far did all of this sheep-related activity that started in Asia Minor and western Asia eventually go? Today, the list of sheep breeds and varieties numbers in the thousands. Many of them are trivial geographic alterations, some real, some imagined, but the full, recognized breeds of sheep number at least 326.

It is interesting to see where the art of refinement has been taken most earnestly, reflecting not only economic interest but also cultural emphasis and almost certainly chauvinism. The United States and Canada have between them eight distinct breeds that were evolved here in a relatively

short time. With imported breeds that have been allowed to remain intact, we have twenty-one. The former USSR developed fifty-eight breeds over a vast area to suit a great range of climates and cultures in Europe and Asia. Spain and Portugal together developed nineteen. France and Italy have engaged in constant refinement and have developed between them an amazing forty-seven breeds. Wales, Scotland and England, dedicated to both mutton and wool, developed forty-one. Australia and New Zealand, both with enormous holdings of sheep, evolved just four breeds, satisfied, apparently, to accept European breeds and keep them as they got them. Thirty-eight breeds evolved on the African continent and twenty-eight in India and Pakistan. In the Middle East, where it all may have started, just thirteen breeds are listed as indigenous.

All these are just the breeds still living. No one can even guess how many hundreds or even thousands of breeds were allowed to fall by the way during the process. No one keeps a roster of the losers no matter how much the winners are cherished. It is believed that in the world today, over a wide geographic spread and in a great variety of cultures, well over a billion sheep are maintained by man.

Their impact on our history has been enormous. The series of historical events known collectively as the Industrial Revolution was spawned, at least in part, by the the huge flocks of sheep that grazed in the British Isles and on the continent of Europe at the beginning of the eighteenth century. When the automated loom was invented and mills built to spin and weave wool and cotton, an agrarian economy was transformed into an industrial one. Masses of people left farms to work in the textile mills and live in unspeakable conditions. The filth and human degradation, the extreme overcrowding, the breakup of the family structure, the pollution of air and water, the outbreaks of disease, the violent and deep-seated social antagonisms, all were born of that new economic emphasis. And the sheep grazed placidly on. We are still reeling from the blow, still trying to recover our universal dignity and deal with the poverty, overcrowding and alienation the concept of the mill and factory gave us. Goats challenged our use of the land and all that it naturally contained. Sheep challenged our use of each other.

Australia and New Zealand were explored and annexed to become pastures for man's flocks. Out of the endless supply of lanolin, the multi-billion-dollar cosmetic industry arose. These and other consequences of the domestication of sheep have all been important factors in man's structuring of his contemporary world. Yet the wearing of wool cloth was a serendipitous development that could not possibly have been anticipated. It came about by accident, then turned the societies of man upside down. Those who argue intentionality in the initial domestication of animals might ponder that.

A word on cultural sequence. The ancient Greeks wondered about domestication just as we do. As far back as 320 B.C., Dicaearchus recorded a concept that we assume went back much further than his own time. He stated a sequence of (1) hunting and gathering, (2) domestication and then nomadic pastoralism and only then (3) agriculture. That sequence was accepted right up to our time as being *the* way it had to have been. But that is not so. Some New World peoples who never domesticated animals went on to agriculture anyway. There were overlaps, and in some areas, it is certain that people were scratching the earth before they were husbanding animals. In many places now, people do both. It is, in fact, rather typical of farms to practice the dual arts of agriculture and husbandry. It is generally only in those few places where pastoral nomads still move through their cycles that there is interest in animals alone. (Where shepherding and agriculture do coexist, one helps the other. Sheep manure is a precious commodity to the garden-keeper. It has twice the nitrogen and potassium of cow manure.)

I am not certain that anyone who has not spent time with sheep-herders can appreciate the intense involvement that exists between the shepherd and his flocks. The well-being of the flock is all, everything else falls by the wayside. All that is done the whole year long is attuned to that single overriding consideration of the flock. Man's fierceness in defending his flocks and his lack of tolerance for anything he even imagines impinging on them are remarkable. To people who keep sheep, it almost seems, every other animal on earth could perish and it would be of no account. No matter what language is being spoken, no matter the racial or national or religious affiliation of the shepherd, he is a part of a universal sheep culture. Sheep, once domesticated, became the focus of this culture, unique and universal in scope. And even though it now competes with many other fibers—natural and synthetic—the wool from domestic sheep has profoundly affected our own culture.

FOUR

Reindeer:
The Only Domestic Deer
in the World

The Cultural Context

The Finno-Ugric race is made up of many tribes and cultures. From Siberia west to the land of the Magyars and north into Finland and Lapland, they have extended their absolute faith in magic and shamanism, their drum-beating, their many difficult languages and their belief that all things have a soul. The reindeer has long been linked with these tribes and cultures, and certainly it, too, has a soul that is indissolubly linked with its body. When a reindeer's body dies, so does its soul, and that is why it is a cause for mourning.

In Norway, early huntsmen carved images of the reindeer as a symbol of force and power. Later, in the Bronze Age, in Vikso in modern Denmark, magnificent ceremonial helmets were made with the same symbolism. Like the horns of bulls, the antlers of reindeer have always been a synonym for a massive fist clenched around the handle of a heavy, broad-bladed sword.

The Koryaks are a northwestern extension of that Finno-Ugric cluster of cultures. One of their names for the northern constellation we call Ursa Major is Elwe'kyen, Wild Reindeer Buck. The Koryaks believe the creator journeyed to the stars to get reindeer for the people. And one of the most sacred possessions of these people, which every family must have, is a drum typically made of reindeer hide. If a shaman is required, he will come without a drum of his own and use the household instrument to overcome evil forces, even those handed down by the gods. The reindeer from whose body the drum was created sacrificed all in a cause that was good.

The Original Animal

The progenitor of today's domestic reindeer belongs to the same species, *Rangifer tarandus,* as the animal man now holds as a meat and milk source and a beast of burden. The lack of a name of its own for the domestic form is unusual but not unique. The reindeer's family is Cervidae, the deer family that has between thirty-eight and forty-one species depending on the eternal vagaries of taxonomy. It is the only deer ever domesticated, although experiments are now in progress in northern Russia with the

largest of all deer, the animal the Europeans call elk and we in North America call moose. (What we call elk in America is more properly wapiti.)

The Cervidae have had wide distribution. They are found in North and South America, Europe and Asia and just possibly in extreme northeastern Africa, although that continent is usually said to be without deer. They have been introduced into Australia and particularly New Zealand, where they have become pests.

Well within recorded history, the reindeer itself had a huge range: Ireland and Scotland up until the Middle Ages, Scandinavia and Germany up until Roman times, Poland until the sixteenth century, and Russia, Mongolia, China, Alaska, Canada, the continental United States and Greenland. In prehistoric times, the same species ranged south into Switzerland, France and Spain. No fossil ancestor has been found in all of Europe and Asia, and it is assumed the species originated in North America. In North America today, that same species is called caribou.

The reindeer is the only species of deer in which both the male and the female bear antlers. There is great diversity in antler form and size over its range, but the species remains the same. The males shed their antlers by November or December, the females shed them in the spring, while the young carry theirs into summer.

There are two forms of reindeer (and this is true as well for caribou), the tundra and the woodland, the latter perhaps better fed and generally larger, up to seven hundred pounds. As their names suggest, their habitat is open tundra to adjacent boreal forests.

The reindeer are the most gregarious of all deer. They gather in herds, and at times there may be twenty thousand animals per square kilometer. This is particularly true of the tundra form, and in North America alone, of both forms combined, at least thirty herds have been identified. There may be as many as two hundred thousand animals in a herd. In 1917, one herd in Canada was thought to contain twenty-five million animals.

The herds are like great pulsing masses. They separate by sex, combine to migrate and breed, then the females separate to give birth in May or June after a 228-day gestation period. The herds congregate again briefly, split apart by sexes for the summer, rejoin to migrate and then disperse for winter. The fawns are precocious. They can follow their mothers within an hour of birth, and some may give up nursing after only a month.

The diet of the reindeer is peculiar. There is not much biodiversity in their range, yet they are very picky eaters. At the coast, they will eat some seaweed; in woodlands, they will eat fungi. They will take leaves and some species of grass but not others. They will eat some twigs, some flower species, but not other closely related kinds. They like cranberry but not heaths. They are not keen on evergreen needles but eagerly take lichen, particularly the one known as "reindeer moss," which may be several feet thick. They will eat real moss only under near-starvation conditions.

Reindeer are able to convert this mass of unappealing but cellulose-rich vegetation into carbohydrates, fats and proteins for use by man as meat and milk, as hide, hair and work energy. They are large animals that must feed themselves in difficult conditions and have adapted well to do so. Perhaps the strangest reindeer peculiarity is their tendency toward a carnivorous diet, more so than any other ruminant. They will scavenge for fish and meat discarded by man, and they will scramble after lemmings, actually hunt them, especially when the lichen growth is down.

Clearly, the reindeer, in order to survive as large animals with high energy requirements in areas where they live, must have an intricate set of chemical signals that tell them what their bodies need. They alter their behavior, including their tastes, and seek what they need when they need it. One of their strangest needs is a near craze for human urine. They will take dog urine, do not particularly like their own species', but are fairly mad for human output. (They eat the snow wetted with urine.) Hunters and herders have used this craving to bait and in some measure control herds. It is also well known that, even though reindeer do not like accepting food from human hands, they will lick those hands endlessly for perspiration. These strange tastes may be due to the lack of salt in their diets.

Their Stone Age Role

For the Paleolithic hunter of ten to twelve thousand years ago, the reindeer was an extremely important source of meat, hide, sinew and bone. An association with man actually approaching domestication that long ago is suspected but not really known.

We can see today the history of the domestication of this species, whenever it began, in the sequential relationships still existing. In the most primitive stages of the association, men hunt wild reindeer as they do other animals in other parts of the world. Elsewhere, in other cultures, there is partial domestication because both man and animal migrate. The later association can also be seen—full domestication—where reindeer are milked and cheese manufactured, the animals pull sledges, carry burdens like any draft animal and are ridden under saddle. Some are harvested for meat and hides. About three million reindeer are maintained as domestic animals today, mostly in the former USSR. That area harvests thirty-two thousand tons of meat and 650,000 hides every year. Domesticated reindeer have been introduced into Iceland, the Orkney Islands, Scotland, the Kerguelen Islands, South Georgia Island, Alaska, Canada and Greenland, and efforts have been made in the lower forty-eight states.

The earliest keepers of reindeer were primitive tribes spread out over enormous land areas under severe climatic conditions. It is small wonder that the record they left is anywhere from difficult to interpret to nonexistent. The bones of wild and domestic reindeer do not differ, so there is no record there to be read. Reindeer herders routinely castrate their stags (by biting—an ancient practice), and the antlers of intact reindeer and castrated reindeer do differ. Where many of the latter are found in a small area, domestication can be supposed.

We know that herders were milking reindeer by A.D. 500 in Siberia, and long, long before that, herdsmen and children got milk by sucking on the does. Milking appears to have developed in two areas, Scandinavia and northern Asia. Cheese production is a modern craft.

Reindeer were used as beasts of burden in the first millennium B.C. It is possible that the use of reindeer for riding, for carrying burdens and for pulling sleds may not have evolved until the example had been established with horses and oxen. Some researchers, however, see incipient domestication as far back as 12,000 B.C., with Paleolithic man attempting and to a degree succeeding in controlling migration.

Herding

It is not difficult to understand reindeer hunters evolving as reindeer herders when we understand what the migration of these animals involves. Reindeer can move at fifty miles an hour when stressed and at normal speeds can cover thirty-five miles a day. A migration may extend over seven hundred miles each way. If a family depended on reindeer meat and fat for food, reindeer hide for clothing and shelter and reindeer antlers and bone for tools, there might well be a desire to slow things down a little and contain the source of all good things, rather than chase it endlessly at high speed across frozen wastes. At river crossings, the reindeer's path is predictable, but for the rest of the time, men and wolves just have to keep up and try to outguess the herd, which might be spooked off on a new tangent by things man, certainly, and possibly even wolves cannot detect. It would be a tiring way to obtain all of one's essentials in a harsh environment. Herding even in its most primitive forms must have seemed a desirable development. A movable feast is one thing, a reindeer migration another.

One clue to the antiquity of the association between man and controlled reindeer herds can be found in the difficult Lapp language. The Lapps have no other domestic food animal, so they have placed all their linguistic eggs in one basket. They have over fifty words that describe reindeer color and markings. They have almost that many words again for antler form and dozens more for age and sex distinctions. With so many defining characteristics, it is possible for herdsmen to distinguish one animal from among hundreds and perhaps thousands. I know of no parallel in the world of domestic animals.

While reindeer culture may be the key to a survival economy in one place, it is far more than that in others. Reindeer meat is of excellent quality, and marketable quantities have been produced in many areas including Alaska. Stags are easy to manage once they are castrated, and reasonable numbers can live off the land even when not migrating. They have long been a critical animal for people living in high northern latitudes of Europe and Asia. Their use may still be expanded somewhat, although it will perhaps always be within their natural range except, of course, on the night before Christmas.

I would guess that in our world south of the Arctic, not many of us have eaten reindeer. To other people, however, who are at least as sophisticated as we believe we are, it is normal fare. In a restaurant in Helsinki, where the waiters wear tuxedos and speak at least four languages, I have ordered from a menu that featured roast reindeer, braised reindeer tongue, reindeer sausage and a variety of other reindeer dishes that in just about any other context would sound impossibly exotic. Reindeer may not be important to us; in fact, it would be surprising if we were to encounter it on a menu in New York or Los Angeles. But to other people, its utilization, up to and including domestication, is a major cultural accomplishment and a matter of great economic importance.

It is interesting to note that the Inuit, the far northern peoples of Alaska, did not domesticate the caribou although they did hunt it. But in the northern reaches of Europe, these multiharvest animals (meat, fat, hide, milk, antler and bone)—along with fishing—made the complex cultures that evolved there possible. They are geographically remote cultures, and it is fair to say that the Lapp people have not much altered the course of history in Europe. But with relative isolation and reindeer, they have managed to survive it intact, and that is a major accomplishment.

Few domestic animals have been similarly limited by geography.

The scenario for most case histories has been one of dispersion. Not so the reindeer, for however intense its use has become, however sophisticated its management, it was and probably always will be an animal with its own special place near the top of the world.

FIVE

The Dog:
The Animal That Forever
Changed
the Emotions
of Man

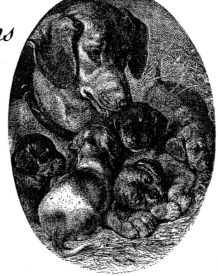

The Nature of the Beast

From the earliest times we can interpret, dogs have been close to the core of human consciousness. They have done far more than herd our sheep, drive our cattle and guard our homes. They have offered us an emotional treasure and an unconditional companionship that has become important to our physical as well as our psychological health. And we have celebrated them in our art, our legends, our myths and in our perception of the cosmos.

In ancient Greece, Homer wrote that Cerberus was a many-headed dog, giving the species a quality of magic at a time when magic was important and the knowledge of it proof of wisdom. Heracles's twelfth labor was to descend into Hades and fetch Cerberus. But dogs were not strangers to Heracles. For his tenth labor, he had to overcome Orthrus, a great dog that guarded a herd of giant red oxen. Later, Orthrus gave birth to the Sphinx.

Still in ancient Greek myth, the dog Maera was the companion of Icarius, who gave wine to some shepherds. Thinking they had been poisoned, they murdered Icarius and threw his body down a well. Maera helped Erigone, his master's daughter, find Icarius's body. Later, he was sent into the heavens as a messenger. And there he became the brightest star that shines, the Dog Star, Sirius. (One of my eleven dogs at the moment is a greyhound named Sirius or Yxerius, and I think of him as one of the brightest dogs that shine.)

In Japanese lore, the dog is one of the five most prominent of all creatures. The story is told of a dog that was traveling with his mistress and one other companion, a silkworm. The dog grew hungry, ate the silkworm and later produced a large quantity of silk in a single strand coming from one of his nostrils. When the dog died, his mistress buried him under a mulberry tree and prayed to the Buddha to thank him for having given her such a wonderful dog. Suddenly, the mulberry tree was covered with silkworms and the woman became rich.

In a Chinese tale, the emperor offered his daughter in marriage to anyone who could slay an enemy general who had been besting his armies. No human warrior dared try, but a dog did and succeeded. When the emperor explained that the princess could not marry a dog, the dog countered that if he were placed under a bell for 280 days, he would emerge a man. On the 279th day, the emperor could not restrain himself and peeked under the bell. The transformation was not quite complete and there stood a man with a dog's head. At the wedding, the groom wore a red cloth to hide his head. Members of a tribe known as the Jung centered in Fuchow still wear a red covering to hide their features.

Eskimos look upon dogs (qimmit) as the dividing line between rich and poor. People without dogs are considered poor. These people of the far north think of dogs as being without souls unless given a human name, often the name of a deceased relative. Such a dog is taken into the home and better fed than the other dogs. Dogs are trained by women and there is a special mystique about how it should be done.

On the American plains, a series of complex cultures arose along the migratory routes of the great bison herds. The men of many tribes belonged to societies with very serious obligations. Members of the Dog Society were committed to the protection of the people, and there was a particularly warlike ritual known as the Dog Dance.

Wherever one turns, from preagricultural times to the present, the dog is there. It has not always been treated well—the degree to which that is true is strange, to say the least—but no other animal that we have domesticated has held a firmer grip on the human heart and mind. Clearly, we are two species that were meant for each other. The dog would not have come into being without us, but what we would be without the dog is difficult to imagine.

The Origin

The source of the domestic dog has been almost universally believed to be in whole or large part the wolf, at least one subspecies, *Canis lupus pallipes*. But it now seems certain that other subspecies had to be involved as well, and perhaps even other canine species. *Pallipes,* a rather small, essentially desert wolf, is still found from modern Egypt to India. I have heard them howling at night in the craggy hills of the Sinai Peninsula. It is as eerie and wonderful an experience there as the song of the wolf is anywhere it is heard. It is a sound that links hemispheres. It is the generic sound of the wilderness that seems to transport one back to another kind of time, another kind of life. (Shepherds seldom share this feeling, however, since the desert wolf preys on their flocks.)

There can be no doubt that in time, larger, more heavily coated Arctic wolves were used to help create the northern spitz group of dogs we know today. That would include the now diminutive Pomeranian, the Chow Chow, and the powerful sled dogs found around the top of the world. The Samoyed from Siberia, and the Siberian husky, Alaskan mala-

mute, Canadian Eskimo, Norwegian elkhound and Finnish spitz would all be included.

At one time, the Austrian ethologist Konrad Lorenz believed that the jackal was part of our dog's history. Because Lorenz was so highly respected, the idea took on currency that we now believe it did not deserve. Lorenz lived to regret ever having postulated the theory and back we all went to the wolf, Lorenz in the lead—the wolf with another but unidentified constituent, that is. And there it would appear to stand today. But some very perplexing questions remain unanswered. No other animal we have domesticated is as indecipherable.

The "where" of the wolf phase of this seminal association of man and animal seems easier to pinpoint than the "when." Somewhere in the Middle East, or between there and the Indian subcontinent, seems apparent for at least one of the earliest wolf/dog transmutations, but when? Some students of the subject have put the dog before the goat or the sheep, or at least contemporaneous with them. If so, its early domestication came about near the transition from the Paleolithic to the Mesolithic ages—between twelve thousand and fourteen thousand years ago in some areas—and we may never be able to be more precise than that. The first dog was whelped in a cave, however; of that much we can be certain. The dog preceded architecture. But evidence seems to make it highly unlikely that this was the only domestication of the dog. The geography of the earliest dogs may be the most confounding single subject in the entire history of the human/animal bond.

Before Domestication

The predomestication association of man and wolf is easy to envision. Wolves scavenge and man discards. (And man scavenges and a rain of rocks could convince wolves to discard.) That would be almost enough to explain the domestication process with this species, but there is this, too. People still eat dogs in a number of cultures, and surely they ate wolves back in the cave. Early Mesolithic hunters undoubtedly stole pups or cubs from wolf dens. And without refrigeration, they would have found it more practical to keep some alive in the care of women and children rather than kill them all at once and lose a part of the meat to spoilage. Just the presence of pups in the cave would have started the process of domestication with no factor other than man's natural love of companion animals to drive it. Wolf cubs are endlessly appealing. They play, they pounce, they chew and lick

and they whine and mock-growl. They are also warm, intelligent, interactive and have large eyes that look to the front like our own. They cuddle when they are tired, and their puppy breath is very attractive to human beings. It awakens something in us. Those were probably enough excuses for man to "invent" the dog.

Early Associations

If the actual sequence in which wolves/dogs were domesticated and kept as hunting partners and companions could be deciphered, we would know a great deal more about our own history as well. At the end of the last Ice Age, there were dogs in Germany and Denmark, and soon after in Switzerland. All that between nine and twelve thousand years ago. Note, they were no longer wolves. They were already dogs. There were dogs in ancient England and Scotland. Before the Stone Age began to phase out, there were true dogs in Russia and France. Bosnia and Italy also had dogs, and by the beginning of the Bronze Age, breeds like the modern collie and German shepherd can be distinguished. Lake dwellers in Switzerland apparently preferred smaller dogs, which suggests that they kept them in their stilted homes.

At least four distinct breeds or types of dogs are known from ancient Europe. There was a wolflike polar dog that could have been used as a beast of burden very early on. And in the British Isles, there were the shepherd-type dogs already mentioned, an ancestral houndlike dog and a small house dog that could have later given rise to the terriers.

At the same time, pariah dogs were found over much of Africa, India and into southeastern Asia, at least as far as Java. In Asia Minor, dog remains that are still somewhat wolflike date back almost eleven thousand years. There was a dog in Belt Cave in Persia almost twelve thousand years ago. Well west of Egypt, in Algeria, there were also dogs, although the time sequence there is fuzzy. In Egypt itself, houndlike dogs would soon be deified and set to guard the tombs of kings. Greyhounds are distinguishable in Egypt from predynastic times. Similar dogs were in Spain, northwest Africa, Malta and the Canary Islands.

The pariah dogs of Asia and Africa have many similarities with the dingo that was carried to Australia in very ancient times. (It had to have been carried by man. There is no fossil record on that continent to account for a placental animal anything like a canid.) There the dingo became a feral hunter of primitive marsupials that were ill equipped to avoid such a clever enemy. The dingo may have reached Australia even before the Middle Stone Age dogs emerged in Europe and Asia. Perhaps that long ago dogs of several types were also in Japan.

On a recent trip to Borneo, I stayed briefly with Iban natives in their rain forest "long house," 206 people in a single structure with their numerous dogs and fighting cocks. The dogs there have a distinct dingo look to them—the somewhat snipey muzzle accented by very wide jaws at the hinge. The upright ears point slightly forward, and the tail carriage is again very dingolike. Interestingly enough, the dogs in this particular settlement were predominantly black and white, whereas most of the village dogs I had seen while traveling across both Sabah and Sarawak in northern Borneo were dingo-color, golden red to fawn. Somehow, black and white genes had gotten into this particular gene pool but had not altered the dingo structure, even if it had robbed the pool of dingo colors.

Now the questions. Was the dingo descended from dogs domesticated in the areas between Israel and India, then transported all the way to Australia by very early settlers, ancestors of today's Australian Aborigines? And how long did that take, in how many stages? That seems unlikely, given the distances involved. Were those same genes carried to Borneo directly, or are the Bornean dogs descended from dingoes that moved north from Australia? Or did the dingo get to Australia from Borneo, and could both the Australian feral dog and the present Bornean dogs be descended from a different domestication than the one descending from *C. l. pallipes*? And if it was a different domestication, was the wolf the ancestor or was there a species of truly wild dog involved? These are questions that need answering, and with DNA study techniques, we may be able to address them seriously for the first time. Speculation and opinion may have to yield at last.

The New World

There is also a mystery surrounding the appearance of dogs in the Western Hemisphere. In Peru, there was a shepherd type, a dachshundlike dog and one that is best described as a "bulldog." We have generally assumed that they were brought there by visitors, since South America as an independent site of dog domestication has not usually been taken very seriously. (If domestic dogs were, in fact, transported to South America *thousands* of years ago, and it seems certain that they must have been if they were not domesticated there, we can only wonder who brought them.)

In a cave site in modern Idaho, dog remains date back at least eight thousand years. How did they get from Egypt/India to Idaho that long ago? The mystery deepens when we move around the world and consider the mastiff. It may have originated in Tibet. Yet, when the Romans invaded the British Isles, they found the "savages" there had a mastiff of their own. Exactly what were the movements of early man? The appearance of the dog doesn't match what we have believed we knew of our own history.

Once the goat set us free to travel with our own store of live food, when and where did we go? Wherever it was, when we got there, we apparently left dogs behind like fingerprints. But why did we go away and then forget that we had ever been there at all? Why did we not have traditional memories of those journeys?

From Wolf to Dog

There are distinct characteristics that make it not only possible but also relatively easy to separate wolf bones from those of domestic dogs. Dwarfism and short-leggedness as found in the dachshund, basset and bulldogs, for example, are clearly the results of domestication. All such grotesque features are, including the "push-face" look. Those are definitely not survival characteristics. The dog's back is generally straighter and shorter than that of the wolf, and its chest tends to be more barrel-like and less keeled than seen in its wild ancestor's cross-section. As a result, the dog's forelegs are turned out at the shoulders, giving it a distinctive gait. The wolf places its hind feet in the imprint of its forefeet, while a dog places its hind feet inside the forefeet marks.

The dog's tail is carried in a variety of positions, but wherever it is in a specific breed or type, the animal's anus shows. That is never true of the wolf, which is evident to the archaeologist in the shape of the vertebra. Dog muzzles are shorter than wolf muzzles, and the teeth are smaller and closer together as a result. The brain capacity of the wolf is half again as large as that of a dog of the same size. And there are at least a dozen more characteristics that clearly distinguish the remains of the dog from those of the wolf.

In all of this, the matter of neoteny is of paramount importance. Neoteny is the retention of juvenile characteristics into adult years. A dog, in one very real sense, is a wolf cub that won't ever grow up. It is possible to find neotenous traits in almost all domestic animals, but in companion animals, it is most apparent in the dog and the cat.

When we speak of species that were surely dangerous to handle in their wild forms, neoteny takes on an additional importance. Juvenile animals are easier to manage than adults in most cases. Animals that tend to act like submissive, food-begging babies even as adults appeal to us and surely appealed to our forebears in the cave, another factor in their domestication.

If we were to accept a single subspecies of wolf as the only ancestor of all of the world's domestic dog breeds, we could move on from that point without too much difficulty except in the matter of our own early movements. There remains that nagging doubt, however, and it should be acknowledged again. What if one of the now extinct nonwolf *wild* canine species (and there were a number that became extinct within our time frame) gave rise to a dingolike pariah dog and it, in turn, gave rise to at least some of today's breeds of domestic dogs? In that scenario, the wolf would be only a contributor to a very malleable and vigorous new species. That will be sorted out in time, but meanwhile the wolf in one or several subspecies remains the ancestor of choice by default, as much as for any other reason. Yet the possibility exists that some dogs are descended from the wolf and some from a species (or several species) of true wild dogs, and if that is so, today's domestic dogs would have to be hybrids.

The amount of crossbreeding that has been done to derive the hundreds of modern breeds has been bewildering. And, again, another species besides the basic wolf could account for the incredible malleability of the dog's genes. We have no other species in our domestic pantheon in which one example can weigh barely 3 pounds (Chihuahua) and another 220 pounds (Saint Bernard, Newfoundland). Just envision a Yorkshire terrier standing beside an Irish wolfhound, borzoi or a Scottish deerhound. Today, they belong to a single species.

As the announcer of the Westminster Kennel Club Dog Show for twenty years, I have sat at the judges' trophy table and watched the AKC recognized breeds, all of them, move by. A year has not passed that I have not studied their astounding variety and pondered the matter of their origin. I understand that contemporary conventional wisdom says that one species is ancestral to all the dogs there are, but I am no longer able to believe that. Conventional wisdom, I fear, is often conventional error.

The Herding Instinct

When and where man was first able to control the natural aggression of his wolf/dog/plus? and turn it to herding is unknown. When it did happen, however, it opened wide the door to economic growth that had begun with the first controllable goats. It could not have been too long before dogs were essential to the process. Some dogs evolved to protect goats and sheep from their wild predators and others to guide and direct them. Dogs that were aggressive toward their charges, stock-killers, were, then as now, quickly identified and killed. Non-stock-killers lived to reproduce offspring like themselves.

Wolves had the herding instinct in their original genetic package. Herding after their own fashion and cutting off easy prey is one of their

hunting techniques. By harnessing that skill, man evolved the miraculous herding dogs, among the most intelligent of all breeds. Eventually, when goats, sheep and cattle were kept in huge numbers, the economic value of herders, guards and drovers was beyond estimate. Even today, in places like Australia, New Zealand and Scotland (and many others in the Middle East, Asia and Africa), the loss of the stock dog would have an enormous economic impact.

One of the dogs currently in my own family is a Border collie, and watching this dog is a lesson in dog behavior unlike that in any other breed I have come to know well. Herding, controlled aggression, is a compulsion. As so many other owners of the breed have reported, if given nothing else to herd, a Border collie will herd the bathtub, the basin and the toilet bowl. They are possessed and collapse at night from exhaustion after having spent the entire day running at near full tilt. Our Duncan, an appropriately Scots name, herds our llamas, alpacas, horses, donkeys, cats and other dogs, and particularly our geese. His drive to herd but never touch is phenomenal. I shudder to think of one in a small apartment.

The Guard Dog and the Retriever

Wolves are naturally territorial and protective of food and their young. It would not have been hard to turn that genetic bent into the watch/guard dog that once protected the cave and now patrols military bases. Wolves bring food home to their young, and in that trait probably lies the beginning of the retriever. Wolves live in a structured pack, and therein lies the relative ease of obedience training. In fact, the wolf contained the dog, our perfect companion, and all we had to do was find it, release it and style it. The species once extracted has proven to be remarkably well suited to our ways of life, whether they work for their keep or *we* work for their keep. Assuming that other unknown ingredient, of course, raises a whole volume of questions. What did this mysterious other species contribute and what the wolf?

The dog today exists in the bewildering variety already spoken of. In the United States alone, the American Kennel Club, the principal purebred dog registry, recognizes 155 breeds and varieties as of 1996. The United Kennel Club, a family-run registry, recognizes 166 breeds, while the Canadian Kennel Club lists 155. The Kennel Club in the United Kingdom lists 186 breeds. Worldwide, however, there are somewhere between 450 and 850 breeds, and it is certain that hundreds of others were

selectively developed down through the millennia but allowed to become extinct. There are breeds today that are close to extinction and their loss seems certain. And it is a loss when a breed of animal vanishes. A whole chapter in our own history, a special view of aesthetics and utility, vanishes with each breed that dies out. What is happening to wildlife *species* is happening at about the same rate to domestic animal *breeds*. Biodiversity is dwindling. The course man took once he had the goat under control continues unabated. The assault on biodiversity is the most perverse thing man has ever undertaken, and future, wiser cultures will be astounded as they uncover the record in our present-day caves and tells.

Of Grave Concern

Far, far too many domestic dogs are now born every day around the world. There is no possible way that the puppies can be housed and cared for as pets in the numbers that appear. At best, these "surplus" dogs are euthanized; at worst, they are turned loose to seek their own fate in a then hostile world. They have an impact on wildlife to an extent that hasn't yet been reckoned. Frustration over this tragic situation has led some people to propose that a moratorium be declared on all dog breeding. It is a well-intentioned suggestion, but it must be taken into account that the majority of the "surplus" dogs whelped, over 90 percent, are random-bred, dogs of mixed ancestry. They are as sensitive, as lovable and as needy as any purebred dog and serve every bit as well as companion animals.

The extermination of purebred dogs as a kind of retaliation against irresponsible dog owners is not the answer. If all purposeful, carefully considered breeding were to stop tomorrow, within eight or nine years, the mastiff-line dogs, mastiff, bullmastiff, Great Dane, Newfoundland, Saint Bernard, bulldog, Great Pyrenees, Kuvasz, Komondor, Bernese mountain dog, rottweiler, and many more short-lived breeds, including all of the other giants, bloodhound, Scottish deerhound, Irish wolfhound, borzoi, would disappear. Five or six years after that, all of the other pure breeds would vanish, too. The loss to our culture, traditions and our sense of aesthetics would be incalculable.

A wiser course is to spay or neuter all random-bred dogs before they can reproduce. Following the basic tenets of domestication, the finest examples of the pure breed lines should be identified and bred, but only at a rate that human society can accommodate. Lesser examples of the pure breeds should also be humanely rendered incapable of reproducing. The two principal purposes for breeding any domestic animal are: (1) in the short run, to acquire desired offspring for immediate use and (2) in the long run, to preserve the best gene pool possible.

Dogs have been used as military and police guards, as home watch-dogs, baby-sitters, beasts of burden in both peace and war, as messengers, as drug, gun and explosives detectors and extensively as cattle drovers, shepherds and flock guards. They have led the blind, guided the hearing-impaired and helped the handicapped to deal with everyday life. They have tracked and trailed children, lost campers and escaped convicts. They have hunted as pack hounds, as pointers, spaniels, setters, terriers and retrievers and served generally as utility animals. But no task has engaged more dogs than the task of companionship. True, dogs have had significant economic value (particularly as drovers and shepherds), but still, today at least, their biggest job, the one for which we as a species are most profoundly grateful, is their capacity for nonjudgmental friendship. That, in itself, is a remarkable contribution to human history.

We have in the dog created a species of animal quite different from our own to depend on us, interact with us at an intensely personal level, to seemingly love us. Far from being peculiar or "unnatural," the proven psychological and physiological benefits of this bonding have been enormous.

The roles dogs play in our families and cultures are really just now being evaluated, instead of being taken for granted. As "role models" for children, they display what we define as bravery, loyalty, courage, intelligence and other cherished social values. It is believed that responsible pet ownership can lead toward good parenting, and the of companionship of a pet is known to be of distinct therapeutic value.

Although there are and have been for four thousand years true "cat lovers," and some cage birds have played a role in the human emotional condition (horses, too, have been "loved"), no animal that we have domesticated has played anything like the role the dog has assumed. The literature on the subject is vast and ranges from poetry that appears to border on the neurotic to psychoanalytical studies that catalog an intense interreliance with profound benefits for man. The dog almost seems an extension of ourselves, and for a great many people, that is not a subject open to debate.

PART TWO
EARLY AGRICULTURE

SIX

Cattle:
A Fierce Giant Subdued

The Symbolic Bull

The worship—or at least the adoration—of cattle has been universal since prehistoric times. As wild animals, before the beginning of their domestication, their progenitors were apparently awesome. The real love affair, however, blossomed once domestication was under way. The powerful male animal, the soon-to-be-sacred bull, was admired and later treasured for its fearlessness, its combativeness and its astounding fertility.

(In fact, an important stud bull today releases enough sperm in a single ejaculation to fertilize three hundred cows. In the time-honored tradition of "Waste not, want not," the managers of beef and dairy herds harness that enormous reproductive power by freezing sperm in liquid nitrogen for later use in artificial insemination, and by the scientific wizardry of the implantation of a fertilized embryo.)

Today, in some Latin countries, the bizarre festival atmosphere of the bullring is a holdover from ancient fertility rites. It can only be viewed as a ballet of death. The combat between man and bull as a test of masculinity is one of the oldest truly savage rituals to hang on into modern times. Originally, sex orgies were undoubtedly attached to such religious rites masquerading as "sporting" events. Or perhaps they were "sporting" events masquerading as religious rites.

What really is involved in the bullfight, of course, is animal sacrifice. Although the occasional bespangled bullfighter gets killed, it is the bull that is invariably slaughtered, a role originally played by a goat, a sheep or a virgin all dressed in white. Other quasi-religious rites in the same countries involving bulls forgo the trappings. The animals are simply tortured and killed. There are no longer any parallels to this extraordinary and anachronistic Latin relationship with the bull. The fact that the spectators are not nude and rolling around on piles of cushions seems to be the only concession made to modern convention.

In another testament to the bull's power and fertility, phallic statues dating very far back often display alarmingly disproportionate penises. That is because although the figure is that of a man, the penis is that of a bull. In Babylon, bulls or bull-like forms guarded the entrances to most important buildings. The bull and the king were often intertwined in mythology and symbology. That symbology apparently lives on in our subconscious minds. Male patients undergoing psychoanalysis, it has been said, have reported dreams that reveal their desire to kill their fathers—who appear in their dreams as bulls.

In Persia, the bull was represented as the force from which the power of life comes. Bulls were sacrificed to Mithra, the god of light. Mithra's companion was a dog, and the dog and the bull were often depicted together. In Hebrew tradition and in Assyrian, too, the image of the horns of a bull embracing the disk of the sun is equated with power.

And the Cow

In dramatic contrast, the cow is the symbol of love and fecundity. She is the creative principle, the great all-giving nurturer, and she appeared as a figure variously admired, beloved or actually held sacred throughout ancient times. She is Isis. She is Io. She is the admired of Zeus. She is Aphrodite. And before Moses could stop him, Aaron erected an idol for the Israelites in the desert, a golden calf. Its worship was almost certainly at least in part sexual in expression, as well as symbolic of devotion to the temporal and material as opposed to the spiritual.

The bull and the cow, no matter where we turn in the past, have symbolized fertility, fecundity, force, power, passion, love, sex, nurturance, milk, the parents, the sacred and beloved of the gods, the sun, the origin, the source, the spring, the givers—all positive attributes that are still the capstones of major economies today. Our association with cattle has been a long and extremely fruitful one for our species. On a personal note, I heard it summed up by a man whose life has been devoted to cattle. His name is Bill Pickens, and he is a Ph.D. reproductive physiologist now retired from Colorado State University in Fort Collins. It was a bitterly cold morning and we were standing beside a feedlot enclosure packed with cattle. Their bodies were steaming in the brisk air. Vapor and dust hung over them in a cloud backlit by the golden mountain sunrise. With a distinctly mystical tone in his voice and a faraway look on his face, Dr. Pickens stared out across the cattle and said to himself, "Damn, but I love cows." I don't think he knows I heard him.

The domestication of cattle appears to have begun in Europe well before six thousand years ago. There were distinct breeds of cattle in Europe by 2500 B.C., which means their domestication had to have begun long before that. The new species would go on to become the most valuable of all domestic animals, producing milk, butter and cheese, meat, fat, horn, hides, manure and motive power. Cattle then as now represent great wealth. In Africa, I was once offered seven cows for my very, very pretty seventeen-year-old daughter. She was not amused. Her mother and I were. We had no intention of getting into cattle-ranching.

The Origin

During the Pleistocene era, there were two hollow-horned ruminants in Europe. The bison, or wisent, as the European form of this animal is known, still survives, although in small numbers, mostly in Poland. The other, the aurochs *(Bos primigenius),* has been extinct since A.D. 1627, when the last known specimen, a captive, died in a Polish park. But the aurochs lives on around the world in our domestic cattle.

Not a great deal is known about the wild ancestors of most of our cattle, including where they originated. They do not appear to have originated in Europe, or at least their ancestors there have not been identified in fossil form. They may have migrated to Europe between Ice Ages, in all likelihood from somewhere in Asia.

All true wild cattle should be considered members of the genus *Bos.* The bison of Europe and North America are in the genus *Bison,* the yak belongs to the genus *Poephagus,* the powerful Asian gaur is in the genus *Bibos,* and the water buffalo of Asia in the genus *Bubalus.* The very different

African or Cape buffalo is in the genus *Syncerus.* The anoa is named for its genus, *Anoa.* But in Cambodia, there is a form known as the kouprey that may be a cross between species of genera *Bos* and *Bibos.* Therein lies the confusion. All of the above genera can apparently interbreed and produce at least a high percentage of fertile offspring. According to our basic understanding of genus and species, they shouldn't be able to do that.

The domestic cattle we have today have been considered in large part the descendants of the aurochs, but at different times and at different places, any of the other wild species could have been used to strengthen or otherwise alter the emerging domestic breeds. The humped cattle of the Indian subcontinent appear to have their own history. There could have

been planned or accidental interbreedings. In fact, considerable DNA evidence now points to two lines of descent. Between 200,000 and a million years ago, the evidence shows, there was a divergence between the European or taurine cattle (to which the aurochs belonged) and the Indian or zebu cattle that we refer to as *indicus.* Apparently, both lines were eventually domesticated by different cultures in different places. The cattle now in Africa were descended from the European taurine line in part, with the humped zebu playing a role as well. That is also true of many lines of beef cattle in North America today.

The aurochs was a formidable animal. It was between six and a half and seven feet tall at the shoulders, putting its head more than seven feet and the tips of its horns between eight and eight and a half feet above the ground. Consider that our forebears were generally much shorter than we are today, and then imagine what an aurochs must have looked like from that eye level.

The giant animal was black or reddish black with a white stripe down its back and white, curly hair around the bases of its horns. Its muzzle was light gray and its coat ran from slick and shiny in the summer to heavy and curly in the winter. There were color variations between males and females, age groups (the calves were red until they were six months old) and geographical races or varieties. That was also true of horn shape and size. The many variations that occurred naturally marked the species as ripe for selective breeding. It was malleable.

Breeding experiments conducted in zoos in Berlin and Munich starting in the 1920s resulted in offspring closely matching early depictions of wild cattle on cave walls and pottery. These reconstituted aurochs reveal interesting traits that reflect where, how and why they were taken into custody. Their body form is not the only thing that flashes back to the Stone Age. Their temperament does, too. They are fierce and unpredictable. They are quick and agile. They are shy, temperamental and suspicious. In a word, due to their great size and strength, they are distinctly dangerous. And these experimental re-creations are considerably smaller than the originals.

In fact, of all the animals man was to domesticate, the aurochs was perhaps the most dangerous. The mortality rate among early herdsmen must have been significant. It was a wonder that man persisted until the cattle he kept were tractable. With the exception of a few breeds and generally the prizewinning bulls of other breeds, domestic cattle today are far smaller than their wild ancestors. That may have been a fortuitous result of the breeding man was doing for other desirable traits, or it may have been that the early husbandmen were working to increase their own odds for survival by decreasing the size of their charges. Size and tractability were certainly considerations, and even today, with the use of the charged bull prods, barbed and electrified fencing and tranquilizing drugs, they still are. Cattlemen like knowing that they will still be alive after their work is over for the day. No farmer wants to hear *ole!* in his pasture. Only in a relatively few Latin countries where "Fighting Bull" is the name of an actual breed (aka *toro de lidia* or *ganado bravo*), do stockmen breed for the original ferocity of the aurochs, albeit in a much smaller package. Everywhere else in the world, the trend for six to eight thousand years at least has been to quiet the species down and make the animals tractable.

What did cattle supply to man that goats and sheep did not? Before tackling the awesome aurochs, man already had the other two species well along in their development. Why cattle, animals that were not only dangerous but also much more labor intensive than sheep and goats, were domesticated when theoretically they were not really needed is something of a mystery. They were needed, as it turned out, but the early domesticators couldn't have known that. They probably had not learned to use milk and cheese, even though goats were already available, and they could not have fully understood the value of cow dung in land renewal unless they were agriculturists and, apparently, they were only just moving in that direction. The invention of the wheel and the plow both followed the domestication of cattle ("oxen") and could not have been anticipated. (The water buffalo in India and later in China were being developed as a domestic animal at the same time as true cattle or shortly thereafter. Wheels and plows may have been developed as much to accommodate the newfound power of one as much as the other. But with water buffalo and oxen both available, man could literally move mountains or their equivalent. And once rice cultivation got under way, he did just that.)

The meat and hides of the wild aurochs were available because the great beasts were widely hunted. But it wasn't until after domestication that their milk could be identified as a valuable product of husbandry (even if goat's milk was already being harvested). That was true of manure beyond agricultural applications. The discovery that it was valuable as a building material probably did not occur until after cattle were being closely held. The importance of manure as a fuel followed closely behind deforestation and overbrowsing by goats, as wood became progressively more difficult to find.

Clearly, the immense value of cattle emerged only after domestication. And it is possible that man first began trying to control aurochs simply because he admired them. If man would come to worship the smaller cattle he eventually developed and equate them with power, light and life, imagine the awe he must have felt for the fierce, giant wild form. Man, with his first domestications, was gaining a measure of control over his own destiny that he had never before had. It was a new degree of hubris he must have experienced. He no longer was totally reactive in his struggle to survive. He had wealth and power. By controlling his herds and flocks, he was controlling, in a sense, nature. Was the aurochs something he needed to control for economic or for spiritual and psychological reasons?

A sidebar to our domestication of animals with dairy potential involves our own genetic makeup. No mammals in the wild state normally have access to milk after they have been weaned. That is as true of us as it is of the gorilla, the capybara and the three-toed sloth. The principal sugar in milk is lactose. It is broken down in our bodies by an enzyme called lactase that is produced in the walls of our small intestines. When lactase is present, the products of lactose digestion can be absorbed into the circulatory system. When lactase is absent, lactose passes through the digestive system without making a nutritional contribution. In fact, undigested milk can cause bloating, diarrhea and severe cramps. For some people, it is a

poison and can cause not only gastrointestinal disorders but also symptoms up to and including permanent blindness.

Depending on race, a large percentage of adults lose the ability to produce lactase, a genetically controlled function. When they no longer need the enzyme because the age of natural milk intake has passed, a genetic signal is given and adult bodies no longer produce it. (Is this natural chemical economy or an "energy-saving device"?) Northern Europeans now generally continue to produce lactase as adults, while Oriental, Amerindian, some southern European, Australian Aborigine and African populations do not. (Consider which populations have traditionally produced cheese.)

For an adult to have used milk, a change in the genetic makeup of the human species was required. Before domestication, the normal condition for adult human beings worldwide was lactase deficiency and, as a result, the inability to gain nutritional value from goat, reindeer or cow milk. Thus, the domestication of these animals effected dramatic changes not only in man's culture, environment and economy, but also in his evolution.

Beyond the Dairy

The great ruminant offered more than products as it came under human management; it offered services. Beyond its ceremonial uses, it would become the most important source of draft and drawing power in the ancient and historical world. The value of cattle and specifically oxen as beasts of burden, as the pullers of plows and drawers of carts and water, cannot be overstated. (Oxen are any cattle trained as beasts of burden, although they usually are castrated males.) Around the world, even today, oxen are the most widely used draft animals. The dominance of the horse

on the recent European and American scenes presents a distorted picture of global animal economics.

An equally valuable service provided by cattle is land management. Herds can be moved to where they are needed to lay down their manure. That product (it is so versatile and valuable it cannot really be called a by-product) is still the most widely used fertilizer in the world. It is organic, free for the harvesting and nonpolluting. It is also an endlessly renewable resource requiring no labor in its production other than the tending of flocks and herds. In short, it is one of the richest animal products in the world.

The grasses that domestic animals convert for our eventual use in products and services evolved under the stress of grazing. Although these animals require it in order to be most productive, grazing has taken on an evil image among the environmentally concerned, and understandably so, but that can be a somewhat shallow view. Grazing is essential; *over*grazing is beyond foolish, it is downright villainous. It is total mismanagement. Properly managed cattle maintain their habitat, since they fertilize as they eat, where they eat. They feed the system that is feeding them and they, in turn, feed man with products and further services.

The Sequence

The predomestication association of man and aurochs is easy to envision. Men hunted them. (Women probably did not if we are to go by the Stone Age cultures with which we are familiar.) They were among the greatest prizes there for the taking. They provided meat by the hundred-weight, and fat, sinew and both bone and horn, and there were hides. There must have been enormous status and pride in the accomplishment. Perhaps even more than with the other animals that man hunted, the taking of the aurochs was a rite of either passage or reaffirmation. It must always have been an event.

As a ruminant, the aurochs was a grazing animal (in the winter probably a browser as well). Aurochs out on open ground, grazing in groups that in some cases must have been large and easily alerted, had to have been both difficult and dangerous to hunt. Man did not yet have horses and couldn't ride in over a ridge like the wind. He was on foot and pitted against tough, aggressive and suspicious prey. A herd of fifty animals has one hundred eyes, one hundred nostrils and one hundred ears. It also has young to protect. There had to have been an easier way than crawling across open ground on hands and knees, trying to look like a clump of grass while getting close enough to strike with primitive and almost certainly not immediately lethal weapons. And those early hunters found it. In a word, it was herding.

Using natural elevations, land features like gullies, cliffs, valleys and riverbeds, and at times augmenting them with windfalls, rocks and brush piles, men could have stampeded herds into manageable holding areas. Fire was an easy tool with which to trigger a stampede, and man already had fire under his control. A second device, a line of hunters beating drums and shaking rattles made from tortoise shells, could have made more than enough noise to intimidate, confuse and drive wild herds toward camouflaged containments.

We assume from boneyards discovered near the bases of cliffs that primitive hunters drove herds off precipices to die on the rocks below. Less wasteful and far more sophisticated would have been the drive into a compound where the animals could be controlled until singled out for slaughter or other use. Once man was holding cattle in areas of his choosing and to some degree of his design, the first step was taken. Religion and just plain bravado would have resulted in interaction with these captive herds, including extremely hazardous physical contact. Braided strips of animal hide used as ropes could have added strength to brute force. Once that "rodeo" was born, domestication had begun.

If man could contain a herd, he could divide it up and decide which animals to slaughter, which to ride or otherwise interact with directly, and which to allow to breed. Cattle bear precocious young that can be separated from the nervous and aggressive adults very early in life. Animals deprived of tutorial alarm calls and the shuffling of their parents soon begin losing their fear, or at least that is so with many species. They become progressively more manageable with every generation. It wouldn't take long before traditions were born among the herders. And once people have traditions involving a specific animal, that animal has been truly enfolded into a culture. Within three or four generations, people wouldn't be able to remember or even imagine a time when they didn't have cattle.

Of course, the time frame was not that brief. When we speak of the span between stampeding aurochs off cliffs and breeding dairy cattle, we are speaking more of millennia than of generations. It has always taken a very long time to truly domesticate a new species of animal.

If hunters six, seven or eight thousand years ago began bottling aurochs up in containments of their choosing, did those areas include enough grass and water to sustain the animals? Originally, in large areas, they may have, but the more totally man managed those animals, the more numerous and inevitably smaller the compounds became. When did our ancestors start providing water and food? Sooner or later, they had to. It quickly must have become a specialized occupation. And whenever that happened, man's relationship to the animals must have changed dramatically. He was truly "keeping" them.

By 4000 B.C., humped zebu cattle were being kept and herded in India and Mesopotamia. At about that same time, hornless cattle began appearing in Egypt, an obvious selection encouraged by early herders not only to keep the cattle from hurting each other but also, perhaps, in self-defense. From surviving artwork, we know that some early Egyptian cattle were already exhibiting color patterns not found naturally anywhere in the wild. They were both piebald and skewbald. (The difference is in the color. The piebald animal is black and white, the skewbald any color other than black, and white.)

The first identifiable domestic cattle in northern Europe appear to have come from Denmark. Evidence of other forms, very like the aurochs but considerably smaller, came from Germany. In Bavaria, yet smaller forms evolved very early on. Strangely, the Romans appear to have had a trade that ran north and south, utilizing larger forms of aurochs' descendants. With the disintegration of the Roman Empire, those larger forms vanished and smaller forms persisted into our times as the domestic breeds we now depend on for so much. Why the Romans ran against the grain of the ever-spreading cattle culture and retained large forms, which must have been far more difficult to handle, is not known. Perhaps it was hubris, or there may have been mystical or religious overtones.

On Crete, at the height of the Minoan culture, hazardous sporting events were staged involving gladiatorial types and cattle. There were bull-leaping and bull-riding, events that were recorded on pottery and metals, including gold. There has been a great deal of discussion about whether the animals used were domestic cattle or truly wild aurochs. Since the animals are generally depicted as spotted or piebald, one has to assume they were domestic stock. Or perhaps they were derived from feral stock, for surely as soon as man began keeping and moving domestic animals around, he began losing some back to the wild state, as he still does today.

The bull, in Minoan culture, was venerated, and a large body of mythology grew up around cattle. Many of the beliefs and practices that came to maturity on Crete probably originated in Asia. In Greek mythology, Minos had a wife named Pasiphaë, and the lady had a problem. The only way she could be satisfied sexually was for her husband's engineer to build a mock cow inside of which she hid to be "covered" by a bull. From this union, the Minotaur was born. The creature had a human body and a bull's head and was unsavory at best. It was said to eat youths and maidens. And there is no doubt that human beings were sacrificed to bulls, just as bulls would eventually be sacrificed in the bullring. The intensity and complexity of these European, Middle Eastern and Asian relationships, both in myth and fact, reflect the role domestic cattle came to play in the affairs of man. In time, Africa, too, would develop cattle-dependent cultures. Today, there are well over three hundred recognized breeds of cattle worldwide, and their varieties number in the thousands.

Cattle are much more demanding charges than either sheep or goats. Once man had cattle, all kinds of considerations about where he could live and during what seasons of the year had to have become dominant forces in the life of the clan and the tribe. The nomadic nature of contemporary pastoral peoples may have evolved as a secondary system for dealing with the needs of the herd. (The Maasai and until recently the Samburu and Turkana in Africa are excellent examples.) It is likely that the early domestication of cattle marked the beginnings of real agriculture, not the least of the factors being the easy availability of just about the best fertilizer in the world. As much as any other outside force, the cow remade man.

The American frontier could not have been settled without the cow. Oxen pulled the pioneers' wagons westward. Combination milk and beef or small "homestead" cows like the Dexter and the Belted Galloway were tied to the wagons on the thousand-mile treks. When the settlers arrived at their destination, plows pulled by oxen broke the plains and cow manure made subsistence agriculture possible. Slowly, herds built up, and the demand for grazing land led to the near extinction of competing bison herds. And while their chief means of sustenance was under attack, the Indians, too, were killed, conquered or confined.

The cow culture that emerged in the American West included the cowboy, the cattle rustler, the hanging judge, the gunslinger, the cattle baron and the sheriff and his posse. Although great herds still roam the West, those who once tended and protected them have all but vanished. Still, they live on in legend and folklore as figures of romance. Indeed, the traditions of the West persist in the American psyche to this day, proof that the cow has been not the offspring but the parent of human cultures.

SEVEN

The Buffalo, the Banteng and the Yak:
Icons of Other Cultures

The Buffalo

Buffalo is one of the most persistently misused words in the animal lexicon. Neither Europe nor North America has had a native buffalo since before the emergence of modern man. There were buffalo in Europe perhaps as recently as a quarter of a million years ago, but in the time frame of domestication, there have been no buffalo on either of those continents.

The so-called buffalo of the American plains and eastern woodlands is correctly the bison *(Bison bison)*. The buffalo of Europe is better known as wisent *(Bison bonasus)*, and is also distinctly not a buffalo. What is the difference between a buffalo and a bison? The same thing that separates the zebra from the horse, the wolf from the fox. They have different gene packages. They are different animals. They were hunted, of course, and many cultures were dependent upon them for survival, but no attempts we know of were made to domesticate either of these bison, which is both surprising and historically interesting.

In Africa, there is the Cape or African buffalo *(Syncerus caffer)*, sometimes erroneously referred to as "water" buffalo. But true water buffalo come from Asia and gave rise to a very important domestic animal. The Cape buffalo has never been domesticated and is, in fact, considered one of the most dangerous animals on the African continent. In herds, it apparently feels secure and generally will not seek confrontation with man. A bull alone, however, is a terror and will reputedly stalk man with terrifying persistence. If only a fraction of the hunters' tales from this century and the last are true, there is no mystery about why serious attempts at domestication were not made or, if they were made and are unrecorded, why they obviously failed.

The Water Buffalo

The Asian water buffalo *(Bubalus bubalis)* has a wide range that includes parts of Pakistan and Bangladesh, India, Sri Lanka and perhaps Burma to the Sunda Isles. Over the millennia, it has been exported as a domestic animal west to Israel, Egypt, Syria, Madagascar and Italy and east to Thailand, Vietnam, Laos, Cambodia, Australia, the Philippines, Japan, and, very importantly, China. They have also reached Central and South America, and there has been an experimental breeding colony at Gainesville, Florida. There are at least ten breeds recognized today, with scores of varieties and synonyms. The world census of domestic water buffalo now exceeds seventy-five million.

The water buffalo, wild and domestic (the latter known as *carabao* in the Philippines, *kerabou* in Indonesia), are large animals. A really big bull can weigh up to twenty-five hundred pounds, although that would be exceptional. They wallow in muddy water whenever the opportunity is there. The muddy coat they acquire protects them against insects, which worry them to an extraordinary degree. During the heat of the day, if allowed to do so, buffalo wild and domestic will remain submerged in the water with just their nostrils showing.

The wild and domestic animals vary little in appearance except in size, and they may be either reddish brown or black, with only a rare white specimen. The spread of the horns is impressive. Triangular in cross-section, they can measure up to four feet along the outside edge. Both sexes carry horns. Generally, the domestic buffalo is somewhat smaller than its wild ancestor and has smaller horns.

Domestic water buffalo are nowhere near as aggressive as the wild form, which is logical. They could not be used with that weight and those horns unless they were relatively mild and biddable. But even the domestic variety can be difficult or dangerous to manage at times, and some breeds are distinctly more tractable than others. Coming upon a wild water buffalo in its natural habitat, as I have done on occasion, is a memorable experience! Eye contact at close range is chilling, to say the least. Experiments have produced a hornless variety, but it is not often encountered, however good an idea it might be.

Water buffalo, as the name implies, require water for wallowing and do not last long where it is not available. That somewhat limits them to moist areas of the tropics and subtropics, although they are found slightly north and south of those belts. They are immensely powerful as draft animals and are used to very good purpose in rice cultivation. In fact, the large-scale cultivation of rice, and the many cultures it spawned, could not have occurred without them. In areas like Europe and the United States, where they are virtually never seen outside of zoos, the enormous importance of the buffalo in other parts of the world is easily overlooked.

In India, where they are listed as a form of cattle, water buffalo constitute between 20 and 25 percent of the total "cattle" census. Yet, they provide almost 60 percent of the nation's milk. A water buffalo cow will routinely produce three times as much milk as a milk cow, milk that is 50 percent richer in fat. Butter made from it is harder, more enduring and less likely to become rancid than butter from a dairy herd. It is pale greenish white in color.

Water buffalo are far more resistant to disease than cattle and generally a wiser choice for hot, moist climates. The fact that some people persist in using cattle in hot, moist localities when water buffalo are available is difficult to understand. Perhaps it is the European influence wherein cattle are traditional wealth and are maintained not only for product and power but also as a status symbol. Colonists have always taken a lot of baggage with them, tradition often being one of the heaviest and most cumbersome.

The water buffalo was almost certainly domesticated in India well before five thousand years ago. Before that, man had hunted the giants for their meat and fat, their very tough hide and their horns, and it is quite likely that the domestication scenario was not terribly different from the one in Europe that produced the first cattle from the aurochs. It had to have been a daring exercise.

The association was there, the hunter and the hunted, and water buffalo do congregate, although not to the extent of the Cape buffalo in Africa, where a thousand animals may be seen in one small valley. But water buffalo must have been herded into traps of some kind, allowing the early domesticators to manipulate their movements despite their size, strength and those awesome horns. With care, young animals could have been cut out of the herd and hand-reared, although it is a bit of a mystery where man would have gotten the milk, except perhaps from goats he had long since held in domestication and had learned to milk. There is a cylinder seal from Mesopotamia from around 2500 B.C. that shows creatures half man/ half god feeding water buffalo from ewers or giving them water. The idea of nurturing these animals was well established by that time.

In northwest India, the water buffalo was undoubtedly first taken under control in one of the continent's forested river valleys, with their extensive swamps. It offered what cattle offered European domesticators—powerful traction, dung, milk, meat, fat, horn and distinctly superior hides. Wherever the wet cultivation of rice emerged (something that started in Lower Egypt, probably during the reign of the Ptolemys, well before water buffalo got there), water buffalo eventually would become indispensable. Rice and buffalo flourish under the same conditions, and combining their powers to sustain human populations was an inevitable step for man to take.

The large-scale cultivation of rice requires plowing and water impoundment. Hundreds of tons of earth and water are involved and would represent an impossible expenditure of human energy. The tireless, plodding water buffalo has provided the power, pulling plows and sleds loaded with mounds of earth to close dikes and control water. In China, the Philippines, in Sri Lanka, in Malaysia, the scene is the same. Miles upon miles of terraced hillsides with huge earthen dams, vast water impoundments and mile after mile of rice paddies.

The spread of the water buffalo toward the west was slow and discontinuous. And they were late in coming. The governing factor was water. Unlike other beasts of burden (camels, horses, asses, oxen), water buffalo cannot be driven over long stretches of arid land. Interestingly enough, although there was an apparently well-established trade between Rome and India, water buffalo were unknown to the Romans. The northern outpost of the domesticated species in modern times is Hungary. It is well known to the Slavs and Romanians.

Any animal with a present-day count of over seventy-five million must be considered an extremely important domesticate. And the water buffalo has proven to be just that. It is difficult to decide which of the gifts it offers man, traction or milk, is most important. Milk would be of less interest at the eastern end of the buffalo's range, more so back in the west. In areas that have a long tradition with this animal, there are separate breeds for each product. It is too valuable an animal to slaughter with great regularity, although some are sacrificed for their hides and some, probably in part as a ceremony, for their flesh. But perhaps its greatest contribution was to cultivation of rice. Without the water buffalo and rice, the vast populations of Asia and the Indian subcontinent could not have flourished, nor the arts and religions that have so greatly enriched the tapestry of human civilization.

The Yak

The wild yak *(Bos grunniens)* today is found in Tibet at altitudes between six thousand and twenty thousand feet. It is a large animal, the bulls sometimes up to a ton in weight, cows only a third that size. They are blackish brown with long, profuse wool. As a wild species, they have been badly overhunted by local tribesmen and today are listed as endangered.

Yaks probably were domesticated in the first or second millennium B.C. but never spread far beyond their wild range in Tibet and China. The domestic form is generally smaller than the wild yak and offers wool, milk and meat as well as traction. Above six thousand feet, the yak is certainly the single most useful of all domestic animals. They can be ridden, and they have enormous endurance as pack animals, handling deep snow and summer swamps with equal ease. They are extremely surefooted. Although fly-covered and rather like an unmade bed in appearance, they are highly regarded by the people who depend on them for product and power.

Yak-cattle hybrids are common over the yak's range. They are called

dzo in Tibetan, *pien niu* in at least one Chinese dialect, *hainak* in Mongolian and *hainyk* in Russian. In almost all cases, the sires are cattle and the dams yaks. The male hybrids are sterile, but the females can be bred back to either yak or cattle. The hybrid can be considerably larger than either parent's stock and the cows give more milk. The hybrids are considered more manageable than the pure yak and are preferred for plowing. The real story of this domestic hybrid may be more in the future than in the past. Still, the unique cultures that evolved, particularly within its Tibetan range, an extremely inhospitable environment, must be in large part attributed to the yak.

The Banteng, Mithan, Gaur and Kouprey

There are several other secondary domestications in the bovine family. The huge wild banteng still survives between Borneo and Burma, but its populations are on the way down. War and hunting have been their relentless foes. Bulls can weigh close to a ton, but even animals of that size are no match for modern ballistics now available to tribesmen. The banteng prefers fairly dry, open areas but does depend on forest thickets for cover. It is a very shy animal and probably always has been. A single male may hold a harem of up to twenty cows.

The harems or herds (unmated bulls form loose associations or "bachelor herds") are ideal for a small-scale drive, and forest thickets readily lend themselves to well-camouflaged run-in chutes and traps. On Java and Bali, banteng were domesticated probably because cattle did not do well in the region. They were secondary, replacements for the cattle that were rapidly becoming the norm of civilization. However, the banteng was one of several regional domestications whose results had little influence beyond the ranges of its wild ancestors.

The mithan or gayal is probably a domesticated form of the powerful gaur *(Bos gaurus),* still found in scattered populations from India to Indochina and the Malay Peninsula. The wild form is in danger of extinction, and further encroachment on its range will leave us its smaller, domesticated descendant and nothing more.

The kouprey is a southeast Asian bovid that is found in the wild *(Bos sauveli)* and as a domestic animal with a very limited range in Vietnam and Cambodia, Laos and surrounding areas. It wasn't even known to science until 1937, and the area has seen constant warfare since then. The wild kouprey may be the most seriously endangered of all wild bovids. It is at least possible that the domestic kouprey is a gaur/domestic cattle cross and the endangered wild kouprey only a feral animal.

The yak, the banteng, the mithan or gayal, the gaur and kouprey are domesticates of very limited influence on the economies of the world. They are fairly recent episodes as domestications go—probably mostly between three and four thousand years ago—and seem to have followed cattle into the fold once that example had been set. They all do much better than cattle in their parts of the world and should be acknowledged for the roles they have played in their small wild and domestic ranges. Unfortunately, the wild forms may be extinct before much sense can be made of their history and relationships. In the world at large, the cattle (aurochs) and the water buffalo are the two species that truly changed the face of continents, economies and cultures.

There are well over a billion domestic bovids in the world, and perhaps 10 percent of the total are water buffalo. The leading-cattle producing countries are India, the United States, Brazil, China, Argentina, Pakistan, Mexico, Ethiopia and France. When the Soviet Union was intact, it was listed as the third largest holder of cattle, but it is doubtful that any of the member states, now independent of that union, would rate anywhere near that high today.

If you combine the cattle *taurine* group, ordinary cattle, the *indicus* group, the zebu or humped cattle with the water buffalo, you have the animals that have had the most profound influence on man, his cultures and his economies. It is true that the goat and sheep came much earlier—they have been twice as long in domestication as cattle—and grandfathered the whole domestication process, but once the bovines were in our midst, the world changed dramatically, perhaps forever.

Wars have been fought over cattle and over range and water to sustain them, cattle thieves have been hung without ceremony or shot on sight, and it is an inescapable fact that at many times in many places, the lives of cattle have been held to be of far greater worth than the lives of human beings. Consider the basis for that fact.

If you were part of a cattle-holding culture, that one animal at its core pulled heavy loads for you, gave milk to your young, sick and old, provided fertilizer (and in some instances building material) and fed your fires so you could cook otherwise inedible foods like wheat, millet and rice. The same animal enabled you to have larger agricultural fields than otherwise would have been possible. At planting time and at harvest, the same beast was there. You ate its flesh, rendered its fat, used its horns, and its hide was the most durable leather you knew. Cattle bought brides and were constants in trade far and near. Cattle gave you status when little else did.

On top of that, you probably firmly believed in its magic, its powers in this world and beyond. That was the cow in some cultures, the water buffalo in others. Little wonder you guarded it above virtually all other possessions. Quite literally, it was the most valuable thing you could own.

There is, of course, a bitter irony to acknowledge. Our debt to domestic cattle is truly beyond measure. Today, their meat is the protein staple in scores of cultures; their milk and the butter, yogurt and cheese we make from it is the basis for much of our modern cuisine. The cow's hide is the standard for the leather industry, which we still see as vital to our lifestyles despite the plastic imitations that have been developed. Oxen remain critical motive power in many places, and cow dung is a precious commodity as fertilizer, fuel and building material in more cultures than we can reckon. Entire economies in states and nations around the world are built in no small part on the cattle culture. When a cow is slaughtered, every single part of its body is put to use in one industry or another. Cattle blood is used in steel processing and road paving. The cosmetic and pharmaceutical industries, gelatin users, pet food manufacturers, all wait for their part, their share.

For all of that, we still treat cattle appallingly all around the world. The most supposedly civilized of nations, for all their churches, synagogues, cathedrals, universities, congresses and parliaments, allow industry to treat cattle in ways that would be ranked as sociopathic torture if inflicted on human beings, outrageous if done to dogs. It is an element of human behavior that is almost universal and in all contexts inexplicable. When this matter has been put right, perhaps we can then make more valid claims to our own humanity.

EIGHT

Swine:
Meat for the Table
of Everyman

The Pig

The pig has been preserved into our time, serving the same purpose for which it was initially domesticated. It is a critically important, highly productive, low-cost maintenance meat animal. Well over 500,000,000 pigs are now maintained around the world in small holdings and large. Some holdings are so small that one or two animals can represent much if not all of the family's wealth.

It is an unusual domesticate in that all of a pig's other attributes, even its skin, which makes a fine grade of leather, are distinctly secondary. This in contrast to cattle, for instance, with milk and power to offer as well as meat, and goats with fiber and milk, too. In the case of the pig, these secondary "benefits" include such arcane specialties as planting or at least pushing seed into muddy ground (inadvertently, one has to suppose) reportedly retrieving, although to a very limited extent, pig-cart pulling in some extremely small areas in the south of England, truffle hunting and battleground land-mine detonation.

Pigs are excellent domestic meat animals for several reasons. They grow very fast (some breeds can be expected to add between two and two and a half pounds a day), they grow very big, they have large litters, more offspring by far than any other meat animal—mammal, at least—and they eat almost constantly with enormous enthusiasm. They are not selective about their diet, which can include just about anything from berries, fungi, nestling mammals and birds, carrion, worms, grubs, insects, acorns or forest floor mast to garden waste, kitchen garbage and, on occasion, even human beings. The ardor they display for both food and reproduction can make them aggressive.

Strangely, the very qualities that have allowed the pig to excel in its principal and one true role have been widely and relentlessly disparaged. Ancient encyclopedias referred to lascivious people as resembling swine who would "rather have their snouts in dung than in flowers," a less than endearing image. An old German sculpture of a pig playing bagpipes represents lust. Gluttony has been depicted as an ugly old hag riding on the back of a pig. Dante had pigs living in a nasty swill pit in a third region of hell. (As if hell were not punishment enough. The implication is that all pigs automatically go to hell.) Clement of Alexandria explained that the ban Moses announced on pigs was based on the association of the animal with lust and greed. And in our time, the word *pig* has been used as a pejorative label for all authority figures, particularly the police.

The pig, when it appeared in dreams, presaged bad news, frequently of a sexual nature. It was thus for an emperor, we learn, because a dream about a hog embraced by twelve lions turned out to be symbolic of his lustful wife's unnatural appetites. In Chaucer's *Troilus and Criseyde,* Troilus, the Trojan warrior, dreamed about a hog, later to learn that his wife had betrayed him.

However, as is generally the case in our symbologies, we have been ambivalent and hence fickle. In parts of both Asia and Europe, the same lustful, boorish animal has been seen as nothing short of divine. As a reincarnation of Vishnu, the hog was a slayer of demonic forces and had the high honor of rescuing the Earth from the bosom of the suffocating sea. In Norse mythology, the boar has been depicted as a thunderbolt and, as a glistening apparition, it drew a sun cart across the northern skies of Scandi-

navia. It also appeared on the helmets of some Scandinavian warriors and denoted power and tenacity.

In Roman mythology, Mars and the hog were often the same entity, and the god was depicted on coins wearing the skin of a pig. When Mars slew Adonis in a jealous rage, the pig was identified with the event. When Adonis ultimately triumphed over his enemy with the return of spring, the image for that sequence was a slain boar.

Christ cured the insane by driving out the evil spirits that possessed them, forcing them to reside instead in hogs. Not a pretty picture, the pig as the ultimate residence of evil. (As a Jew, Christ would have had less than affectionate regard for pigs.)

As difficult as it is to reconcile these contradictory views, the pig was actually sacred in some cultures, and so the eating of pork often had ritualistic overtones. Yet, the taboo against pork as food and also against the pig itself exists as strongly today in the worlds of Islam and Orthodox Judaism as it ever did. When Muslim mutineers were seriously challenging imperial Great Britain in India, the rumor was spread that the bodies of Muslim warriors slain in battle would be gathered up by the British troops and sewn inside freshly obtained pigskins. These would-be warriors of heaven would thus spend eternity wrapped in filth, corruption and shame. Another purposeful bit of disinformation had it that the paper cartridges routinely bitten open by troops in the process of loading their muskets had been manufactured with lard as a sealant. Muslim troops were not about to bite lard-encrusted cartridges! Such stories affected the outcome of battles, and the revolt itself, we are told.

The admonition against eating pork for the early Jews, and later by extension for the Muslims, is said to have been due to the fear of trichinosis. Pork was thought to be "unclean." But without refrigeration in Mideastern temperatures of over a hundred, any meat, fish or fowl would become "unclean" very quickly. Chicken, for instance, would be poisonous in a matter of hours and reek to the high heavens. Fish would have suffered a similar fate.

In fact, pork had been a staple in the Jordan Valley for millennia before Moses issued his edict, and it probably had achieved ritual status as a food among many pagan sects. The pig itself, because of its demonstrable reproductive powers, may have been a bit of an icon off as well as on the table. The Jews had a prejudice against any food used in the rituals of other peoples, just as they eschewed other people's idols. There was also the traditional animus between nomads (the Israelites) and settled clans like swineherds. They didn't like each other and treated each other's cultures with disdain.

The ban against eating the flesh of swine could have been part of the Israelites coming into being under their own banner of monotheism, something they felt very strongly about. They themselves had arisen, after all, from pagan tribes and had this "better idea." Much had to be cast away if a totally new intellectual and social order was to be built up from it. More than ritual was involved; eternity was at stake. The pig probably just went out with the bathwater. It had been too long too close to the affairs of the zealots of other faiths. That, at least, could be part of the story. To mix zoological metaphors, the pig as a food animal may have been more of a scapegoat than anything else.

In Israel today, however, when the truly orthodox Jews aren't looking, or the Muslims, pork is sold under the counter as "white beef." Bacon is called "zebra." I have had both served to me in Israel by Israelis. Since a pig farm isn't something one could expect to find in the Israeli countryside, it is amusing that after all this time, there is an underground network smuggling in and distributing not guns or bombs but bacon. Treating that enterprise as an abomination is one of the few things that Jews and Muslims apparently agree upon.

The hunt of the wild boar was more than sport. It had originally been hunted for meat, of course. But long after its domestication, it is still hunted in the wild form, sometimes with dogs, sometimes not, sometimes by mounted hunters, sometimes not. And not infrequently, mechanized vehicles are used, equipped with radio communications. However, boar hunting was once a highly ritualized affair and eventually came to symbolize the pursuit of evil by priests. Yet, King Arthur had the head of a boar on his shield, and in heraldry, the boar, although not too often used, was equated with power. At a later time in imperial India, "pig sticking," killing wild boar with javelins from horseback, was almost as royal a sport as the wholesale slaughter of tigers from elephant back and running horses to death in polo chukkers. And somewhat farther afield, more charitably, the Gahuku-Gama people of the New Guinea highlands stage pig festivals and establish pig commons where the clans can graze their pigs without contest whatever their other problems might be.

An extremely unsettling aspect of both the fact and the imagery of the hog arose during the American Civil War. There are hundreds of harrowing stories about the cries of the wounded left on the field after dark following the murderous onslaughts that characterized that war. What was seldom reported by either side, almost certainly out of regard for the families of the dead and missing, and what history seems to have mercifully forgotten, is that those cries of agony sometimes came from incapacitated men being eaten by hogs. This same grim scenario may also have been enacted in earlier wars in Europe and Asia.

Up until the middle 1800s, there are records of hogs being tried in courts of law (sometimes dressed in human clothing with human defense attorneys appointed by the court—one of the most bizarre charades in the entire human-animal relationship) and then executed by hanging. Considering the shape of the pig's head and neck, that must have been a nasty bit of business. Frequently, the charge was murder, especially of children. Man has not maintained very many even occasional man-eating domestic animals, and although one does not want to overstate the frequency or the threat of this aberration in the farmyard, it has and does happen. Large boars can be dangerous, while smaller pigs are kept as pets, at least for a while, by a few devoted enthusiasts. Again, ambivalence.

The Sequence

As has probably always been the case in the domestication process, there was a long and important association between man and the wild boar before domestication was attempted. Man hunted wild pigs over wide areas of the world and must have known the animal well. But the overlap of keeping swine and hunting swine that has continued into our time is unusual with a major domesticate. It is not unique; the wolf and the reindeer are examples, but nonetheless it is unusual. And there is an added facet to the story. Feral domestic pigs have bred themselves back into wild stock, creating more different kinds ("degrees") of wild pig than there ever were before both inside and outside the true wild boar's original range.

Pigs, wild and domestic, belong to the order Artiodactyla, the even-toed ungulates, along with the hippopotamus, camel, deer, giraffe, antelope, cow, sheep and goat. Their family is Suidae. (Peccaries, also javelinas, the pig's closest relatives, are in a different family, Tayassuidae.)

The family Suidae almost certainly evolved in Eurasia and was widely distributed in extremely ancient times. The sequence of pig species as they evolved, the famed "pig sequence," is used as a dating device today for paleontologists and physical anthropologists working with prehominid remains in Tanzania and Ethiopia. The pig was here before we were. Man found them waiting and soon enough learned to hunt them for meat and fat, and to a much less urgent degree, for tusks and skin.

From Eurasia, the early pig species, on their own, reached Britain, Ireland, Sardinia, Corsica, the Philippines and the Celebes, Japan, Taiwan, Sri Lanka, Sumatra and Java, and spread throughout Africa. That was long before our own appearance. Once we were in the game and the pig was domesticated, it was carried to North, Central and South America, New Guinea and other southwestern Pacific islands and both New Zealand and Australia. In many areas, especially on islands, swine have been allowed to establish feral populations and exist in highly destructive numbers against which native wildlife has little or no hope of survival.

Whaling ships released pigs on selected islands like the Galápagos and Hawaii (the Sandwich Islands) so that their feral descendants could be hunted and supply fresh meat to future voyagers and, not just coincidentally, offer a little sport to relieve the tedium of long sailing journeys. It has proven to have been a devastating practice, creating problems for wildlife and plant conservationists. Typically, feral pigs are now killed wherever they are found to give dwindling native wildlife and its habitat a chance for survival. It is not known how many species of plant and animal have been driven to extinction by introduced feral animals, largely pigs, rats, cats, dogs and goats. Certainly, it is a substantial number. Insofar as the pig is concerned, where it evolved *naturally,* the problem did not come into being. The pigs' predators evolved, too. But where they have been superimposed on natural habitats as feral domestics or as wild boar transplanted for sport, they have been overwhelmingly destructive.

There are four full species in the genus *Sus.* The pygmy hog comes from the southern Tibetan region, the Javan pig from that island plus the Celebes, Moluccas and Philippines. The bearded pig is found on the Malay Peninsula, Sumatra, Borneo and adjacent island groups. *Sus scrofa,* the European wild boar, in one or probably more subspecies and varieties, is the ancestor of most of the domestic pigs we now have in our farmyards. Our pig is assigned to that species today. A separate Asian species, *Sus vittatus,* may have been used simultaneously in that part of the world, but the

European species gives our modern domestic pig its scientific name. How much cross breeding eventually was done cannot even be imagined. Local subspecies and varieties or races of the European and the Asian boars were used as well. What the final mixes contain is unlikely to be sorted out because many of the wild forms used are now extinct.

In their natural state, wild pigs live in fast-moving and frequently aggressive "sounders," or herds. They prefer forested land with a good lower story of brush, but they will also feed out in the open if it isn't too far from cover. They are hunted by every major predator in their range, from wolves to tigers, from lions and hyenas to leopards and bears. That would account for their having substantial litters. The attrition of constant predation had to be a factor in the swine's evolution. The pressure of natural predation on pigs, plus the added pressure put on them by early hominids and their descendants (including us), forced the wild pig into a pattern of eternal vigilance and, where necessary, tough resistance. But eventually the stage was set for domestication, which the pig's other predators, obviously, never attempted.

Pigs are omnivorous, an added advantage not available to most strictly vegetarian prey animals. And they are smart as well as fast and strong. They are at least as smart as domestic dogs, and when they are aroused, they can attack in concert, presenting a formidable phalanx of aggression and slashing tushes.

Because they do live in groups of anywhere from ten to forty animals —sounders of a hundred or more boar have been seen in Europe but that is on the upside; in eastern Poland, I have seen sounders of twenty-three or twenty-four animals, never more than that—pigs are easy to drive into chutes and pens and pitfalls set up in the underbrush. Although aggressive and dangerous in close quarters, they were still easier to manage than giants like the aurochs and the water buffalo. Their rapid reproduction—as little as 100 to 110 days' gestation, with litters as large as twelve—made them ideal for even the most primitive agronomists.

There was another reason for domesticating the pig and removing as many as possible from the wild. Pigs are extremely destructive to agriculture, and men who took the wild boar into custody not only gained a ready supply of meat but protected their produce as well. If there was one single meat animal that it was logical for man to take in charge, it was the pig. As for efficiency, pigs convert 35 percent of the food they eat into meat and lard. Sheep are considered efficient at 13 percent.

The Scenario

Inevitably the questions, where and when. There is probably no single "where," and the "when" almost certainly covered a wide swath of our own history. The earliest pig domestication may have occurred in the Neolithic era, with dates from six to eight thousand years ago, but there are now other suggestions. Findings in Turkey point to ten thousand years ago. That would take the pig all the way back to preagricultural times, or very close to them. Some researchers believe the pig, not the dog, sheep or goat, was man's first domesticated animal.

Tradition has it that man began settling down about ten thousand years ago after a history of endless wandering. It has been the conventional belief that the end to the hunting-gathering cultures came about when man learned to domesticate grains. Perhaps that was not universally so. In northern Turkey, the remains of the earliest settlements reveal not wheat and barley, but small pig teeth. In the initial stages of domestication, swine lose size and have smaller teeth. Pigs, then, and not grain may have given man the reason as well as the means for settling down. Pigs are notoriously uncooperative when being herded, and swineherds would be happier in one place as opposed to "on the road."

It is highly likely that the pig domestication scenario was played out in many different places because the essential pig living the essential pig's life was found in so many places in Europe and Asia. The local subspecies were very much alike in almost all regards and had the same gift to offer, an enormous amount of meat for relatively little work.

Sheep, goats and dogs were probably already being held and selectively bred in many of these wild pig areas, and an ongoing process of domestication would seem to have been inevitable. It is amazing that it doesn't seem to have occurred in Africa, where a good many forms of wild pigs evolved. Pig domestication, however, does appear to have been a European and Asian happening that also involved the Middle East until eating pork became a religious issue there.

Just as cattle would eventually be divided into essentially meat animals versus essentially dairy animals, with still other breeds used more often for power, and goats were broken out into meat, fiber and milk breeds, and sheep into various wool-grade animals versus meat animals, pigs would inevitably become specialized, too. There was a big difference, however. Pigs in all forms are basically meat animals and always have been. The forms they have taken reflect not their use but the easiest means of local maintenance. There are herding pigs, there are sty pigs and, in parts of Asia, notably China, an assortment of house pigs. In Asia, many of these backyard varieties are now grossly deformed by their breeding and can barely walk, much less respond to the demands made on herded animals. It is generally believed that the dog and the pig were the first two domestic meat animals in China, and that has allowed a lot of time for bizarre forms to evolve.

Pigs today are commonly referred to as bacon types and lard types with a third subset obvious, meat animals. They all refer to pigs as food alone. But, unfortunately, in the modern agriculture–animal husbandry world of Europe and North America, the very intelligent pig has been forced to become a meat machine without any regard at all for its well-being as a sentient creature. Production is everything: pounds of weight gained (can that 2.03-pound daily weight gain be made into 2.7 pounds with the same quantity and quality of feed?) and the number of offspring produced versus time and food invested. It is cruel and unusual punishment for an animal that has meant so much to man for so long a time.

No domestic mammal is *routinely* treated with such profound cruelty as the pig, cruelty that is accepted as some kind of perverted norm in even our most sophisticated societies. People who are horrified by stories of Mexican rodeos, bullfights, pit dog fights and fighting cocks accept without any apparent concern equal cruelty displayed on most modern pig farms. It is difficult not to believe that wild boar chased by Neolithic hunters through the forests of Germany and Poland until they were stampeded into camouflaged pits filled with sharpened and fire-hardened stakes had a better deal than today's pampered, pedigreed pigs so grotesquely fat and deformed that they can barely move.

PART THREE

THE BURDEN-BEARERS

NINE

The Elephant:
Man's Most Powerful Servant

Wild or Domesticated?

There are two proboscideans left on this planet, *Elephas maximus,* the Asian elephant, and *Loxodonta africana,* the African bush elephant. Some authorities give species status (*L. cyclotis*) to a generally western African forest elephant sometimes called the pygmy elephant. But it is probably a subspecies. It is markedly smaller and has more rounded ears.

In the past, there were mammoths and mastodons in North and South America, Europe and parts of Asia, where most of their kind vanished millennia ago, at the end of the Pleistocene era. Some lived on long enough to be hunted by man or man's ancestors. In terms of man's "use" of animals, however, other than in hunting them, just the two surviving species matter. Man did not ride the woolly mammoth nor did he go logging with the mastodon for a bulldozer.

But just exactly what man *did* do with our two contemporary elephants revolves around an important question. Has he, in fact, ever *domesti-*

cated either elephant? Despite the endless references to his having done so, it is my opinion that he has not. Man has *utilized* elephants to a remarkable degree, but that should be viewed as something entirely different from domestication. He has not controlled breeding and therefore has in no way altered the original animal that he took from the wild and continues to take to this day. An elephant taken, kept and worked for ten or twenty years and then released is the same animal and (here is the point) so are any young it produces.

Typically, the owner of a working cow elephant in Asia who wants her to produce offspring turns her loose to mingle with nearby wild elephants. After a suitable time, or after scouts have reported her mated, a handler or mahout who specializes in such problems goes out and coaxes the cow back into captivity. It is a highly skilled subspecialty of elephant handling. Not everyone has a taste for it.

The important consideration, however, is that the breeding was, from the owner's point of view, entirely random. He could not control the dominance pattern among the wild elephants that alone would dictate which bull became his cow's mate. Relying on politics within a wild herd is not at all the same as domestication, which entails, as we understand it, gene manipulation by selective breeding. A Jersey cow does not look or behave like an aurochs, a Poland China sow does not look like a European wild boar and Chihuahuas and cocker spaniels do not much resemble timber wolves. A working elephant, however, looks exactly like a wild elephant. It is the same animal brought in from the wild and put to work. It has been utilized, not domesticated.

Why aren't elephants routinely bred in captivity like other "domestic" animals? There are several reasons. Bulls that will cooperate and breed in captivity are quite rare, and those that will function as studs-on-command tend to be very dangerous and difficult to contain. There may have been docile working bulls that would act as studs and still allow themselves to be handled, but I have never heard of them. There are approximately thirty breeding bulls in American zoos, but that is a high point in the captive maintenance of elephants. The only stud I ever knew personally was in a zoo in Portland, Oregon, and he tried to kill me and everyone else he could reach. He was just plain murderous.

The standard, everyday working elephant is by no means an easy animal to control. A male (nonbreeding) I worked with on a film in Sri Lanka had a lifetime record of ten victims. He had killed nine mahouts who had somehow displeased him, and on a particularly bad day, he had picked off a pedestrian he passed on a village street. They were both on the way to work.

Rama was a handsome, huge, extremely cagey, immensely powerful royal tusker, but he did have his off days. He was so valuable, however—probably worth at least $5,000—that when he did kill his mahout, a new and hopefully wiser handler took the man's place. To put that dollar value in perspective, a mahout at the time earned $12 a month. In the forests of Asia, you don't shoot a $5,000 animal for killing a laborer who is earning $12 a month. Those are simply the facts of elephant utilization. As an added point, Rama's owners probably had never met him or the people he had killed. Working elephants are frequently owned by a syndicate of urban businessmen. They invest money in working elephants and lease them out to lumbering companies or wherever else they are needed.

On another assignment, also in Sri Lanka, at the site of the bridge in the film *The Bridge on the River Kwai,* I arrived at a sawmill that had just been leveled by a bull working there. He was not a stud, just your run-of-the-mill working animal. He had become distressed over something and tore the building down and flattened or overturned several vehicles as well. When he had expressed himself to his satisfaction, he walked across the flattened corrugated metal roof of the building and wandered off into the forest. A specialist was already on his way to track the bull down and coax him back into chains.

The working elephant can, then, be extremely dangerous, and breeding bulls are far worse than most, if and when they can be identified in the wild and captured. One problem is that you cannot know in advance whether a bull will breed in captivity. Since most will not, and since capturing mature bull elephants is costly and dangerous, the practice has evolved of allowing random breeding to prevail, not the selective breeding we associate with actual domestication through gene selection and emphasis on valuable or endearing characteristics.

The second most common fallacy concerning elephants in the service of man (the first is that they are domesticated) is that only the Asian species has been involved in whatever has gone on, however you choose to characterize it. In all likelihood, the African elephant was utilized before the Asian species, or at least it goes as far back as a working and war animal. It was probably in use in the Nile Valley in the earliest dynastic times. By the fourth century B.C., Aristotle was able to describe what was already an "ages old" tradition, the capture and training of elephants in Africa.

Also in the fourth century B.C., Ptolemy Philadelphus set up camps in what is now the Sudan and Ethiopia to capture and train elephants. By 277 B.C., we know, the Carthaginians had working elephants. The thirty-seven elephants Hannibal took across the Alps in 218 B.C. were African, as were the war elephants later trained by the Romans. All of this was activity in fairly recent times, but it was built on very ancient traditions.

As recently as the early 1900s, elephants were trained and photo-

graphed with native handlers in the Congo. But why they did not become an important economic factor in Africa, as they did in Asia, is a mystery. Given the amount of work trained elephants can do and the cultural riches they bring to a people, it is nothing less than amazing that in Africa, they somehow slipped out of man's grasp. It is to Asia we must go to find the real story of the unusual relationship between a smart, inherently dangerous undomesticated animal and the economic and cultural imperatives of man.

As Seen by Man

The elephant in Asia, as a symbol of divine wisdom, goes back farther than we can reckon. Ganesha, in Hindu mythology, generally is depicted as a god with an elephant's head. Rajas typically were referred to as "elephants" or "lords of the elephants," while throughout Asia elephants were sacred to the sun, and the Buddha himself was said to be "like a well-trained elephant." There are thousands of depictions of elephants from ancient times in Asia everywhere they were known. It is the persistent symbol of strength, memory, authority, intelligence and industry.

The intelligence of the elephant is typically overstated, in all likelihood. They are probably somewhat more intelligent than dogs, although they can be highly focused and bring their intelligence to bear on a fine point. A well-trained elephant in forestry work or in associated chores knows a standard 115 vocal commands and physical signals. There are over ninety pressure points on an elephant's body through which a skilled handler can signal commands using a pointed stick or ankus. Elephants are incredible problem solvers when it comes to managing heavy weights and shifting loads on a truck or sawmill bench. They use their trunks, their tusks, their feet, their mouths and their foreheads selectively once they are given a chore. And they always find a way to do it. As for its fabled memory and *never* forgetting, *never* is a long time. And elephants live a long time. Seventy years is not that remarkable, although it *is* old age.

Elephants are creatures of habit, and if they are trained to work until 2:45 P.M. every day (typical) and then to be walked to the river where their mahouts scrub them with rough coconut halves, it is best to stick to that routine. Elephants have killed their mahouts for taking liberties. The bond between the handler and his elephant is strengthened, in fact, by the scrubbing routine. It is good for the elephant's skin, and even more important than that, it is beneficial to the mahout's longevity.

There are a number of techniques for capturing elephants, actually removing these enormously powerful animals from their wild herds and enslaving not their genes but the animals themselves. *Keddah* are wild elephant drives still occasionally staged in some remote areas like Assam and the Chittagong Hill Tracts of eastern Bangladesh. A wild herd is driven into a corral by scores of noisemakers beating drums, blowing whistles and carrying flaming torches. Special mahouts riding elephant-catching *koonkis* or "bullies" cut selected animals out of the herd once they have settled down in the corral. They are then abused day and night and not allowed to rest until they lose the will to fight. Again using *koonkis* to guide the animals in training, they are broken to take basic commands within a few weeks. It is a cruel, heavy-handed process, but the task of a man, at his size and strength, actually bullying an animal the size of an elephant into submission is formidable. I watched part of the process in the Hill Tracts in Bangladesh, and the young cow was obviously depressed. The wounds that had been inflicted upon her were deep and festering. It is a cruel practice. Dominance is achieved by sheer brutality.

Since elephants have not been selectively bred, there are no breeds, as such. Instead, there are grades of elephants, quality ratings, and the value placed on each animal strongly reflects these traditional and somewhat subjective descriptions. The terms that are used are in dialect and vary from place to place.

The *makhana* is a mature but tuskless Asian male elephant. His value is limited by the kind of work he can do. Tusks can be extremely important for an elephant handling heavy tropical hardwoods. Tusklessness in Asian bulls is much more common than in African bulls.

The *koomeriah* is the royal tusker most highly regarded in the forest, sawmill or procession, religious or secular. It is the most highly valued of all elephants and is characterized by long, heavy and relatively straight tusks. Its color is dark gray with pink pigment spots likely on the trunk and forehead. The skin is heavily wrinkled and the base of the trunk is broad and powerful. The tail, too, has a broad base where it attaches to the body, and the end of the tail carries many heavy hairs. Very important is its overall conformation, the body solid and square on legs that allow it to be set not too high off the ground. "Not much sun shines under a *koomeriah's* belly," it was once explained to me in India. The back is broad and straight and the flatter the better, the ears large, the head massive, the eyes clear without significant discharge. The pads of the feet are hard, and the nails are smooth and readily polished.

A step below the *koomeriah* is the *dwasala,* insofar as it differs in any way from the ideal. If the animal has smallish tusks, or is outsized with long or thin legs, or has an arched back, it still may be an important working animal, but it is less highly regarded.

At the bottom of the elephant beauty contest is the *mreega,* which is best described as deerlike. It is still potentially a powerful animal and can do a lot of work, but it is not the animal you would want your cow to breed with during her honeymoon in the forest. You would hope for better than that for any cow of your own.

It is true that these ratings of elephants correspond to breeds in truly domesticated animals and carry a heavy burden of aesthetics, but they are also practical ratings given to animals that are viewed as working machines. Unfortunately, they are chance happenings. In a *keddah,* they try to drive as many wild *koomeriah* as possible into their corrals, but chance ultimately has the say.

The men who work elephants in the forests and sawmills and who control them in parades are far less sentimental about the animals they deal with than are the people who watch them do it and later write children's books about it. The mahouts are realistic about their living bulldozers because they know they have minds of their own. The mahout is exposed to those minds and their whims every working day. A certain amount of dominance by the handler is essential; too much or too little is potentially fatal. The mahout lives on a razor's edge, more so than the managers of any other working or food animal.

In circuses and zoos, elephants kill more handlers and keepers than any other animal. People who work with elephants watch for mood swings whenever they are with their charges.

The two elephant species we have left on Earth are probably doomed. In Asia and Africa, human populations are clearly out of control. With a growth rate of 8.1 babies per woman in Kenya, for example, how long can the elephant herds have? Ivory poachers are probably the biggest single threat, but so is the spread of agriculture, encroaching upon their domains.

Wild elephants, in fact, make difficult neighbors. Their digestive systems utilize only half of the food they consume, and so their demands are enormous. Each adult elephant requires between three and four hundred pounds of food a day plus sixty gallons of water. Even a few elephants feeding through a single night can wipe out an entire village's food supply. When bored, they will topple a tall tree that may take more than a century to regrow. They will eat a few leaves and move on to knock down another tree. They are wasteful and destructive because they evolved to migrate over vast areas, where their extravagant ways were not concentrated and therefore of little significance.

Since elephants are rarely bred in captivity, and then in only small numbers, captive breeding programs may not be able to preserve the species. When the wild gene pools vanish, so will the species not long after that. Again, the demand for ivory, a hard currency in much of Asia, and man's incomprehensible unwillingness to control his own species will be the causes.

TEN

The Camel Family:
Reluctant Facilitators

The Image

The camel of the Middle East traditionally has been portrayed in two contradictory images. In one context, it has long been the symbol of the humble of the world, stoically accepting the burdens placed upon it, and therein lies a kind of quiet nobility. In another context, however, the one-humped or dromedary camel, at least, has been the symbol of the very essence of lasciviousness. Lust and ill-temper are the traditional associations. On the subject of temper, Beryl Rowland, in her book *Animals with Human Faces: A Guide to Animal Symbolism* (1974), quotes this saying: "The camel curses its parents when it has to go up hill, and its Maker when it has to go down."

In the once-upon-a-time lore of India, a man who attempted to rape a beautiful maiden was turned into an ugly camel as punishment. The superstitious in India believe that a ghost will not enter a house if camel bones are buried beneath the threshold. In North America, where the camel family was extinct before man arrived, it is said that a camel is a horse designed by a committee.

In Peru, llamas and vicuñas were considered sacred animals of the mountains. Llamas were often depicted in legend as participating in caravans that moved only at night, transporting the Earth's treasures from one place to another. In some versions, they were guided by a llama-herdsman, while in others, they moved on their own, doing the work of the gods without human intervention or guidance. There are tales in the Andes of the tragic consequences to man of hunting or otherwise harming llamas.

The Animals

The family Camelidae was once found in the wild state from the Arabian Peninsula to Mongolia and widely in southern and western South America. The camels of North America were animals of the Pleistocene era and earlier, known to man only in fossil form. Before the advent of man on Earth, the camel family was spread over vast areas of the world. At one time, the ancestors of the guanaco in southern Argentina and those of the Bactrian in Inner Mongolia had to have walked the intermediate Earth.

Man has had two seemingly contradictory effects on the camel family. The original wild forms have all but disappeared, their range contracting with each passing decade, either because they have been hunted out or their habitat has been usurped by man and his ever-growing herds and flocks of domestic animals. The second effect has been in counterpoint.

Camels have been moved around the world even to areas where they were almost certainly not known even in their heyday. There are now camels deep inside Africa and across the top of that continent all the way to the Atlantic Ocean. They are found in Australia, in Europe and across Asia, of course, while llamas are in North America in increasing numbers, all in some way serving the real or imagined needs of man.

The camel family actually originated in North America. Initially, they were no larger than a hare (Eocene) and later were about the size of sheep (Oligocene). But by the Pleistocene era, they were huge, much larger than the descendants we know. During periods of glaciation, they apparently migrated westward on land bridges across the then much diminished Bering Sea. Some descendants clearly had made it down into South America, where a different course of evolution was charted. Then, for reasons that probably have to do with climate, the North American camels, along with early horses, immense ground sloths, dire wolves and saber-toothed cats became extinct.

The four South American camelids today are the guanaco *(Lama guanicoe),* the llama *(L. glama),* the alpaca *(L. pacos),* and the vicuña *(Vicugna vicugna).* The vicuña and the guanaco are considered wild animals. Since the ascendancy of the Inca, wild vicuñas have been rounded up, sheared of their extremely high-quality wool and released back into the wild. Early efforts were not made to control their breeding, and hence they were not domesticated. Later, the Jesuits took on that project but were expelled from Peru before succeeding. There have been other efforts recently, and we may reasonably predict that the vicuña will be the next animal to be domesticated (the moose *could* beat it). The vicuña's extraordinary wool will serve the luxury market.

The true domesticates, the llama and the alpaca, are believed to be the descendants of the guanaco. The llama is the only beast of burden with an indigenous ancestor domesticated by the native peoples of the Western Hemisphere. The alpaca is not a beast of burden but a wool and meat provider, yielding one of the finest of all natural fibers and some pretty fair meat that tastes somewhere between pork and lamb. Since the author maintains alpacas as pets, it is not something pleasing to contemplate. Llamas are also sometimes eaten.

The one-humped or dromedary camel was known as a wild animal in the Arabian region until about two thousand years ago, but all that remain there now are domestic animals and their descendants, part-time or semiferals. In parts of Kenya, it is common to see camels feeding in open areas near the road. They may mingle with domestic animals and sometimes with hoofed wildlife. They appear at first glance to be wild animals them-

selves, but close examination reveals a halter, a neck bell, a decorated rope collar or some other sign of management. It is believed that there are no wild dromedary camels left anywhere except possibly a few multigeneration escapees. In such cases, *wild* versus *feral* becomes a matter of semantics, not zoology, and that has been true since about the time of Christ.

The two-humped Bactrian camel was a wild species originally found from former Soviet Central Asia all the way to at least Inner Mongolia. But like the dromedary, the Bactrian is probably only found in the wild today as an escapee. There are occasional stories of truly wild groups of up to twenty or more animals. It has been suggested that there may be as many as three hundred truly wild Bactrian camels left somewhere in the remote foothills near the Gobi Desert, but that is not certain. There may, in fact, be no truly wild camels left in the world except the vicuña and guanaco of South America.

Interestingly, the one-humped camel as a fetus has two humps, one of which is absorbed before birth. That has led to speculation that the dromedary is only one more domestic form of the original wild Bactrian and should be acknowledged as a subspecies or even geographical race and nothing more. In Turkey, hybrids are regularly produced. They generally exhibit one hump, but are heavier in build than the dromedary.

Domestication

The "where" of domestication is open to speculation. For the dromedary, it could have been in central or southern Arabia. In fact, it was probably one or the other. And it seems to have started between three and four thousand years ago. Since wild and domestic dromedary camels do not differ as markedly as other domesticates from their wild forebears, it is difficult to tell what one is looking at from remains. When the dromedary was domesticated, it quickly spread west into the Nile Valley and hence across North Africa, south and east into India, up into Palestine and Syria, Iran, Iraq and Turkey, and from there outward. During the Hellenistic and Roman periods, the dromedary was in Europe, albeit probably never in large numbers except for, eventually, Eurasia.

The history of the Bactrian camel is even more vague. The species undoubtedly had an enormous range as a wild animal. The first depictions of the two-humped animal in the company of man date from four to five thousand years ago. Bones are unreliable, depictions in art more revealing.

The true "where" of the first domestication of the Bactrian camel is quite likely unknowable. The possible places are many, far spread and difficult to pin down. The idea was such a stunningly good one that once it had been accomplished, it spread like a storm across those parts of the world suitable to the species and accessible by overland travel. It is likely that nomads, or at least seminomadic peoples, were responsible in both cases, and their history is as misty and as difficult to identify as their distant caravans over a far ridge passing on a moonless night. We think we hear men's voices and the *thonk* of wooden bells, but we can never be quite sure.

The Original Association

Camels are fast, very fast, and have enormous stamina, much greater than man's. For a hunter on foot (and this was thousands of years before gunpowder), the camel must have been a very difficult target. They have a keen sense of smell, and as open flat-land running animals, they have excellent eyesight. They are also found in herds, which means every animal may have scores of eyes, ears and nostrils working in its defense.

The Bactrians form several kinds of herds. There are bachelor herds, all-adult female groups with newborn young and mixed herds of females with young up to two years of age led by a lone bull. Camels live up to fifty years and have plenty of time to learn all the tricks of survival. A wily old bull knows all there is to know about keeping his females and offspring out of harm's way. Any one of these herd types would be extremely difficult to stalk in the open, and driving herds by means of fire would be hard to do with either species, except in the few areas when the bands moved

onto grassy and brushy flats. Deserts and other arid regions don't burn very well.

The Bactrian camel gives birth between the middle of March and late April, after a protracted gestation period, as long as 440 days. The dromedary births any time between February and early May. The young are up and running in a few days, so there is only a small window of opportunity there. One can suppose that if there were an area, a valley perhaps, into which pregnant female herds moved for the birthing period, there would be some vulnerability before, during and immediately after parturition. Still, camel stalking would not be a sustaining activity for a human population over the course of the year. Many more calories would be expended than gained, and that equation just doesn't work. There has to be more profit than loss, a given in human survival.

The one point of vulnerability of camels would seem to be water. They can subsist on desert vegetation and brackish (even salt) water for months on end, but sooner or later, they come to a river. Although wood to build traps was scarce (and still is) where wild camels roamed and is needed as fuel, traps could have been set where they came to drink. Somehow using water as bait, nomads, a couple of thousand years before Christ, managed to contain and control camels and explore their potential. In terms of human needs, it was an enormous step both forward and upward.

The Value

The camels that were trapped near water, if indeed that was the way it was done, were animals that thrived in areas where man could scarcely go on his own. Man could live near the desert before the camel, but not in it.

The last pluvial age was immensely wet, and water tables in the Near East and the southern Mediterranean were at a probable all-time high. However, the last postglacial age (from 10,000 years ago on) was very dry, and an agricultural disaster lay in wait. With little knowledge of land use, and with the intent to own all the goats and sheep in the world, the new agriculturists and husbandmen in those areas set themselves up for a terrible fall. When their flocks denuded an area, there was nothing left to come up in the devastated plant life's stead. That made ideal conditions for the camel. For most higher forms of life, the goat was a terminal species. After it had been there, nothing remained except, of course, the camel. It was the only animal of use to man that could go a notch beyond the goat, and it could take man with it, feeding on the poorest fodder, and going long stretches without water. Man could now travel between wells and oases and survive.

Initially, as a hunted wild animal, the camel was taken for its meat, hide, bone and wool. It is not possible to say that no one ever looked at a wild camel and thought of it as a potential beast of burden, but it is more likely that young animals taken and kept for later slaughter were playfully jumped on and briefly ridden by young "cowboys" in the clan and an idea was born. From that idea, the caravan emerged, and man was at last able to travel to otherwise unattainable locales. And as camel caravans snaked across continents and subcontinents, man was also able to trade in goods and ideas. The important incense trade expanded once camels were available to carry loads of goods and riders. The spice trade, too, depended on camel caravans. With camels, nomadic tribes gained both economic and political power that they had not had since other tribes had settled down and stopped wandering.

Sometime after 1000 B.C., but before 500 B.C., the northern Arabian camel saddle was invented, and that increased the efficiency of camel packing and riding by quantum leaps. In a relatively brief period of time, camels became of importance to city dwellers as well as nomads. In addition to their role in trade, they were essential in warfare, they stimulated exploration and conquest, they were an important form of wealth and status and facilitated cultural exchange between East and West, all this centuries before man readily took to the sea. "Ship of the desert" is not a casual play on words. That is what the camel was and still is. Its domestication and utilization was a seminal cultural accomplishment, one of man's greatest.

One has to travel in arid regions, in true desert, to appreciate what the camel meant to man almost from the beginning. *Forbidding* hardly describes the land. In many areas, roads are useless. The drifting sand literally parades mountains across the landscape. The dunes are said to "walk," and that is an accurate description. The heat during the day, the freezing cold at night, the shifting sand underfoot, the uncertainty of finding water and the distances between oases make life impossible for man without the speed, endurance and carrying capacity of camels. Living with and without camels in a desert region is like living on two different levels of reality. The incredible advantages of possessing camels must have been apparent immediately, and people without them must have been quickly reduced to a lower status.

Camels pull carts and wagons, draw water from wells, pull plows, thrash wheat, provide the power for milling linseed for oil, operate irrigation devices requiring heavy-duty pulling; they do just about all of the things beasts of burden generally do to facilitate agriculture where agriculture is possible.

There are no camel breeds as such, but the Indians, at least, identify types. They have hill and plain camels, with the plain camel further divided into riverine and desert varieties. The riverine form (it is not a species or even a subspecies) is robust and rather slow, an ideal baggage animal. The desert camel is held in the highest regard, rather like a thoroughbred horse. It is the fastest camel of all and has great stamina. In India as elsewhere, the camel is first a beast of burden, then a milk and fiber animal, only lastly a leather and meat provider. In many areas, camels are not slaughtered unless there is a strong ceremonial component to the event. In China, the Bactrian camel has been known for a couple of thousand years longer than the dromedary, but both forms are in use there.

There are aspects of the camel that are not positive and have made it a second-choice animal where oxen, horses and asses could be used efficiently. Camels smell bad even to people who love them. Males can be obstreperous and even dangerous (a substantial Bactrian bull can weigh close to three-quarters of a ton). They are not particularly intelligent or responsive, they are frequently ill tempered and difficult to train, and they are slow breeders. The young can't really be used for four to five years. Unless an area is really arid, camels are subject to a number of diseases. There is a lethal insect-borne disease called surra, there are anthrax, rabies, a highly contagious camel pox and the inevitably fatal *kumree*. Camels are not easy keepers or particularly endearing. At times, they are difficult with other animals when held in close confinement, but they can do what other beasts of burden can't begin to accomplish. That has been enough to make them shapers of culture and civilization, and one of the most important domesticates in human history.

South America

At one time, it was believed that the llama was the descendant of the guanaco and the alpaca of the vicuña. It is now generally accepted, however, that the guanaco is the ancestor of both domesticates; the llama developed as a pack animal with pretty rough wool and the smaller alpaca as a fine fiber animal not robust enough to be significant as a bearer of burdens.

All evidence suggests that Peru was the place of domestication and three to four thousand years ago the probable time. There are hints today of how it could have been accomplished. Wild vicuñas are driven along alleyways made of stone walls into stone corrals, where they are sheared before being released. Guanacos could have been handled the same way and simply not released, and thus the llama and alpaca could have been selectively derived.

An interesting sidebar here: It has been suggested, since the New World domestications came long after that process had been perfected in the Old World, that Old World visitors in *Kon-Tiki*-like craft brought the idea to western lowland–coastal Peru. It caught on there and moved into the highlands, so the theory goes. There is not, however, very much to be said for or against that idea until we have perspective on very early oceanic travel. In the meantime, there would appear to be no good reason to deny Peru the honor and her Inca peoples the credit.

Llamas are not large or very robust, and about a hundred pounds is their maximum load. For that reason, caravans are now often very large, with dozens or scores of animals in the charge of one or two herdsmen, and that has probably been the case from the earliest days of this animal's use as a bearer of burdens. How is it possible for one or two men with perhaps a boy or two to manage so many animals? The answer is to be found in one word, *dogs*. Llamas were taken in from the cold eight to ten thousand years after dogs were. But there are no South American canids from which the domestic herding dog might have been derived. It certainly didn't come down to the Inca from the maned wolf. What about, then, those early transpacific travelers? Or if North America was a site for independent dog domestication, how would Stone Age Amerinds have made the sea or land journey to Peru? They couldn't have. The visitors would have had to come from farther away than that and been sophisticated in ways we understand imperfectly.

There are two alpaca varieties recognized in Peru, the Huacaya and the Suri, but they are both of the same species. The latter has a longer coat, and although both have wool of fine quality, the Suri is the preferred type. There are an unknown number of llama varieties (ccara and lanuda are examples), based very often on local preferences. Research is under way now to determine how many varieties are really valid. The huarizo is an alpaca/llama cross. The pacovicuña is a cross between an alpaca and a vicuña. Neither is of any real economic significance.

The influence of the camel family on human history was determined largely by the accident of geography. In the Middle East and Asia, the two Old World camels, the dromedary and the Bactrian, were presented with limitless horizons. Thousands of miles east and west, north and south, the level of cultural exchange was enormous, and the riches in both material and intellectual accomplishments forever changed the course of civilization. Wherever the camel carried man, his goods and his ideas, new worlds were born that were spread farther still when technology enabled man to establish regular sea routes.

In South America, however, the llama and the alpaca were held in check to the east by the impenetrable rain forest of the Amazon Basin, and to the west by the vast Pacific. Their horizons were very limited, and as a result, the brilliance of the Inca world never met the Mayan or the Aztec worlds, let alone more far-off cultures. And in their isolation, they were all vulnerable to the merest touch of the outside world. Diseases and parasites destroyed whole populations that had never had an opportunity to develop immunity. Those who survived became a captive people, and their greatest accomplishments, peculiar to only their place, responsive to only their needs, went down with them to reemerge only centuries later as tourist rites.

If that appears to be harsh judgment, it is the judgment of history. It is interesting to speculate what might have happened if the camelids of the New World, like those of the Old, had been able to bring the glittering islands of high cultural accomplishment face-to-face with their equals. What then might have happened if the move across oceans had been away from the Western Hemisphere instead of inexorably toward it? There is further irony in the fact that although camels still are of enormous importance locally, on the world scene, the caravan has been replaced by the cargo jet. But the keepers of the camel have been enlarged rather than diminished. The fuel the jets require lie in vast oceans of crude petroleum under the sand over which the caravans traveled for so many centuries.

ELEVEN

The Horse:

Energy and the Servant of Man

The Image

In its time, in its many places, the horse, the ultimate symbol of man and animal joined as a single unit of energy, has had innumerable faces, some of them clearly contradictory. It is almost as if man has not quite been able to believe his good fortune in being master of an animal this large, this powerful, this fleet. Perhaps because it has allowed man to be more than himself, more than he could ever be alone, the horse has had a dominant role in myth, legend and superstition and, not surprisingly, in our dreams.

The horse, sleek, muscular, body gleaming, eyes burning, mane blowing, tail flowing, steel-hard feet sending bolts of lightning searing through the clouds of heaven, has been itself a god and the steed of gods, the sun, the sea and the wind among them. It is a phallic symbol, the sign of power and virility, and therefore a model and an object of veneration.

The mother goddess of the ancient Britons was Eona, a horse. Demeter, the Greek fertility goddess, had the head of a mare, and around her grew a cult that penetrated deep into the heart of diverse European cultures. It lasted up through Roman times and beyond. The horse's hoof, itself a phallic symbol, causes springs of fresh water (or semen) to flow from the earth wherever it strikes. The shape of the horse's foot is symbolic of the female genitals.

In the Bible, the horse is a symbol of power most often associated with warfare. In Revelation, even the heavenly host is equipped with horses. Moses warns the Hebrews that if they elect a king, he must not gather horses unto himself or buy them from Egypt, which probably meant he should not be warlike and build an army. Some kings heeded the advice that came down to them from the time of the Exodus, some did not. King Solomon's stables held four thousand head, or was it forty thousand? It is not clear. Throughout the books of the Bible, the horse appears again and again, usually in ceremonial or military roles. Supernatural afflictions were frequently delivered by horses. The Hebrews are forbidden to eat them. They are unclean; their hooves are not cloven.

The number of arcane beliefs that center on the horse is bewildering. It is the most fabulous of all domestic animals. Horses can see ghosts (is that what makes them *spooky* at times?) and horses are ghosts. See a white horse on New Year's Eve and wish on it and you will have a lucky year. See a white horse and you will soon see a redheaded girl. The converse is also true, they say. Newlyweds must never drive a pair of white horses if they want their marriage to work. It is lucky to dream of horses in India, Great Britain and the United States. But in Canada, if you watch a span of white horses drive out of sight, your life will end within the year. Witches and the Devil have appeared in the form of a horse. A coal black stallion with forefeet lashing out whinnying madly into the night is the very stuff of nightmares. (Nightmare, incidentally, is not derived from a female horse in the night. It derives from the word *mare,* an evil spirit believed to sit on one's chest during sleep, thus causing a nightmare.) Such images appear as leitmotivs in European lore and mythology. But, then, that is true wherever the horse has gone.

The ancients had a wide variety of horse-centered beliefs and legends. Heracles owned man-eating horses. (Meat-eating horses don't exist. They are fictional animals.) The wooden horse enabled the Greeks to take Troy, of course, and Achilles inherited the immortal horses, Balius and Xanthus, from his father. Athena had a surname, Chalinitis, which described her as a trainer of horses with the use of a bridle. The Roman goddess Epona protected horses as her principal chore. She was a kind of Lady of the Stable. Selene, the moon goddess, was drawn across the heavens in her chariot by two magnificent white horses. (In the interest of accuracy, they were sometimes represented as mules and at other times as cows. Ancient myths are like that. They are inconstant things at best.)

Since man brought the horse under control, the myths and beliefs have burgeoned. They have been copied, adapted and altered to suit an enormous variety of cultural contexts. But certain tonalities have remained constant. The horse is fast, noble, valiant, faithful, splendid, dangerous, highly sexed and thus to be emulated, and unbelievably powerful. In every context, the horse is handsome, awesome, beautiful. It is amazing, then, that man has treated his own and his gods' beloved steed so badly. They eat horses in France and Belgium, which is hardly a rewarding experience, for the horse.

The Animal

The horse belongs to the order Perissodactyla, the odd-toed ungulates. The rhinoceroses, the tapirs and the equines, which include the horse, are all that is left of this ancient and once very large group of often very large animals. The horse's family is Equidae. In modern times, the family has been represented by the horse (one or possibly two species), three asses and four zebras, one of which, the South African quagga, became extinct in this century. These are thin pickings given the former glory of the group and particularly when we remember that the wild horse is almost extinct except for zoo populations. A small population of very primitive horses in northeastern Tibet, in an area known as the Riwoche region, has been located and will be under evaluation for several years, at least. It *could* be a distinct species, a kind of equine missing link. The members of this small isolated herd hidden in a remote valley reportedly look like the horses in Stone Age wall paintings.

It is generally believed that almost all of the horses seen in the wild today, excepting perhaps the Riwoche horses, are either feral or have been hybridized by feral horses. Certainly that is true in the New World. The animals that survive represent the end of a major evolutionary line, which stretches from the present all the way back to the Eocene era.

Horses originated in North America, but along with camels, they migrated westward across the land bridges of the Bering Sea and became extinct in the Western Hemisphere. They developed from cocker-spaniel-sized creatures of brushy areas to the steeds we know today, from the Shetland pony and the Thoroughbred to twenty-one-hand (eighty-four-inch) draft horses. They started as browsers and ended as grazers. And that is why they learned to run.

The perissodactyl foot is made for running, and that has been most highly developed in the horse. Tapirs run on four toes, rhinoceroses on three, but the horse on one. Tapirs live along watercourses in thick forests and jungle, rhinoceroses and horses in flat or undulating grassy areas. (The few remaining specimens of the Asian rhinoceros species do move in deep cover much of the time. The African species are savanna animals.) Without the benefit of cover, the group generally had no choice but to run. The horse, without the rhinoceros's awesome bulk and impressive nose horns, had to learn to run the fastest of all.

It has been estimated that for a human being to punish his feet the way a horse does—a half ton of animal slamming down at a full gallop, and clearing an obstacle and landing on one forefoot, therefore on one toe—that person would have to have a foot the size of a tennis court. Whether or not that statement is precisely accurate, it does convey a picture that is. The horse's foot is a remarkable device. The horse itself, heart, lungs, legs, feet, energetics, all considered, is an incredible running machine.

The Original Association

Widespread Bronze Age man (outside of Tibet) probably knew two forms of wild horses. In Mongolia, there was the pale yellow Przewalski or Mongolian wild horse, and in southeastern Europe, there was the light brown to gray tarpan. Both had black manes and tails. The latter form probably became extinct early in the 1600s, and the former lives on today in zoos. Both animals are believed to be substantially unchanged since they were first encountered by man. It is likely that it was the tarpan that gave rise to the domestic horse, although it is not given a different species name from either the domestic animal we know or the remaining Mongolian horses today.

As they did with the aurochs, the principal ancestor of today's cattle, European zoo men (especially in Germany in the 1930s) experimented with breeding for seemingly primitive characteristics to "re-create" the original animal. It wasn't something that could actually be done, but they were apparently successful in approximating the extinct ancestral forms. There are still some of the man-made "tarpan" in Poland, and I encountered them in the extreme eastern forests there.

They are bold but gentle and seek physical contact with man. I once walked along a forest trail accompanied by one of these constructed throwbacks with its head between my arm and my body, a position he assumed on his own after nudging me in the back to announce his presence. How fairly this represents the true wild tarpan I do not know, but however much these animals may look like wild tarpan, I doubt that they act like them. If they did duplicate ancient behavior in German zoos sixty years ago, there is no mystery about domestication. Bronze Age man simply walked over and put a rope of braided hide around a tarpan's neck and walked off into the future with him. Surely the truth was more violent than that.

Horses offer the hunter a lot of meat, tough hides useful in scores of ways and tail hair ideal for braiding into rope. Here again, however, like wild cattle and wild camels, was a fast, alert, tough animal that lived in herds and took off in an instant at speeds that would make any thought of pursuit foolish. Man has never domesticated an animal anywhere near as fast as the horse. In order to capture or kill even a single horse, men would have had to drive whole herds into chutes and corrals, using grass fires and noisemakers. For mass and extremely wasteful slaughter, herds were driven off cliffs.

Bone piles at the foot of cliffs tell us that this was done. Herds could also have been tricked into capture by barricading water, as may have been done with camels. One way or another, groups of animals were stockaded, separated, slaughtered for food and hides and eventually put to work. The wild horses available for manipulation were undoubtedly very tough, and capturing and breaking them must have quickly become highly skilled trades, probably with significant social standing. The cowboy is an ancient occupation.

Domestication

The where and when of this extraordinarily important domestication have been under discussion for centuries. There is an enormous amount of information, although no uniform interpretation of what it all means. As so often happens today, the quantity of data has outstripped our ability to interpret it. But as far back as the closing centuries of the last Ice Age, the wild horse was an important meat and hide source for the burgeoning population of Europe. That was between twelve thousand and thirteen thousand years ago. We will never know when the first young daredevil threw himself onto the back of a foal or yearling and thereby anticipated the future. And we certainly don't know exactly where and when domestication became a concerted effort with a real goal in mind.

Excitement has centered on a small ivory carving of a horse's head found in the Saint Michel d'Arudy cave in the Pyrenees. The horse appears to be wearing a rope halter. The piece is carved from mammoth ivory and comes from the Paleolithic, the Old Stone Age, fourteen thousand years ago. That is very much earlier than the traditional time given for horse domestication. There is a great deal of speculation and disagreement about this piece. If it is a halter and the piece is as old as believed, then we know almost nothing about the early history of the domestication of this most important animal.

Juliet Clutton-Brock, the British authority on domestication, suggests that wild horses were becoming rare in Europe by 7000 B.C. Could there have been too much hunting pressure, too many herds driven over cliffs? The human population was growing. By 4000 B.C., there is evidence of horses in the company of man. That is eight thousand years after the mysterious mammoth ivory carving found in the cave in the Pyrenees. Since 6000 B.C. is generally thought to be about the time serious efforts were being made to bring this tough, wild animal under control, we simply have to set the Saint Michel d'Arudy carving aside for the time being. A discrepancy of nearly eight thousand years is too difficult to explain.

Where?

There is a group of Neolithic sites north of the Black Sea known as Sredni Stog. They are scattered over the steppes, and it is often suggested that this was where the domestication of the horse really began. At a late Neolithic site called Dereivka near the Dnieper River, a large number of horse bones have been recovered. At least one horse whose remains were found there would have measured about fourteen and a half hands (fifty-eight inches), which is about the size of the Mongolian wild horse today and of the reconstructed tarpan in Poland.

The early uses of the horse in captivity were almost certainly consumptive—meat and hides and then, slowly, draft power. Some researchers believe that horses were not ridden until 1000 B.C. That would mean the horse was a breeding captive for fully three thousand years without being ridden, and that seems highly unlikely. The macho temptation would have been too great. Man could not have sat on the idea of riding a horse for three millennia. Some young buckaroos full of wine and themselves would have taken the step shortly after the horse was in captivity, certainly after they were breeding in captivity and there were foals less skilled in the art of being wild.

The horses of Dereivka could have been wild animals and not

domesticated at all. Thus far, there is not enough evidence to pin down a place for their first domestication. At first, the horses in captivity did not differ enough from the wild form to leave a clear record in the bone caches. Eventually, the horse in captivity would get smaller and then, much later, much larger. It has proven to be a species with a fairly cooperative set of genes. On my farm, I have Belgian draft horses, massive animals, and a miniature horse now fully grown that can still walk between my legs. Both are the products of selective breeding and demonstrate just how malleable horses' genes have been.

Once the horse was put to work as a draft animal, the idea spread rapidly. From Anatolia, part of modern Turkey, to the Negev in modern Israel, to western Asia to the British Isles, to North Africa and the Iberian Peninsula, the horse was on the move, undoubtedly carrying man on his back.

At least we can be sure the three-thousand-year-old remains from Ireland are from domestic horses. There is no record of fossil horses in Ireland. They had to have been brought there by man. Clutton-Brock tells of a mare's skull from Norfolk in England that dates from the Bronze Age. This mare of long ago had survived so long that her teeth were too far gone for grazing. She could not have lived that long on her own. She must have been carefully fed. A pet, perhaps, or some kind of goddess?

As a rule, horses from northern latitudes tend to be cobbier and have shorter legs and ears and shaggier coats than the specimens from warmer climates. There they have tended to develop the long, sleek legs, the short, shiny coats and the smart, upstanding ears we admire in our champion horse breeds today. But all domestic horses were apparently de-

rived from one single wild species and spread out from there. As they were moved by man (or as they moved him) from one place to another, they adapted to the weather conditions and were also forced to adapt to man's taste by his control over their breeding. It was a fairly simple process for man. If you did not like the way a horse looked or performed, or if you did not like his disposition, you ate him.

No one knows when man first made the connection between copulation and birth. They are events separated by eleven months in the case of the horse. But the connection did not have to be understood for there to have been selective breeding. And even if it was understood, it is certain there was no understanding of genes. Man would naturally keep those animals with the most endearing and useful characteristics around longer, giving them greater opportunities to breed.

With the domestication of the horse came a variety of cultural adjuncts. Between 1000 and 1500 B.C., sleds and carts or wagons were established technologies. Almost certainly, animal-drawn plows were in use by then, too. Oxen would have been harnessed first, then horses and asses and later mules. The first horseshoes were probably slipperlike fittings attached with leather thongs. They were used by the Romans. Actual horseshoeing—nailing metal shoes in place—probably came into practice between A.D. 800 and 900. By the middle ages it was standard practice. In more recent centuries there have been horse-drawn vehicles of every

description, from circus calliopes and fire wagons to omnibuses and the stage coach. The trappings of no other domestic animal have so greatly cluttered up our lives.

Benefits

The differences between a culture with horses and one without are profound. Consider the values to a people of speed, mobility, communications, vast military superiority, efficient agriculture and not, just incidentally, elegance of transport and self-image. From the beginning, horses would have been war machines. And that lasted up until World War I, when machine guns, tanks and aircraft began to replace them as the ultimate weapons of intimidation.

It was not long after the horse's potential had been explored that horselessness was akin to poverty. In areas like prehorse North America, the differences did not exist and so there were no equine "haves" and "have-nots." Once the horse arrived, however, the concept of horses equaling wealth quickly became the reality of the times. As for those adventuresome explorers on horseback, although most people today don't particularly like the idea, they had an added advantage. If things got rough in new and strange lands, they could always dismount and eat what they rode in on.

The horse in uncounted ways changed the lives and fortunes of mankind. Consider the sequence just in North America alone.

By 1494, there were horse-breeding farms on the island of Hispaniola based on stock brought there by Columbus. The Spanish exploration and conquest of the mainland depended on horses from those farms. Later, the British brought horses to Virginia, and when they moved out of their coastal settlements, it was on horseback. Eventually, the Spaniards coming in through Mexico and Florida and the British from the East Coast introduced the horse to the Plains Indians and their cultures exploded. The Indian wars were fought on horseback, except in the dense forests of the East.

Exploration of the West depended on horses, and transportation, although oxen and mules were used to some extent, was also very horse-dependent. Most plows were drawn by horses on the first farms in the region. And until the invention of the telegraph, the fastest form of communication was the horseback rider. Newly opened regions were protected by mounted cavalry. When the cattle culture arose in the West, the manipulation of huge numbers of animals over vast areas depended on the cowboy, who was, of course, mounted on horseback. The American West as we know it could not have evolved as it did without horses.

Transport in and between all American cities was also on horseback or in horse-dawn vehicles. Trams, fire trucks, the whole expanding American scene was horse-dependent. That dependence is gone, but the horse is still deeply embedded in our culture. Everything from western movies to horse racing, from the ghastly anachronistic rodeo to elegant recreational riding and Olympic events, is horse-related. And when the internal combustion machine began replacing horse-drawn vehicles, we rated those machines (as we still do) in units of horsepower and put the engines in the front because that is where horses used to be.

TWELVE

The Ass, the Donkey and the Mule:
The Priceless Plodders

The Image

When Cleinis of Babylon tried to make the ass the sacrificial animal of choice in tribute to Apollo, the god rejected the gesture and demanded that only sheep, goats and heifers be used. That Olympian put-down was not a high point in the history of this splendid animal. Apollo apparently had a problem with the ass. When King Midas chose Pan over him in a musical contest, Apollo changed the king's ears into those of an ass, and it bothered Midas no end. Even being rich didn't help.

But asses were sacred to Dionysus because one carried him across the water on his journey to the oracle at Dodona. That was a leg up for the evolving donkey. And Priapus was the son of Dionysus and Aphrodite. That was impressive lineage, and the young god became the patron of reproduction and the powers of nature. Sacrifices to him included asses, Apollo notwithstanding.

Mary, Abraham, Joseph, Job and Moses were among those who rode asses through the pages of the Bible. But the most famous passenger any ass ever carried was, by far, Jesus of Nazareth. For Jesus, riding an ass was a symbol of humility in a world where prancing steeds and fleet desert camels had long been in use. In time, however, Jesus' chosen mount became a symbol of degradation. Condemned prisoners on the way to the gallows were required to ride a donkey to their violent destiny, sitting backward, hanging on to the animal's tail. And prostitutes were ordered to ride a donkey nude through the village for their punishment.

The ass, like almost all domestic animals, took on one mantle after another. To the Church of Rome, Jesus' mount inexplicably became a symbol of lust. (There have been many wearers of that crown.) The Hindus perceived the ass in much the same way. In the ancient world, the ass or donkey was the sign of stubbornness, stupidity and ignorance. But for the Greeks it was the symbol of wisdom, and it was the sacred animal of Bacchus, the god of wine. Pan himself sometimes wore asses' ears (although goat's horns, ears and hindquarters were his usual costume) as a badge of insight and fine-tuned musical sensitivity. The Phrygians worshiped asses even as others damned them. And today the word *ass* is not a flattering epithet.

There is nothing new in any of this. Domestic animals, as they reshaped cultures and economies and redefined man's role and potential, were required to be all things to all people real or imagined. And much of what was believed ranged from the sublime to the downright ridiculous. Thus it ever was.

The Animal in the Wild

The three wild asses that have existed since the history of domestication began are the kulan or onager *(Equus hemionus)*, the lesser-known kiang *(E. kiang)*, and the African wild ass *(E. asinus)*. The last named also bears the species name for the domestic ass, otherwise known as the donkey or burro. The name *burro* is simply Spanish for donkey. There is nothing to distinguish between the two. A jackass is a male ass or donkey. The shortened name *jack* is sometimes used and is equally correct. Jennet is the female. It is believed that the African form is the ancestor of all existing domestic donkeys.

In the wild, asses generally have flourished in semiarid to arid areas. They can go longer without water than either horses or zebras. Their social organization is very zebralike, although they can do with less food in harsher conditions than their pretty striped cousins. The asses are uniformly sure-footed, more so than the other equids, but are the slowest of the lot. They are deliberate and extremely hardy.

Why the African wild ass should be the only one of the three to be

domesticated is a mystery. Frederich Zeuner, one of the true historians of domestication and author of one of the few standard references on the subject, says that is not the case and places the onager as an intermediate form between the true wild ass (African) and the horse. Clutton-Brock and others do not agree, and like so many other historical accounts of domestication, the same data may lead to different conclusions.

The original range of the African wild ass was not that vast in terms of human contact, probably Morocco to Somalia and to some extent the Arabian Peninsula. The kiang's range was even more limited, Tibet and contiguous highlands, generally at nine thousand to ten thousand feet. The onager, on the other hand, ranged from modern Syria (where it is now extinct) and Iraq all the way to Manchuria and at least western India. That exposed the onager (or kulan, among its dozens of names) to an enormous number of advancing cultures and the opportunities for domestication would appear to have been endless.

There are those like Zeuner who believe the onager was domesticated in the ancient world by the Sumerians and others, but that would not appear to be likely, for there are no identifiable descendants. Donkeys bred to African wild asses produce fertile offspring. Donkeys bred to onagers and kiangs do not. Donkeys or horses have also been bred to onagers in modern times to produce small mules, which are infertile. Wild asses everywhere have been badly overhunted for sport and for their hides. Quite literally, the domestication of the African wild ass to produce the donkey is the only conservation effort that may ultimately offer any of the ass species a chance for survival. The donkey is an animal that has been taken in from the cold.

Where and When

There were probably three races of the African wild ass. One was a northwestern form now extinct; it did not survive the Roman occupation. The second, a northeastern form, the Nubian, is now almost extinct, and the Somali form is also surviving in very reduced numbers. There was a European race at least in Italy, but they were extinct well before domestication began. That European form apparently once ranged all across the continent, even onto the British Isles.

It appears almost certain that the African wild ass was first domesticated in either the Nile Valley or Libya. There are tomb depictions that go back at least as far as 2600 B.C. Between 3000 and 2500 B.C., the bones of asses occur in deposits from Bronze Age Palestine, and there is a pottery figure from Jericho. Damascus is "the town of the asses" in cuneiform, according to Zeuner, and from that period, the spread of the ass as donkey and burro was an endless march around the world.

Ferals

Feral burros are so common in many places that they are considered pests. In Australia, shooting burros from vehicles has traditionally been considered an easy entertainment for an otherwise dull Sunday afternoon. It is target practice. In the United States in the Grand Canyon and elsewhere, rescue teams have had to be organized to save burros from elimination. They are said to be of danger to the habitat, which can be a real problem for native wildlife in arid and semiarid areas. In island isolation without predation, donkeys do represent a threat to the habitat, and in the Galápagos and other remote archipelagoes to which they have been transported, shooting is generally the solution. Treating donkeys as vermin somehow does not seem right. But feral horses are treated the same way in at least nine of our western states.

Whatever went into the initial domestication and however well (or badly, in all likelihood) the animals were treated, something worked. I have been involved in two Grand Canyon rescues, and the donkeys are exceptionally easy animals to deal with. They are gentle with children and are generally gregarious, constantly nuzzling for treats and allowing themselves to be held and petted. The sound of their braying close up is one of the most astounding in nature. Hence their affectionate designation as "desert canaries." The two that live in a field immediately adjacent to my study are true pets and are hand-fed every day. One of them, the male we call Pedro, was wild-born in the Grand Canyon.

Their appeal and eventually the need for donkeys are easy to see. They are hardy, undemanding, surefooted and able to handle fairly large loads over very rough terrain and in any temperature man is likely to encounter. They are easily managed as individuals and in groups, and they easily herd with other livestock. The fact that they are stubborn is a minor point and not really a deterrent. Size variations are quite surprising for hoofed livestock. The handsome and highly regarded Poitou ass developed in France is about the size of a horse, while there are dwarf donkeys no bigger than sheep. Gray is the usual color, but black and white lines have been developed, even one that is piebald. Coat style depends almost entirely on where the animal is asked to live. Donkeys grow coats according to ambient conditions.

The donkey has been called the "poor man's horse," but that term is relative. Many a poor man has been greatly enriched by an animal willing to carry him almost anywhere he has wanted to go and bear his burdens as well.

The Mule

A mule is a cross between a male donkey (jack or jackass) and a female horse (mare). It is by definition unable to reproduce and, in fact, the term *mule,* when not applied to this specific cross, means any infertile animal, particularly one that is that way because of hybridization. There are rare references to fertile mules. They are usually contested, but some may have existed. In 1984, in Nebraska, it is believed that a female mule did give birth to a foal. It is, however, so rare if it does occur as to leave the definition of *mule* intact.

When the sexes are reversed and a male horse (stallion) is bred with a female donkey (jennet), the offspring, also sterile, is referred to as a hinny. Mules are far more commonly encountered than hinnies. They are perceived as better working animals. There are also crosses between zebras and horses, and zebras and donkeys. Collectively, their offspring are referred to as zebroids, individually variously as zonkeys, zebrorse, zebrule and several other designations. They are infertile, rare and of no economic importance.

Mule breeding began at least in biblical times, and western Asia seems the likely place. The mule, although it is extremely stubborn (it makes the donkey look like a volunteer), is surefooted, large enough to carry heavy loads, patient and easy to ride or drive. Alexander the Great's hearse was drawn from Babylon to Alexandria by a team of sixty-four mules. The Roman army used mules extensively, as did the armies engaged in World War I. The mule has served man well throughout much of his history.

City dwellers today can be born, grow old and die without ever seeing a live mule, and without really knowing what one is except that it looks vaguely like a horse or a donkey. In fact, the difference between an ass and a donkey is also bewildering for some people. There is none, of course, if the ass referred to is the domestic animal. Despite the lack of recognition in modern urban settings, both donkeys and mules have been extremely important in agriculture and transport on every continent except Antarctica. Dependence on them becomes less with each decade that passes, but their role in our development cannot be easily overstated. With the mechanization of the farm and rural transport, there are about twenty-one million tractors now in use around the world. Working donkeys, however, are believed to number close to forty million.

PART FOUR

THE CONTROLLED HUNTERS

THIRTEEN

The Cat:
Goddess or Devil?

The Image

Above all else, the domestic cat is perceived as a hedonistic material-ist, a sensualist and a voluptuary as well as a relentless hunter and a steely-eyed assassin. By and large, it is all of the above. The fact that the first three terms are approximately or nearly synonymous really doesn't matter. As orchestrated by the cat, and they are, they resonate with new dimensions of meaning, and even the slightest nuances justify their seemingly redun-dant use.

In Egypt, not long after its initial moves into the realm of domestica-tion, the cat was actually held sacred. It was endowed with magical qualities that must have contributed to a lifestyle of which we can be sure the cat heartily approved. One suspects the domestic cat of today retains a tribal memory of those "good old days" and is waiting patiently, as only a cat can, for redeification.

The Egyptian goddess Bast was a cat, and the habit of referring to the cat as "she" remains firmly fixed in many, perhaps most, cultures even today. And it is interesting to note that a pejorative word for a woman is not "queen," the appropriate nomenclature for a female cat, but "bitch," the equally appropriate word for a female dog.

Bast rode in a chariot drawn by cats. Woven through Egyptian mythology and religion like a golden thread, she was involved with the sun, the moon and the three dominant religious figures, Horus, Ra and Osiris. A city was named for Bast (sometimes Bastet, Basht, Pasht or Bubastis), cats were protected, and they were embalmed when they died. It was a capital offense to kill a cat. There is a record of a merchant visiting Egypt who was stoned to death because he somehow was the agent of a cat's death. Ceremonies in Bast's honor frequently involved sex orgies, and one assumes they were noisy affairs if they were supposed to propitiate the goddess in whose honor the people were sacrificing their elemental selves.

Alas, in Europe, the cat did not fare as well. The Devil frequently was depicted as a cat, and felines were the familiars of witches. More than just black cats were considered bad luck. Heresy, sorcery, orgies both heterosexual and homosexual, witchery, all manner of diablerie were laid at the cat's door. Godhood was replaced with its exact opposite. Orgy participants reportedly kissed a cat's posterior before joining in the group debasement and debauchery. For some reason, the cat became heaven's detritus, a much-shrunken role from which it is still struggling to emerge. It may never be a goddess again, but as a companion animal, it is adored by millions. Yet again, we see something that is apparently unavoidable. Once an animal is domesticated and folded into a culture, there is enormous ambivalence about the role that animal is supposed to play. Perhaps the reason and the universality of that reaction stems from man's ambivalence about his own nature and role.

The Original Animal

The classification of the wildcats is in a perfect muddle, but we only have to deal with one species that is often feral, unfortunately, but no longer wild. Today, there is a very widespread group of small (five to ten pounds) wildcats ranging over Europe, Africa and Asia that belongs to the genus *Felis*. They have literally scores of names both vernacular and scientific. In theory, the domestic cat could have come to us from any of them. It can breed with all of them, we believe. It is like them in behavior in almost every way, and since a high percentage of our domestic cats are tabbies, they even look very much like this general grouping.

These European, African, Asian wildcats are generally solitary hunters who are skilled at their trade, but they will take carrion. They are tough, tenacious and daring. I have watched an African wildcat dash in among a congregation of crocodiles feeding on carrion on the banks of a river. The cat literally snatched pieces of meat from the jaws of crocodiles twelve and more feet long, ran off into the bush to consume its prize and then came back again. It was an awesome display of skill and chutzpah.

The Beginning

Traditional wisdom has the African wildcat *(Felis silvestris,* although sometimes identified as *Felis libyca)* as the primary ancestor of the domestic cat. Whatever we should call it, that theory seems likely to be about right, at least at the beginning.

The most probable place of domestication was Egypt between 1000 and 4200 B.C., a comparatively recent event. At about that time, the Egyptians invented the concept of long-term, large-quantity grain storage, the silo. For the rats and mice of the Nile Valley that was an excellent idea, and they must have invaded human settlements in enormous numbers. The African wildcat, the saw-scaled viper and the cobra would have followed their favorite prey. The mongoose almost certainly was already being kept as a pet of sorts, and the cobra and the viper, staples of its diet, would have suffered from that fact. And although some people worshiped snakes, they might not have wanted the objects of their veneration as house companions. It is not true that indigenous people necessarily take to all the wildlife that shares their habitat. On more than one occasion, I have seen people scream and scatter, later to return and throw rocks at a cobra that had popped up in their midst. In addition to its fondness for rodents, the cat had a great deal more to offer than the cobra in the way of cuddling and companion-

ship. And it certainly was preferable to the irritable, singularly dangerous saw-scaled viper.

Undoubtedly, kittens were taken from dens and nests and became socialized toys. Those that acted ferociously as adults were released or otherwise disposed of, and those that tended to be softer in disposition were kept and would have bred. Endearing characteristics, the grandparents of genetic selection, would have been exposed and then fostered. And so the domestic cat evolved.

The cat as companion and mouser has moved on around the world with man for centuries, and at various times, in exotic coats and styles, it has been an item of trade. Cats have always had a way of getting lost and becoming feral, breeding successfully in the wild condition. Almost without a doubt, other species of the genus *Felis* would have been crossed into the new species. What these true wild forms had to offer the domestic cat that was new and different is difficult to identify. But domestic cats moving in and out of the feral state may have transported other species' genes back and forth with them. That does not alter the fact, however, that the *African wildcat* was the most likely principal ancestor of our feline companions today.

The Dollars and Sense of It

There have been a few more-or-less minor mammal domestications that are without real economic significance except for the sale of the animals themselves. Shelf pets like hamsters, gerbils and other small rodents are obvious examples, but the cat is the most important economically insignificant of all domestic mammals.

Of course, cats have worked long and hard as mousers. They are good as pest-controllers, although probably not as good as the mongoose or even some dogs like the Jack Russell terrier. Still, however good they are, that is of slight value when one compares cats with goats, sheep, pigs, cattle, water buffalo or horses. Even dogs have helped support major economies as herders and drovers.

What, then, accounts for the enormous popularity of cats? Somewhere between fifty-five and sixty million of them are now household pets in the United States alone. And their true value can be summed up in one word: companionship. Cats are very effective as companions at relieving stress. If there is a significant economic niche for the cat beyond the sale of kittens, pet food, toys and litter (a multi-billion-dollar figure in the United

States annually), it is not possible to measure it because it is in presumed reduced medical and psychiatric costs and therefore reduced lost time in the workplace. There is simply no way of putting a dollar value on the domestic cat's therapeutic value. The figure would of necessity rely on supposition and traditionally held beliefs. It is there, however, even if it can't be quantified. As the owner of nine cats, I can testify to just what their value is as companions, and it is that role the cat has played in part or totally from dynastic Egypt to the present day.

A Tribute: Borneo

Kuching, a remarkable, modern city, is the capital of the Malay state of Sarawak, located in far northwestern Borneo. In the Malay language, *kuching* means cat, and it is generally believed that the city was named for the domestic cat. The name *could* be a bastardization of *Cochin* in India or *Cochin China* in Vietnam, concocted by the imperial British, who were once very much in evidence on Borneo, but the cat hypothesis is probably right.

In the northern part of Kuching is an amazing new town hall high on a hill overlooking the city. It is in the shape of a temple and is truly splendid. Almost its entire first floor is occupied by the Kuching Cat Museum in which the roles the cat has played in the world's cultures and our emotions are celebrated. Thousands of images from every imaginable culture and in everything from crystal and ceramics to bone and stone are displayed with the most modern museum techniques and excellent interpretive graphics in both English and Malay. It is really a most unusual tribute in a rather unlikely place, unlikely unless you think about it for a moment. The Malay people love their cats. Why not such a monument on Borneo? Where better?

The Ferals

There is an unfortunate drawback to the cat's fabled self-dependency: their ability to survive, however briefly, in the wild state. Cats as ferals generally have short lives. Dogs, foxes, owls, disease, wheeled vehicles, people with guns and bows all prey on the hapless cat. But cats can mate at seven or eight months, so they don't have to live long to produce a good many more unfortunates. The reproductive potential of even one pair of intact cats and their offspring, even if their individual life span is only two years, is awesome. Were they all to live (an impossibility), the number of kittens that would be produced in seven years is about 150,000.

Every animal man has domesticated has in time produced ferals, animals living back in the wild state full- or part-time. Feral donkeys and horses are considered vermin in many places, feral dogs spread disease and attack livestock, feral camels thrive in arid areas and can stress the habitat they then share with native wildlife, honeybees can become dangerous so-called killer bees, but cats have a highly developed skill. Like mongooses that have been transported and then allowed to go wild, feral cats hunt native wildlife. Because they climb so well, nesting birds high or low are endangered by their need to feed themselves. The full impact of a feral cat population on reptiles, small mammals and birds is hard to measure, but it is considerable. And where wildlife is having a rough go of it, cats can add an unendurable level of stress. Feral cats, much as we may cherish their domesticated cousins at home, can constitute an unforgivable environmental insult. And the cats, like most other feral animals, suffer the effects of having part of their survival skills dulled by our unnatural selection in creating their forebears.

The result is both ironic and tragic. Millions of cats in the United States alone are collected and killed (euthanized or euthanatized are the euphemisms for slaughter that are generally used, those and "put to sleep" or "put down") because there are no homes available for them. The cruelty in allowing a half-wild animal to exist, to impact wildlife and then to be destroyed because it is trying to survive is a terrible way to define ourselves. Once an animal has been domesticated, it becomes man's responsibility forever, and that includes control over reproduction. In the case of cats, that, by definition, means two concerted efforts—spaying and neutering and never abandoning them.

The cat has run the gamut in human estimation and enjoyed and suffered the extremes of fate. It remains one of man's all-time favored and abused domestications.

A Matter of Size

Because it is such a recent domestication (dogs have been in our charge at least three times as long), we may not yet have a real handle on the cat's genetic potential. Except for the occasional obese specimen or freak, all domestic cats weigh in at about the same, give or take two or three pounds. A dog in the mastiff line, however, may weigh a hundred times as much as some of the smaller toys, although they belong to the same species. Horses run from very small ponies to massive draft animals of almost a ton in weight. If that kind of variation is ever achieved in the domestic cat, we will have to do some careful reevaluation of its role in our lives. A feral tabby cat the size of a very large leopard or jaguar would be troublesome to more than chipmunks and songbirds. It would have lost much of its fear, and fear of man is the only thing that enables man and large predators to coexist. Variability in the size of cats is something we have not yet had to deal with except as fanciers of the pure breeds. It may be a consideration for the future.

FOURTEEN

The Mongoose and the Ferret: On Silent Patrol

The Mongoose

Most people mistakenly think of the mongoose or ichneumon as a member of the weasel group, a variety of the family Mustelidae, when, in fact, the many mongooses belong to a wholly different family, Viverridae, along with the genets, civets and related animals. Both families are in the order Carnivora, along with the bears, hyenas, cats, dogs and pandas/raccoons.

Thirty-two of the viverrines are called mongoose, and they originally came from Africa, Asia and extreme southwestern Europe, although they have been spread around, often unwisely, to other parts of the world. They are agile, graceful creatures and are keen, skilled hunters, best known in their Kiplingesque guise as cobra-killers. Indeed, some species are agile enough to hunt venomous snakes, and some do specialize in what would be for most other animals extremely high-risk prey. They are not immune to snake venom; they are just a whole lot smarter than snakes and generally faster.

The mongoose's move from wild hunter to household companion is not difficult to imagine because it goes on even today, perhaps in much the same way it did in Egypt in pre-Ptolemaic times. It is unlikely that the Egyptian mongoose, a robust three-foot-long animal that ranged as far west and north as southern Spain, was ever actually domesticated in the sense that it was genetically controlled. There is a far more probable scenario. The mongoose (at least this one of the thirty-two species) was allowed houseroom and utilized as elephants were used, for what they could do for man. But they were not selectively bred into any special patterns or styles. They didn't have to be to perform their duties. They could be taken from the wild, harvested as needed. It was just man acting in his role of hunter/gatherer, this time a gatherer.

Fierce little hunters though they are, at least some mongoose species are easily tamed. I have gone bird-watching in Sri Lanka with a guide who walked around with an adult mongoose peering out from between the buttons of his shirt. In India, I have seen people with mongooses in jacket pockets or simply in hand or on their shoulders. In Africa, I have seen them as household fixtures that make frequent calls on newcomers to their turf, asking to be hand-fed tidbits.

In parts of Africa and Asia, the problem of seriously venomous snakes in and around dwellings is very real. In northern Kenya, on the shores of Lake Turkana, the people in a thatch hut next to ours had a nasty surprise one night when a cobra dropped into bed with them from the rafters overhead. There ensued a very noisy thirty seconds with considerable thrashing about. No one was hurt, although the retreating cobra had, one can assume, frayed nerves.

Rodents, of course, are an ever-present problem around a home, stealing and spoiling food, biting babies, starting fires by gnawing wires, carrying fleas that, in turn, carry plague—all manner of nuisances. A mongoose deals equally well with either snakes or rodents in its perpetual interior and exterior hunting forays. It is, therefore, a welcome guest and offers the added advantage of being surprisingly "cuddly." "Affectionate" may also apply, because they do seem to enjoy and very actively seek human contact, and that is an endearing characteristic.

In Egypt, the mongoose's many virtues led to its being declared sacred. By Roman times, they were kept in large numbers and apparently were more or less a fixture in homes and huts of many economic levels. They were cheap pets because they could always feed themselves, which was the idea behind having one around in the first place. There may have been a retail trade in them. Roman ladies kept them as pets, which means that they were stylish. It was probably more unusual to find a home without a mongoose than with one. They appeared on at least one coin (struck in Panopolis at the time of Hadrian, A.D. 76–138), and one is depicted in a mosaic in Pompeii. There were many other representations as well.

But as human population density increased (it was a worldwide phenomenon) and, correspondingly, the problem of snakes under the bed decreased, the popularity of the mongoose declined. It is still a pet frequently kept by Europeans and Americans living in mongoose country. Although the Egyptian mongoose is the only species we have records of, it is extremely likely that, then as now, other species were taken and kept for all the same reasons in other parts of Africa and many parts of Asia.

When transported, the mongoose has become a very real problem. The fierce little hunters will take birds (including domestic poultry and fowl) as readily as they will attack reptiles and other small mammals. In isolated island groups, they can raise havoc on small farms that depend on poultry to a large degree, and as exotics without natural controls on their numbers, they put heavy pressure on native wildlife.

Here again is a case of man utilizing an animal that is compatible and useful without truly domesticating it. There is a world of difference. There are no physical points of distinction between a wholly wild mongoose and one sleeping on his master's pillow. That cannot be said of the dog or even of so recent a domesticate as the cat.

The Ferret

There are sixty-four species of predators that constitute the so-called weasel family, the Mustelidae. Together in this grouping are the weasel, stoat, polecat, ferret, ermine, mink, otter, fisher, marten, grison, wolverine, badger and skunk.

There are three species in the genus *Mustela*. The New World black-footed ferret (*M. nigripes*), which is now seriously in danger of extinction, comes from the western states and the plains region of western Canada and has never been domesticated. The other two species are called polecats; *M. putorius* is the European polecat and *M. eversmanni* is the Asian or steppe polecat. One or both of these polecats gave us a domesticated animal often called the stoat or, in the pet trade in the United States, the ferret or fitch ferret.

It is highly likely that the European polecat was, in fact, the sole ancestor of today's domestic ferret. Some hold to an old theory that the ferret came west to Europe from western Asia and there are some skull characteristics that seem to support that idea. However, today's domestic ferret is so much more like the European species (everything from reproductive patterns to color patterns included) that Europe does seem the likely place of domestication.

When? Evidence begins appearing in the records of the fourth century B.C., but that seems late. The stoat had probably already reached the Middle East by 1000 to 1500 B.C., which would indicate domestication in Europe even before that. There are a number of references in classical literature (Aristotle, Pliny and Strabo are among them) that seem almost certainly to refer to the polecat, but we will probably never really fix the date nor, for that matter, the place of its domestication.

Although the mongoose and the ferret belong to two entirely different zoological families, it is likely that the man-animal scenarios were similar. Young animals can be found and captured easily, and if young enough, they can be socialized. The difference is in the result. The mongoose was never actually domesticated, but the polecat was to become the domestic ferret we know. In both cases, captive or domesticated animals were useful in rodent control.

There is an additional "service" that ferrets provide. They were, and are today, used in a sport called ferreting, particularly in Europe. Ferrets are sent into holes to drive rabbits out into a net. Hunters even shoot over ferrets that start rabbits, making them bolt from cover. To my knowledge, mongooses have not been used in this way.

Neither mongooses nor ferrets constitute major domestications or utilizations by man, but both are venerable and interesting animals. So many other animals could have been used the same way they were that it is puzzling not only why these two were chosen, but also why more weren't. Across the whole spectrum of domestication, perhaps man tried more often than we realize to come up with the few workable species that we have evidence of today. Trial and success mark history well; trial and error leave few if any scars.

PART FIVE

SMALL PACKAGES

FIFTEEN

The Cavy and the Dormouse: Small Feasts

Rodents

Rodentia is the largest of the mammalian orders. It contains at least 43 families and 1,687 recognized species so far, although there are many more than that. New ones are being singled out and renamed every year. Certainly, as their habitats vanish, any number of species will become extinct before they are even identified. They will have come and gone and we will never even know they were here.

More than half of the mammalian species on earth today are rodents. Their actual numbers are astounding. Many single rodent species surpass all other mammal groups combined in numbers of individuals. In terms of food, rodents are potentially of enormous importance. There are millions of tons of them on Earth at any one time. As the prey of other species, they have a significant advantage over larger food animals. When they are used for food, there are no leftovers, there is no waste; electricity and refrigeration are not required.

Man has trapped and hunted rodents for as long as we can reckon our species to have existed. Along with reptiles and insects, they were probably man's earliest prey. Capybara (the largest of the rodents), squirrels, rats, cane rats, mice, dormice, cavies and many, many more have been staples in the diet of hunters and gatherers for millennia. And in other cultures, they have been welcome add-ons or fall-back prey when bigger kills could not be made.

Most rodents are so small that the scale we live on is not perceptible to them. Unless we cast shadows and trigger their hawk/eagle reaction, they concern themselves more with snakes and predators at or about their own level. That makes trapping them an easy task. We must assume that mousetraps and miniature deadfalls were part of a very early technology. A trap I own from a coastal East African tribe (the Giriana) has no moving parts, just the natural elasticity of a bent branch, a crudely woven basket no more than six inches long and a single piece of natural-fiber "string." There would be no surviving artifacts of this kind of fragile, biodegradable technology, so dating it is not practical. But it is safe to say that man, as true man and probably in earlier forms in the process of becoming man, has always eaten rodents simply because they were safe to attack and have always been at hand in huge numbers.

Animals as important as rodents have been well represented in man's consciousness. They were also thought to have medicinal value in many early pharmacopoeias and a few that are still extant. Mouse dung applied as an ointment to a Roman gentleman by his wife kept him from seeking the attention of other women. (I can see how that *might* work, unless he bathed soon afterward.) Rats have been described and feared as devils and the like, and mice have been seen either as adorable storybook characters, cartoons to admire and emulate for their industriousness, or as a plague. Predictably, the range of human reactions to rodents has been enormous.

Although man has domesticated or at least held in captivity a variety of rodents for use in laboratories, for their pelts and as shelf pets, he has apparently taken only two of the almost two thousand known species under control for food. Two more, *Cricetomys gambianus* and *Thryonomys swinderianus,* two- to three-pound rats from West Africa, are in the process of being used that way now. The meat of these two species is being marketed and is highly regarded. These giants have been hunted for as long as we can know, but now they are being bred in captivity. It will be interesting to see if they increase in size and weight as a result of controlled breeding, the way, for example, turkeys and chickens have. Rodents are an ideal food animal to breed in captivity. They breed like, well, mice and have a short gestation period—a matter of a few weeks. They mature quickly, do not require a great deal of space and accept and thrive on a wide variety of readily obtainable foods. Their meat is highly palatable.

The Guinea Pig

The domestic cavy or guinea pig *(Cavia porcellus)* is one of seven species in its genus. The wild forms are found in Colombia, Surinam, Brazil, Venezuela, Guyana, Bolivia, Chile, Argentina and Peru. It was in Peru, apparently, that one of the six wild species—the domestic guinea pig is now a separate species, one of the seven—was developed into that new species, one never before known.

The Spaniards found guinea pigs (the name is interchangeable with *cavy*) being used as a regular dietary item by the Inca when they arrived. In Ecuador recently, in the Indian town of Otavalo, in Imbabura Province, my wife and I were frequently offered roasted guinea pigs on spits. (We declined.) We watched the live animals being traded in the market, and since the sellers were operating out of disposable sacks in the streets (as well as in the open-air market square nearby), raising the little animals is apparently a cottage industry today as it almost certainly was when the Spaniards arrived to save souls. Interestingly enough, many New World tribes ate dog as a staple, but the domesticators of the guinea pig did not. In fact, the Inca despised the dog-eaters, so reported the conquerors.

The Inca (and the pre-Inca; it may have been a domestication the Inca found waiting for them as their culture emerged) kept their little treasures pretty much to themselves until the Spanish reached their highlands. By then, the guinea pig was being bred in a variety of colors and coats not seen in any wild form.

The Spanish were responsible for the spread of the guinea pigs to the many other regions where they had influence. We don't know if they were a significant dietary item anywhere else, but they became pets and laboratory animals so identified with medical research that their very name has come to mean, in English at least, any subject of experimentation.

As for that name, how did a pig that isn't a pig at all and is native to South America come to have an African name? There are two theories. The first holds that there was confusion over the names Guiana or Guyana and Guinea. The second proposes that the Spanish carried some of the animals to West Africa, where they had a presence, and it was from there that the first specimens made it into the English-speaking world. It could have happened either way.

Today, in many South American villages, guinea pigs are released to live as half-wild (not quite feral) temporary commensals (which means "sharing the same table") in and around the house. They are not labor-intensive. As babies, they are really quite appealing, born fully furred with eyes and ears open. They may be used as toys, a kind of wriggling stuffed animal, and then killed when the menu calls for them. Bred in bewildering variety, they are also kept as cage pets in more advanced countries, where, presumably, they do not suffer the same fate.

The Dormouse

There are sixteen small rodent species called dormice. They range widely in Europe, western Asia and Africa, and some of them are considered crop pests. They are essentially nocturnal and crepuscular (dawn and dusk) animals of the woodlands. One species, *Glis glis,* is the fat or edible dormouse. It is a western Asian and European species quite different from the African animals. It was introduced into England in recent times, but it is not a native there. Its name means sleeping or dozing mouse and it makes a memorable appearance in Lewis Carroll's *Alice's Adventures in Wonderland*.

Unlike the guinea pig, which was domesticated and styled to become not only plump tidbits but to suit man's desire to keep pretty and exotic pets, the dormouse (not a very pleasant-tempered little animal) was simply "kept." And so the species joins the list with the elephant and the mongoose, the utilized, as unlikely a grouping as that might be in all other ways.

The Romans held dormice in specially designed enclosures, and for the final fattening, they were kept in the home in jars made for that purpose. They were fed on nuts until they were very plump and then eaten. Since the dormouse is fattest just before going into hibernation for the winter, we can assume they were a late-fall delicacy. There is no evidence that an attempt was made to domesticate them. In fact, just shortly before Christ, about 14 B.C., so said Pliny, their consumption was outlawed in Rome. Why that occurred is not really known, but perhaps it was an effort to reduce conspicuous ostentation. Certain birds and presumably all shellfish were banned at the same time.

Neither the guinea pig nor the dormouse could be considered a major cultural breakthrough for man. When we think of goats and sheep, pigs, horses and asses, cattle and dogs, camels and water buffalo, the guinea pig is not all that significant, and when we think of the elephant, the dormouse, too, tends to pale as a creature of the wilderness put to use. Still, man dipped into the incredible diversity that is the animal kingdom and found in both rodents a few bits and pieces that helped him to survive.

SIXTEEN

The Rat, the Mouse and "Shelf Pets": Lesser Accomplishments

The Original Rat

In earlier cultures, when animals were tried in criminal courts for supposed crimes against man, the rat was exempted. It was tried in ecclesiastical courts. Its fate was in the hands of God and the Church.

There are seventy-eight species in the genus *Rattus* in the rodent family Muridae. They are the true rats in today's terminology. Any number of other rodents are called rats, too, animals like the cane rats, mole rats (naked and otherwise), *pack*rats, kangaroo rats, *musk*rats, the beautiful cloud rats, water rats, spiny rats—an amazing variety, but they all belong to other genera. It is *Rattus* that nearly did our species in and which both plagues and blesses us to this day.

The dreaded black rat *(Rattus rattus)* (aka roof rat, wharf rat and house rat) triggers in us a tribal memory that is chilling at the very least. Little wonder it was tried in ecclesiastical courts. It has probably killed more human beings than any single war or natural disaster in our history. The black rat bore the flea *Xenopsylla cheopis* that bore the bacterium *Yersinia pestis,* the cause of bubonic plague, "The Black Death."

The black rat or plague rat probably originated in the Malaysian region, but it has been spread so widely by man that other origins are suggested frequently—China and the Middle East, for example. But it was probably the Malay Peninsula and the thousands of islands in the region that produced the disquietingly smart, adaptable animal that went to sea in ships and just about conquered the world. It is still traveling by ship and is still found around the world.

Actually how many people have died of plague carried by rat fleas borne by black rats will never be known. Where it struck in the Middle Ages, whole cities ceased to exist. Entire populations vanished. In Europe alone, over a quarter of the population perished, at least twenty-five million people. In modern times, just between 1892 and 1918, eleven million people died of rat/flea-borne plague in India. In Uganda, between 1917 and 1942, sixty thousand people died. It has been one of the most appalling sequences of tragedy in human history. And the records we have are largely for Europe and the Middle East. Since the plague was a true pandemic, a worldwide disaster, the total numbers must have been staggering.

The catastrophe of plague has not been blamed on a bacterium, nor on the flea that bit people and injected the bacterium. The villain had to be something that we could see slinking in alleys and across rafters overhead, or scurrying inside walls, where we could hear them and shudder in disgust. Thus, the black rat was identified as the ultimate enemy of civilization. Not without good cause did the residents of Hamelin hire the Pied Piper to rid their town of the rats that infested it, although they would have been better off had they paid him for the job.

The black rat did not prove to be omnipotent, however. It was a skillful climber, but an even more skillful burrower was on the way, also as an uninvited passenger aboard ships moving between Asian ports and those of the rest of the world. *Rattus norvegicus,* the brown or misnamed Norway rat (also barn rat and sewer rat, although that could be the black rat, too), probably came from northern China and spread around the world as its black cousin had before it. It was an even tougher, more adaptable animal than the black rat, and it drove its competition out. The brown rat is the rodent we now find in our cellars and attics, on our farms, in our suburbs and cities. It does at least a billion dollars in damage a year in the United States alone by spoiling stored food, killing young livestock and poultry, attacking children in their beds and by chewing the insulation off wiring and starting fires.

The Domestication

Today, we know that the climbing black rat was unseated by the burrowing, even more successful brown rat. We know it was the black rat

that carried plague around the world, and it is the brown rat that is now doing so much damage to our enterprises. But most of us can't bear to look at any wild rat long enough to make or care about a distinction. Rats are simply loathsome for just about everybody but the naturalist. And yet we have domesticated them.

The rat, then, is a fascinating exception to a rule of domestication. Man took unto himself an animal he absolutely detested and feared as he has no other animal through much of recorded history. The mouse is the only other exception to the general rule that man has domesticated and "improved" upon animals he has known in the wild and admired or even worshiped. In the case of the brown rat and the house mouse, man did know them in the wild, but had expended a huge amount of energy and inventiveness trying to kill them wherever they were to be found. Then, about three hundred years ago, he began to cherish them. It was an amazing turnabout, the strangest in the history of man and animal interaction. It is the ultimate love/hate relationship in the story of domestication.

The positive feelings some people have for even domesticated rats are not universally held. But, as it turned out, they do possess endearing and valuable characteristics. The domestic brown rat retains the same species designation, *R. norvegicus,* as the wild form. It is generally white, albino, in fact, with pink eyes, or parti-colored, "pinto," brown and white. In recent years the pet industry has developed other self- or solid-colored varieties. Untold millions of white rats are produced every year for use in biological and biomedical laboratories. Zoos breed them by the ton to feed to their bird and reptile collections, and they are also bred for use as pets. They please an awful lot of people who do not have the room to accommodate larger pets. Given any help at all, they are incredibly fussy, clean animals. Enthusiasts claim they are demonstrably affectionate.

In captivity, as in the wild, the rat leads an accelerated existence. Maximum life span is around two thousand days (that is on the long side), the onset of puberty may be as early as forty-five days, and gestation is as short as twenty-one days. Litter size is generally eight to twelve but has been known to be as high as twenty-four. The young can be weaned at twenty-five days, and females can produce offspring until they are eighteen months old. What all that amounts to is an awful lot of rats in the wild or in the domestic form. The rat is, of course, of lesser importance as a domestication than the horse or cow. And it retains an unsavory connotation in our language, as, for example, "you dirty rat." The term "to rat on," meaning to betray, stems from the belief that rats desert sinking ships. But, then, who doesn't?

The Wild Mouse

The mouse was a prophetic creature to our ancestors. A mouse in the sickroom meant impending death, and the sign of mice in the house generally was a bad omen. Mice were thought to embody human souls. A

red mouse was a soul that was pure, a black mouse a soul sullied by sin. Saint Gertrude was the patron of souls, and she was usually depicted as in some way associated with mice. Pliny tells us that mouse ashes mixed with honey cure earaches and sweeten the breath when used as a mouthwash. In England, various concoctions of cooked mice were thought to be good for whooping cough, bed-wetting, head colds and smallpox.

Less beneficial was the tale of the archbishop of Mainz, Hatto by name. During the tenth century, there was a terrible famine and crowds of starving people descended on the archbishop to beg for food, of which he had plenty. In response, he had the mendicants locked in a barn, then had the structure burned to the ground. Almost immediately, there was a plague of mice, and although Hatto fled to the so-called "Mouse Tower" in the middle of the Rhine, the mice followed him there and reduced him to a skeleton.

As is the case with rats, a large variety of animals is known by the generalized term *mouse:* the dormouse, pygmy mouse, jumping mouse, hopping mouse, deer mouse, spiny mouse, brush-furred and broad-headed mice, harvest mouse, field mouse, but, again, as it is with rats, they all belong to different genera.

The mouse genus that is of special significance to us is *Mus.* Thirty-six of the world's mouse species belong to this one genus. *Mus musculus,* the house mouse, is the species of interest. We do not know where it came from. This small rodent became so ubiquitous as it tagged along with man that we don't know what its original range was. Ernest Walker's *Mammals of the World* gives it as "perhaps naturally distributed from the Mediterranean region to China." One thing is certain; it is now found everywhere man is, virtually without exception.

Roughly three hundred years ago, man "tamed" and domesticated the house mouse, although white mice, albinos, were known in Rome, and Pliny spoke of them as bringing luck. Again, as with the rat, albinism is common. (It is actually counterproductive among wild mice for obvious reasons. It makes them too easy to see, and a large number of animals hunt mice.) Today, even after this short time (the mouse is one of the most recent

of all domestications), different colors, patterns and coat styles are being bred for and predictably achieved. There is an attractive array of solid or self-colored and parti-colored mice now available.

The use-to-man scenario for mice is the same as for rats. Every year, untold millions are bred for the laboratory and to feed other animals, both pets and zoo dwellers. Millions more are cage pets. But man is still just as active in his efforts to destroy wild specimens of *Mus musculus* as he is intent on breeding more and even prettier domestic animals of the same species. In one form, they please us mightily (if you are an enthusiast), and in the other, they cost untold hundreds of millions of dollars in spoiled food. The number of tons of wheat and sugar and other dry, bulk foods that have had to be discarded because of mouse urine and droppings can't even be reckoned, but the total, if it were known, would be staggering. *Mus* and man have made strange bedfellows.

Before leaving the subject of mice, we should at least acknowledge the special world of the thoroughly anthropomorphized mouse. Walt Disney was not the first artist or writer to use the inherent "cuteness" of mice to tell a story, but his first animated films in the late 1920s constituted a platform from which would emerge in the 1990s a multi-billion-dollar industry employing scores of thousands of people. Mickey Mouse, it is safe to say, is not only the best-known animal, he is also the best-known single creature the world has ever known. That is, surely, a singular contrast with the mouse in any other form.

Shelf Pets

Besides guinea pigs, rats and mice, man has taken a number of other rodents into his charge, not as food but as cage or "shelf" pets. I don't think any of them can be described as truly domesticated, but hobbyists are breeding them in very large numbers and eventually, with some species at least, the gene pool will be under control and significant variations will be achieved.

The full list of rodents being retained as pets can't be reckoned. Among the most common are:

Mesocricetus auratus, the golden hamster of Syria.
Chinchilla laniger, the chinchilla of northern Chile.
Meriones unguiculatus, the gerbil of eastern Asia.

Squirrels, flying squirrels, chipmunks, grasshopper mice, mole mice, harvest mice, deer mice, wood mice, lemmings and lemming mice, voles, meadow mice—all manner of small wild mammals, usually rodents, have to varying degrees been "tamed" or at least made reasonably manageable by man. Perhaps this is all a result, in part, of his desire to have dominion over the animals in his environment that he can easily control. Whether or not the animals are "happy" with the arrangement doesn't seem to figure into the equation. If well cared for, there should be no cruelty as we would understand it, but we can be reasonably certain that the animals, given a choice, would prefer to remain in the wild. Their lives would surely be shorter there, however, and all would end up as some predator's meal. None of them qualifies as a domestic animal and it is doubtful that many of them ever will. They are at a disadvantage. The most hated mammal in the world has beaten them to the draw. The rat is already there, our rodent of choice.

SEVENTEEN

The Rabbit: Food for All

In Legend

Strange as it may seem, the rabbit, an animal with a very high cuddle-factor today, is a somewhat sinister beast in many of the old legends. Its name should not be invoked aboard a ship at sea if a safe port is to be reached and, wiggly nose and all, it can be a dreaded familiar in the world of witchcraft. Miners heading for their pits, we are told, turned around and went home if they saw a rabbit. There is an admonition to leave a black rabbit alone, for it is the soul of someone's grandmother unwilling to retire from Earth.

Yet there is the superstition that a rabbit's foot brings good luck if you stroke it. Saying the word *rabbit* upon awakening on the first day of the month is also supposed to assure good fortune. And, of course, there is Peter Rabbit. Beatrix Potter did a great deal for the rabbit's image, raising it to the level of icon. The "bunny" we know today is the epitome of cute. Once again, an animal that man has domesticated has provided us with a mixed cultural metaphor. You can have it any way you want with rabbits. Just pick an end of the good/evil spectrum and believe what you will. No one will argue with you.

The Original Rabbit

The rabbits of the world belong to the order Lagomorpha and not to the rodents, as so many people seem to believe. They are, in fact, more closely related to the ungulates, hoofed animals, than they are to rats, mice, squirrels and their kin. The family Leporidae contains roughly forty-nine species of rabbits and hares. The European rabbit, *Oryctolagus cuniculus,* is generally accepted as the ancestral form of the millions of rabbits now held as domestic animals around the world, however varied in shape, color and size they may be. There are forty rabbit breeds recognized in the United States alone, and they are shown in at least 170 distinct varieties. The size differences between breeds are significant. A Flemish giant can weigh between fourteen and twenty pounds—probably the world's largest rabbit—while a Netherlands dwarf in any of its thirty varieties will weigh as little as two pounds.

Where and When

The European rabbit originally was restricted to the Iberian Peninsula, modern Spain and Portugal. When man made his influence felt in that area, one of two things was likely to happen. Either the rabbit would be hunted out and become extinct, or it would be domesticated and flourish. The latter came to pass and eventually man spread the rabbit almost everywhere he went.

The Romans did not selectively breed the rabbit they carried away with them, however, in any attempt to produce breeds and varieties. (This was true, too, you will recall, of the dormouse.) They just fattened them up in enclosed areas and ate them.

Rabbits are remarkably fecund. A single doe may produce thirty offspring in a year. Forty-seven percent of rabbits born are female, so the number that can be produced by a doe and her offspring is very quickly quite spectacular. Rabbits reach sexual maturity in as little as five months, and have an abbreviated gestation period, thirty-one days on average. Females do not have periods of estrus but will breed anytime they are not pregnant. Hence, their reputation, both male and female.

Unlike other mammals, rabbits do not ovulate until after they have mated. The lagomorphs are atypical in many ways. Their eggs are huge,

larger than those of human beings. The male's testicles are located in front of the penis rather than behind it, as is the case in other mammals. If conditions are not right for producing young, does will resorb their embryos. They sometimes reproduce parthenogenetically, without mating, and all young produced this way are female. Some rabbits have gall bladders and some do not. Either condition is considered normal. Rabbits and their kin are strange animals.

By keeping rabbits in enclosed fields and probably by supplemental feeding with garden scraps, the Romans were able to enjoy their rabbit pies and stews throughout the year, allowing selection to occur naturally. They did not design their rabbits, they simply *had* them. Their enclosures were known as *leporaria*. Other species of rabbits and possibly some hares may have been kept by the Romans, too, but again, they were not selectively bred. It was just easier to shoot rabbits in an enclosure than in the wild.

After the Romans

Medieval monks were probably the first people to start the process of actual domestication. They almost certainly bred for size for obvious reasons. Since the fetus of the rabbit was not recognized as meat by the

Church, the rabbit was particularly desirable to have around. Its unborn young could be eaten during periods of fasting.

Rabbits burrow with considerable zeal, and no doubt both the Romans and all who followed them in either the rabbit-keeping or rabbit-breeding business lost a great many of their charges that dug their way to freedom. These escapees established themselves back in the wild, but we can't refer to them as feral because they weren't domesticated in the first place, at least before the Middle Ages.

Rabbits Today

Rabbits are now raised all over the world as an easy supplemental source of protein. They mature quickly, are easy to handle and will eat scrap garden greens. I don't know of any place where they are the staple diet, but they are used far more in some places than others. There are a great many Americans who have never tasted rabbit, but very few Europeans. Almost certainly because of Beatrix Potter and all that has come after her in the way of the veneration of "the bunny rabbit," a great many people find eating rabbit aesthetically repugnant. It almost has the intensity of a taboo.

Rabbits frequently are kept as pets, but that is more common in affluent societies than in marginal economies. If you are hungry, animals like rabbits quickly become more attractive as food than as denizens of a private backyard petting zoo. What is one man's bunny is another man's supper.

In their many breeds and varieties, rabbits have a following all their own and are shown in 4-H and FFA fairs as well as at specialty shows. There is a considerable traffic in the purebred show animals and the standards of perfection are high, distinct and fine breedng stock is jealously guarded.

Rabbits killed for food (hunted, kept or domesticated) have contributed their pelts as well. In the fur trade, rabbit is used for some children's garments and as trim, but it is not really a significant fur. It sheds, breaks easily and is not warm or durable enough to be important despite the millions of incidental skins used. Leg-hold traps set for more valuable fur-bearers inevitably catch any number of wild rabbits, but many of them are discarded as not worth the effort to prepare for sale. This kind of waste, not to mention the pain, is one more reason for finally making the ban on leg-hold traps universal.

There is no doubt that rabbits in the wild can be pests, from the little cottontails that nibble in our gardens to the jackrabbits that were introduced to Australia and multiplied by the millions. But I don't think that justifies their wholesale slaughter. Rabbits have been stoned, clubbed, crushed by deadfalls, snared and strangled, captured in box- and leg-hold traps, speared, shot with arrows, darts and guns, chased by dogs, hunted with cheetah and hawks, killed by the billions. They are usually first game for young hunters-to-be. The word *game,* incidentally, comes to us from the Old German *gamen,* which meant *glee.* A game animal is one we take glee in killing.

For all of that brutality, cruelty and the great deal of waste involved in hunting as well as trapping for recreation, as opposed to survival, the rabbit remains a significant minor domestication. They are attractive animals with many endearing characteristics, so their appeal is unlikely to abate. In fact, as man's numbers continue to increase, rabbits may follow along. They are easy keepers as food in marginal economies as well as pets, and space limitations may mandate an even more important role for them in the future than they have had in the past.

EIGHTEEN

Fur-Bearers: In the Name of Vanity

The "Fur Coat"

By definition, mammals are fur-bearers, even if some species—whales, manatees, elephants and hippopotamuses, for example—don't have much in the way of real fur after they mature. Without doubt, early man retained the skins of the animals he hunted for food. Hides, as leather or fur, constituted his first "fabrics." In colder climates, the hide may have come close to being the primary objective of the hunt. As the glaciers came down across Europe, body covering was essential for survival, as was, of course, a steady supply of consumable protein. Curling up to sleep on a cold cave floor while snow and sleet fell outside surely called for skins to sleep on and to pull over one's naked body.

Man developed other fabrics very early on. We don't know exactly when goat hair was twisted and woven together and used to replace animal skins as apparel, but we can be reasonably certain it was near the beginning of the association. In some cultures, beaten bark (quite rough and not terribly warm) was used as a kind of cloth, and in time natural fibers like cotton and wool came into use. The making of fabrics is a process that began before agriculture and has continued up into our time. Today, synthetic fibers are also woven into fabrics.

Throughout all of this time, woven through all of this technology, men and women, far more often the latter in recent times, have continued to wear fur. What was once the essential practice of anything but refined cave people became, in the last few centuries, an ultimate expression of wealth, sophistication and style. In some cultures, select furs, notably ermine and sea otter, were reserved for royalty. More and more people today, however, have come to see the practice as the ultimate expression of cruel indifference, and fur-wearing is on the wane in most modern societies. It is apparently an idea whose time has passed. It came early, but is now perceived by many as a cruel anachronism.

We don't know where or when man first began keeping fur-bearers captive for their pelts, or why the experiments failed, assuming many or at least some did. And we don't know how many species were tried and abandoned. But we can reconstruct some episodes in part.

The Fox

The fox was kept in captivity in Neolithic Switzerland. At some sites, fox bones are more numerous than those of dogs, and there is every indication that the little canines were eaten. They would have been *Vulpes vulpes*, the red fox, an animal that traces back to the Pleistocene era in the Old World, so it was there waiting when man evolved. A great many fox bones have been found in Jericho, indicating that they were used for food there, as well.

We can assume that man retained the pelts of the foxes he ate, and that at some point, the practice of eating foxes gave way to other protein. Whether man then continued to keep foxes for fur, or if he abandoned fox-keeping for thousands of years, is not known.

There is reason to believe, however, that the first kept foxes of Switzerland were at least on the way to domestication. There are bone anomalies, and diseases like arthritis are evident, which would have made survival in the wild difficult to impossible. Clearly, they were kept, and since they were smaller than the local wild foxes, they could, in fact, have been fully domesticated.

The reason man would keep foxes and other fur-bearers for their pelts rather than trap or hunt them is obvious. Animals grow fur as protection against the elements. Furs, then, are at their luxuriant best in winter, when they are needed. Some fur-bearers become positively ratty during the hot months of spring and summer; they "blow" their coats. Winter, however, can be a strenuous, even dangerous time to work a lonely trapline. It is far easier to keep the animals in captivity and kill them in the winter, when their pelts are at their best, all in the safety and relative comfort of a farm.

In recent times, foxes have been raised in captivity by the millions. In the latter part of the last century, silver mutants of the red fox were being farmed in the Canadian Maritime Provinces. There have been other mutations selected for, as well, and we must consider the farm-raised fox to be domesticated. They are selected for color and quality and bred purposefully to provide a cash crop. Not too many silver or blue mutation foxes are encountered in the wild.

Once upon a time, in the 1930s and 1940s, bulky fox-fur coats were the rage. Movie stars were photographed wearing them over bathing suits. Single and double fox pelts with artificial heads and glass eyes were also standard items of apparel, worn as scarves. These days, fortunately, such garments are seen as artifacts—things of the past.

A Small and Valuable Weasel and Others

The mink (*Mustela vison*) is a member of the family Mustelidae and is thus a cousin of the badger, skunk, weasel and otter. Since the 1880s, it, too, has been raised in captivity as well as trapped. Its fur has been one of the most sought-after in the world for centuries. In this century, the mink became a status symbol. Until quite recently, to own a mink coat was to have "arrived." The mink, like the fox, has been bred by the millions in a number of mutations and is carefully selected for fashionable and therefore valuable colors. It must be considered a domestic animal. Little is known

about its earlier history. It probably never was thought of as a significant source of food except by starving people.

The Russians have profited handsomely from one of the most valuable of all fur-bearers, the sable, *Martes zibellina*. In the late 1700s, a single provincial fur market in Siberia might have handled several hundred thousand sable pelts a year. Today the animals are hunted by expert marksmen for the most part, but some have been farmed as well. Their status as domestic animals has not been evaluated to my knowledge, but it is unlikely that they could be properly considered to have crossed the domestication line.

The North American muskrat *(Ondatra zibethicus)* is also raised commercially for its fur but not in the numbers the fox and the mink have been. Its fur is much less valuable, but the animals are still trapped by the millions. It is not considered a domestic animal.

A substantial South American rodent called the coypu *(Myocastor coypus*—nutria, to the fur trade) was imported into the United States at least as far back as the 1930s and farmed in Louisiana. However, it is doubtful that the coypu or nutria has ever come close to being domesticated.

Other fur-bearers commonly used in the waning fur business may have been kept in captivity at some time but cannot be considered domesticated in the true sense of the word. They include beaver, otter, sea otter, marten, fisher, wolf, coyote, Arctic fox, hare, leopard, jaguar, cheetah, snow leopard, clouded leopard, tiger, ocelot, margay, lynx, bobcat, serval, several jungle cats, civet, genet, several bears, wolverine, a number of seals and sea lions, any number of squirrel species, skunk, ermine, various monkeys, notably the colobus, and many more. It has been an ongoing slaughter since prehistoric times and most commonly has been directed at carnivores.

Many of the species used in the fur trade are now rare, threatened or endangered. And as habitat continues to vanish, the problem will intensify. The natural trend would be to keep an increasing number of species on farms for slaughter, but it is more likely that the fur industry will die before any further species are actually domesticated the way the fox and the mink were. Both fox and mink farming, once common activities in the United States and Canada, have essentially moved to Korea, where most of the pelts used today come from. Even the fur-farming trade journals once published in the United States and Canada no longer exist.

The ethical indignation over the use of animal furs extends with nowhere near the same intensity to the use of leather. The distinction is seen by most people to lie in the realm of original intent. Most leather used in the world today comes from animals that have been eaten, and most of the people in the world are meat-eaters. Leather such as alligator, ostrich, lizard and snake are incidental luxury items. Cowhide and pigskin are leading leather sources along with water buffalo skin and horsehide. No wild species contributes anything like the volume of tannable hides taken from our major domesticates.

The Cheetah

Aside from its occasional use as a fur animal—its fur is of very poor quality—the cheetah *(Acinonyx jubatus)* has lived in captivity since at least dynastic Egypt. It is the mildest-mannered of all wildcats and is readily conditioned for life around human beings. Attacks on people by tamed cheetahs are almost unknown. In fact, the same thing can be said of wild cheetahs. Suprisingly, this fastest of all four-legged animals is not difficult to catch. It quickly settles down and is easily tamed and housed.

During the Middle Ages, the cheetah was highly prized and was used much as falcons were, for coursing and hunting. It was obviously a rich man's sport. The cheetah was called "hunting leopard" then, although with its nonretractable claws, it is not closely related to the leopard, or any other cat, for that matter. In the 1500s, it was recorded that Akbar, the fabled Mogul emperor, apparently one of the most ostentatious people who ever lived, owned as many as a thousand cheetahs at one time, nine thousand during his life span of sixty-three years, it was said.

The cheetah was never domesticated because it wasn't until the last few decades that we have known how to breed them in captivity. Akbar's great horde of cheetahs all had to have been wild-caught. The cheetah's breeding "code" has two secret elements.

The first secret is a cryptic estrus; there is no way of observing directly that the female is ready to be bred. It was only recently discovered that the female's estrus can be determined by the behavior of males who are penned next to her and appear agitated. The second cheetah secret is polyandry. One female must breed with two or more males in order to be impregnated.

The cheetah breeding code was first discovered by a physician in Italy and then again by the film actress Amanda Blake and her husband, Frank Gilbert, on their private experimental cheetah-breeding compound in Phoenix, Arizona. Before their deaths, the Gilberts had bred up to seven generations of cheetahs. The species is now routinely bred in zoos, something that was considered impossible barely a quarter of a century ago.

PART SIX

THE FEATHERED DOMESTICATES

NINETEEN

The Chicken:
At Every Table, in Every Pot

Origins

There are four species of jungle fowl in the genus *Gallus*, the red, Ceylon, gray and green. All of them could have played a role in the creation of the modern chicken, but the credit usually is given to *Gallus gallus*, the red jungle fowl. Its scientific name has been retained for our barnyard version.

The red jungle fowl has a vast range: India, southern China over into Southeast Asia, the Philippines, Java and Sumatra. It was from somewhere in that large area that the domestic chicken originally came. The green jungle fowl, *G. varius*, is also from Java and from Bali and adjacent islands, so it could have played at least a minor role in the process. As the chicken under the control of man was moved toward the west, the Ceylon jungle fowl, *G. lafayettei*, and the gray, *G. sonnerattii*, in southern and western India, probably also contributed some genes to the original red jungle fowl domesticate. We don't know what the mix was by the time it finally worked its way west and north into the Middle East and Europe, but that trail appears easy enough to reconstruct:

Vietnam	By 8000 B.C.
Indus Valley, then Sumeria	By 2000 B.C.
Egypt	By 1350 B.C.
China	By 1122 B.C.
Greece and her colonies, then the Roman world	By 700–500 B.C.
Persia and Mesopotamia	By 600 B.C
Britain	By 100 B.C.

The means by which the jungle fowl was brought under control are easy to imagine. Nestlings are not difficult to locate and capture. If taken young enough or even before they hatch, fowl tend to imprint on the first living things they associate with. Early man could have more readily had chickens (and ducks and geese) around his dwellings than any other animal. They would not have required penning, and would not have represented an enormous loss if individually taken by a fox or wildcat. (Birds are in that sense a high-risk "crop.") They would have come and gone, mated with wild jungle fowl, and wandered back to nest or reappeared later with a clutch of young following behind. Their association with man could have initially been a very casual affair.

I have observed wild jungle fowl only on Sri Lanka, but their behavior is not substantially different from the other three species. The birds are shy and secretive if born wild and allowed to mature that way. They are very alert because their many predators are terrestrial, aquatic, arboreal and some come in on silent wings. The jungle fowl are essentially land dwellers and run rather than fly away if approached. That is in part because they choose brushy or forested areas to peck around in and quick flight is not always an option available to them.

In very rural areas, local "domestic" fowl look suspiciously like their ancestral stock and are "half-wild." I have noted that on Borneo, in India, Pakistan and Bangladesh, Sri Lanka and in the Philippines as well. In India, the hens that peck around in every village and in every yard are called *desi* hens and are nondescript. Exotics like the Rhode Island red are not unknown and are highly prized, but most of the chickens I have met on my travels in Asia have been half-wild *desi* hens.

The transition from wild to domestic would not have been laborintensive the way major mammal domestications must have been, and certainly not as dangerous. Again, it would have been gradual and natural, and it suited both the free-loading chickens and protein-hungry human encampments.

When and where the first domestication took place cannot be determined for certain, but recent findings in genetic typing at the City of Hope Medical Center in Los Angeles suggest Vietnam as the place for this important development, and the time suggested, as long ago as ten thousand years, is much farther back than was believed until very recently. But since it was so easy an association and probably so gradual, there may not have been an actual starting point in time, and it was almost certainly something that happened in a number of places simultaneously. It is likely that no single people or culture actually domesticated the chicken, but rather the fowl just became the chicken in Asia as a natural thing once man began to settle down and give up his nomadic lifestyle. Seeds scattered around a human habitat could have lured the wild birds in until they became scavengers and were just there. For people without written records, it does not take long for a cultural trait to be venerable, something that just is and always has been and therefore should always be. That is why oral tradition is notoriously inaccurate when it comes to time.

Before domestication, man hunted the fowl for food and must have used its colorful feathers (black and red, particularly, in the case of the red jungle fowl) as decoration and probably in religious rites. Certainly, the best feathers, the cock's lustrous black tail plumage, would have been used to denote rank and affiliation. Few things in nature that are so decorative last as long. Flowers die, leaves wither but feathers can be passed from generation to generation if treated with sufficient care and reverence. Then there are the eggs, too. Without doubt, man sought them and ate them as soon as he found them. They are a rich and valuable supplemental food, an ultimate gastronomic lagniappe for the hunter/gatherer.

What man's first motives were for keeping chickens around is not known. Perhaps merely that it was easier to keep them than to catch them. And fowl are a multiple-crop animal. First, of course, there is their highly

palatable flesh, then there are feathers and eggs. And beyond that, there is sport, which should not be underestimated in the case of the chicken. Finally, there is their use in sacrifice and other ritual practices like foretelling the future.

We don't know how long people have been wagering on fighting cocks, but it is a very common activity in many of the areas where wild jungle fowl are still found. Even in the domestic form, the males are extremely aggressive toward each other, and in that characteristic man found a cruel sport. Thus, chickens were kept for a number of reasons, two totally different kinds of food, adornment, status, religion, divination and recreation. They offered more different kinds of rewards to their hosts than almost any other domestic animal.

In the New World, the domestic chicken came ready-made. In 1520, Cortés, in the process of conquering Mexico, introduced a flock from Europe. It numbered, we believe, around fifteen hundred birds.

Today, the number of chickens kept by man is in the vicinity of eight to ten billion. Feathers and manure are important side-products, but chickens now are kept primarily for their flesh and eggs.

Their close confinement in the industrial world is harsh and cruel, and the trend has been to make the birds as much like machines as possible. Their beaks are clipped and they are often stacked in small wire enclosures with no opportunity to move around like living creatures. The science of feeding flocks is highly advanced; the birds are sent to slaughter weeks after they have been hatched (in incubators, not in a nest). Veterinarians are trained not to treat individual birds, but only the flocks. There is no consideration whatsoever given to chickens as individual animals except by fanciers of the show breeds and people who specialize in the rare breeds that are "commercially extinct."

There are at least two hundred breeds and varieties of domestic chickens on record, but most of them are now extinct or extremely rare. The first poultry show we know of in the United States was held in 1849. Among the many good meat and egg producers, there are some true freaks. The creeper has legs so short that it waddles like a duck. The Japanese phoenix has tail feathers up to eight feet long and clearly is for show only. The Araucana lays eggs with blue shells.

Commercial producers of chickens and eggs do not go by breeds but by trade names. The great days of the farmyard chickens, the Brahmas, Cochins, Jersey giants, Langshans, Anconas, Rhode Island reds, Andalusians, Chanticleers and Columbian rocks have passed except for private fanciers and domestic animal historians.

In most of Europe and in North America, today's descendants of the red jungle fowl are plugged into a system of factory farming in which humanity exists not at all. To feed the population of just one large city, millions of chickens are killed and shipped every day. They are, unquestionably, one of man's most valuable and readily available sources of food. It is impossible to imagine what we would do without them. Yet immeasurably more care is lavished on chickens when they are dead than when they are alive. It is the ultimate separation of man and his deeds, a total indifference to the well-being of an animal on which we are so dependent for our own well-being.

TWENTY

The Turkey:
For Special Occasions

The Origin

The wild turkey is strictly a North and Central American bird. There are actually two species: *Meleagris gallopavo,* the common turkey, which ranges over much of the United States into Canada and down into Mexico; and *M. ocellata,* the ocellated turkey, which ranges from southern Mexico to Guatemala and Belize. The common turkey is generally considered the ancestor of our domestic bird.

It is almost certain that the turkey was already domesticated when the Spaniards arrived in the New World. The first Europeans to describe them referred to white hens, and that meant the birds were truly domestic. Neither species of wild turkey is white. Whatever the first people to breed turkeys were selecting for, they triggered a secondary characteristic, the white color. It was probably an accident at first but it held because it was undoubtedly an endearing characteristic.

There was also a spiritual component to the whole association. The Mayans believed that the wild turkey symbolized the south and was the appropriate sacrifice to a great god of the South named Nohol. Their descendants today still forecast the weather by observing turkey behavior. If the birds take dust baths, they believe rain is coming.

When I visited the people of a small Mayan settlement in Quintana Roo Territory in eastern Yucatán, there were artifacts all around them. They lived there among ruined pyramids and temples that are yet to be investigated. Domestic turkeys and chickens pecked around the crumbling splendor. Pigs and chickens were brought to the Mayans by European invaders, but the turkeys were reminders of something extremely rare, an original New World domestication.

Traditional wisdom has it that turkeys were first introduced into Europe around 1524. By the 1570s, they were being raised in substantial flocks, many in Germany. It was in the 1580s that the bird was used, or at least first referred to, as part of a Christmas feast. It had found its niche. A turkey of large but not extraordinary size can yield ten times as much meat as an average chicken, so the two birds have come to play very different roles. Chicken is an everyday dish, while turkey remains something of a special-event bird. It is an extremely popular winter holiday food in the United States, and it has become traditional fare, of course, on Thanksgiving and Christmas. It is festive, as the chicken probably was long ago.

There were no wild jungle fowl in the New World and no pheasants (the ring-necked pheasant was introduced to North America from Asia at the turn of this century). So the turkey was one of the few gallinaceous (fowl-like) birds most readily available, and it was by far the largest. Turkeys offered another advantage: they were always at hand. Unlike other large birds, cranes and geese, for example, the turkey does not migrate. Quail and grouse would have been other candidates for domestication, but the Indians seemed to have settled for the larger, reliable turkey. Like many of the gallinaceous birds, turkeys mature quickly and reproduce very well.

Although the North American aborigines had no other record of domestication (except possibly the dog), the turkey was an easy task. Wild turkeys are very poor fliers (domestic turkeys don't fly at all, which is ironic since the flight muscles or breast meat is the most favored portion and the birds are bred to have huge breasts), so they could be run down and "herded" into enclosures. It would have been relatively simple to trap turkeys and "keep" them, and easy enough to start choosing which to eat and which to allow to breed. The results would have inevitably been a domestic species.

There are seven varieties of domestic turkey in America today: the Bronze, Narragansett, White Holland, Black, Slate, Bourbon Red and Beltsville Small White, and at least six of them originated in the United States. It is possible that the White Holland was developed in Europe. The Bronze is the largest turkey of all. The toms can weigh as much as thirty-six pounds.

There is inescapable irony in the story of the turkey. Despite the fact that they are our sacrifices of choice for some of our most reverential holidays (Thanksgiving and Christmas), they are produced under conditions no better than those of a chicken factory, and, like chickens, are hardly afforded our recognition as living creatures at all.

Other Gallinaceous Birds

Any number of birds in the order Galliformes could have been candidates for domestication. That would seem to be particularly true of the families Tetraonidae (the grouse and prairie chickens), Phasianidae (pheasants, quail and jungle fowl), Numididae (guinea fowl) and Meleagrididae (the turkeys). It is surprising that so few species from this large order have made it into modern times as domestic animals. Besides the chicken and the turkey, the others must be considered accomplishments of minor importance. How many efforts were made and why they failed or were abandoned is apparently not ours to know.

The peafowl *(Pavo cristatus)*—only the male is a pea*cock*—is a wild bird on the Indian subcontinent, Sri Lanka and Burma. Because of the cock's spectacular tail feathers, the birds were probably brought under some degree of domestication early in recorded history, and perhaps before that. Those feathers were surely coveted by anyone who saw them, and they were an early and valuable item of trade. In fact, like ivory, they were a form of currency. For anyone who had not seen a live peacock, the male's tail feathers must have seemed to have mystical powers.

The Romans ate peacocks (what rare, ostentatious and expensive food didn't they eat?) and kept them as decorative birds in their gardens. Today, all around the world, fanciers breed albino and other exotic forms for the simple pleasure of having them to look at. That pleasure can be somewhat mitigated, however, by the peacock's very unpleasant crepuscular voice, rather like that of an angry fifty-pound Siamese cat, inevitably broadcast before dawn on low branches outside bedroom windows.

Peafowl are tractable and they do not have to be penned. They are now inexpensive to obtain as mature birds, eggs or chicks. They are still found in the wild, of course, but they are considered domestic birds in captivity. Exactly when or where the Indian moguls or their predecessors of high station first adorned their homes and gardens with captive peacocks is not known, but from that day to this, someone, somewhere has "had them around."

Guinea fowl *(Numida meleagris* and sp.) are extremely common in many parts of Africa, and I have seen them scurrying around in sometimes very large flocks every day I have spent in the bush. By 500 B.C., the Greeks and Romans, and surely the Egyptians, kept and ate them, and in some minor way, that has lasted into modern times. They are now kept in the semiwild state in many parts of India. They appear on menus in East African lodges catering to tourists and, to some extent, Africans eat them, too. They are kept on private land in Europe and America but generally not as a source of food. They are nowhere near as tender or tasty as chicken. As for domestication, they have been "kept around" for millennia, but there probably has been little purposeful selective breeding. It is true that three varieties are common in the United States, pearl, white and lavender. That fact may offer proof that domestication is under way.

There are about 185 species of birds in the family Phasianidae, including the ancestor of our chicken, the red jungle fowl. Many of them, the quail, partridge and pheasants particularly, are considered prime upland game birds and have been bred in captivity, moved around, stocked and then shot. An example is the ring-necked pheasant *(Phasianus colchicus),* which originated in Asia but is now almost "native" in North America, Hawaii and New Zealand. Indeed, it is likely that most Americans don't even realize that the familiar pheasant is not a native species. Pheasants live in large numbers in the wild, but whether birds introduced and stocked for hunting should be considered domesticated is a moot question. Probably not, because little change occurs during their period in captivity before being released for use in target practice.

The story of several quail species parallels that of the pheasants. They have been hunted, held in captivity and eaten since the period of Egyptian ascendancy. The Greeks and Romans do not appear to have appreciated them as food, but in later times, probably in the Middle Ages or a little earlier, they came to be thought of as delicacies. The only difference today is that various species of quail are marketed as farm-raised birds in the United States, Europe and Japan to a much greater degree than pheasants are. Still, it is not a major food industry. The quail, particularly *Coturnix coturnix*, which remains a wild bird in North America, in southern Europe and western Asia is probably in a transitional stage between exploitation and domestication. There appears to be little difference between wild and farm-raised birds yet. The same is true of the bobwhite *(Colinus virginianus)* and the Japanese quail *(Coturnix japonica)*, whose one-third-of-an-ounce eggs are considered a delicacy.

Since New World peoples succeeded in domesticating the turkey, is it surprising that they didn't with the quail as well? The Mayans called the quail *bech*, and while it wasn't a major player in Mayan lore, there are tales of interaction with a god known as Halach-Uinic. The quail was a very

ambitious bird, it seems, and as a trickster on at least one occasion got itself into trouble. As a result of this, it was condemned to be a ground-nester and vulnerable. The story goes that before it lost favor with Halach-Uinic, it nested in trees. The Mayans, then, knew the quail and surely hunted it for its pleasing flesh. They had a relationship but it did not lead to domestication.

There had to have been an element of chance in the choice of which gallinaceous birds were domesticated by man. The chicken became the premier domestic fowl not because it was necessarily easier to tame and breed selectively, and not because its flesh was more palatable than other birds in that order. For people without refrigeration and who generally lived in small social units, chickens were a practical size. Certainly, that could have been a factor—enough meat to go around but not a lot of spoilage. Once man had settled down (nomads can't keep chickens very well—they don't herd, they scatter and get picked off by predators), he probably began moving toward somewhat regular meals of reasonable proportions. Nomads depending on hunting and gathering are more likely to be gluttonous when serendipity strikes. The size of the chicken probably fit very well into that trend, too. But it was surely also a case of the right bird in the right place at the right time, when people were ready to have domestication happen in their midst. The bird at hand became the bird in hand and the course was set.

TWENTY-ONE

The Duck, the Goose
and the Swan:
Fine-Feathered Friends

The Mute Swan

In ancient lore, the swan was sacred to both Apollo and Aphrodite. But, more importantly, it was what gods and legendary figures became as a kind of ultimate life event, a graceful disposition of the soul.

Cycnus was many things to many people. He was the son of Poseidon and was killed by Achilles at the Battle of Troy. When stripped of his armor, he turned into a swan. He was also said to be the son of Apollo, and he and his mother, Thyria, became swans. As the son of Ares, Cycnus was killed by Heracles. And, here again, he became a swan. In another myth, he was the son of Sthenelus and Apollo transformed him into a swan. (Sthenelus also ended up as a swan.) One way or another, Cycnus, blame or credit whomever you will, was destined to be a beautiful white creature of infinite grace.

In still other legends and traditions, Leda was visited by Zeus, who had disguised himself as a swan. As a result, she laid two eggs, one of which became the beautiful Helen, while the other produced the twins Castor and Polydeuces. The Greeks had very lively imaginations.

There is an almost universal series of traditions in which the move between bird and man is in the other direction. In the oft-told "swan maiden" legend, swans become human beings. Such stories come from Romania, throughout the Slavic world, from places as disparate as Iceland and Finland to Persia, Sri Lanka, China, Japan, Australia, Polynesia, Melanesia and Indonesia. The theme also appears in Celtic and Teutonic tradition, in both west and east Africa, on Madagascar, in *The Arabian Nights,* and very prominently in Indian tradition. It appears in the lore of Ecuador and is in the mythology of Guiana and probably widely through South America. In Ireland, and to a degree in Scotland, swans are assigned magical qualities by tradition.

The connection of the swan with human fate, and as an alternative habitat for the human soul, probably goes back to the cave. In parts of Siberia, it is believed that if a man kills a swan, he will soon sicken and die himself. It is taboo to injure a swan in the Hebrides and in parts of Ireland. It is no accident that Tchaikovsky composed one of the most beloved of all ballets, *Swan Lake.* All of this because of the awe inspired by eight species of birds closely related to the geese.

It is ironic that the swan, universally viewed as the epitome of grace and beauty, apparently is nowhere near as fine a food as either ducks or geese. I have never eaten swan (nor do I intend to), but I have seen it repeatedly referred to as "like leather" and oily. Swans out of the water are anything but graceful and they can be very aggressive. Years ago, when I lived in East Hampton, New York, there was an elderly "local" gentleman who killed a swan every year for his Thanksgiving dinner. One year, he was found dead, his face battered, and his clothing and the ground around his body scattered with feathers. His death was declared the result of an attack by a swan, no doubt a cob, or male, defending his territory and mate.

The Swan of Swans

Of the eight swan species (mute, trumpeter, whooper, whistling, Bewick's, black, black-necked and coscoroba), only the mute swan *(Cygnus olor)* can be considered domesticated. It ranges as a wild bird (and now perhaps a feral one as well) across the northern half of the Old World from Iceland to Siberia. It has been introduced into the Western Hemisphere and Australia. In every area where the mute swan has been kept as a "domestic" bird, we can assume some have returned to the wild, and that wild or feral birds are almost indistinguishable from those kept in captivity.

Are swans domesticated? Possibly, but not much more than that.

Probably as a result of inbreeding, there is a melanin-deficient form sometimes referred to as the Polish swan. Their cygnets are white instead of gray, and their legs and feet, gray during their immature stage, remain that way instead of turning black. It could be a new, distinct domestic form or just a variation found in some populations. But even if swans were actually domesticated, they were allowed to come and go and live semiwild lives. Swan identification marks date from about 1230.

Swan-keeping began at least as far back as Greece in ascendancy. By the tenth century, swans were being kept in Britain. The rules for keeping swans, especially in England, are well defined. Those who tend them are known as swanherds. The post of king's swan master dates back to at least 1361. Edward III appointed Thomas de Russhams to the job. By the late 1400s, the ownership of swans was a prerogative of royalty and those to whom the king granted special rights. The king dined on swans. The royal swans today are still distinguished with a mark applied to their bills while they are cygnets. There are swan pits, also known as swan houses, where "domestic" swans are kept. The tradition of swan-keeping is old and well established and has a vocabulary all its own.

The ownership of the swans on the Thames River today is divided between the queen and the Worshipful Companies of Dyers and Vintners. The marking of the cygnets is a colorful ceremony and as much a pageant as the changing of the guard at Buckingham Palace. Like so much of what goes on in England involving the royal family, the swans on the Thames and the events surrounding them please the tourist industry mightily.

Today, on rivers, lakes and ponds across America, and wedging in tight swan skeins across the sky, the mute swan is a regular part of the North American landscape. It is impossible to know how long any particular swan population has been living back in the wild, but escapees no longer require human intervention. They are considered feral instead of wild because their ancestors are thought to have been domestic birds. Again, however, domesticated or kept and utilized? It is a species in which the distinctions are blurred, but tradition does consider them a domestic species, both in captivity and in the feral state. As for their use, swans are to look at and photograph and little else.

The Duck

About 115 species of birds in the family Anatidae are considered ducks. The other birds in this large avian family are the geese and the swans. And there are a few species in which the distinction between ducks and geese is at least vague.

Wild ducks have been hunted for as far back as we can trace the habits of man. Since most species are ground nesters, young ducks have always been readily taken, and ducks in molt have also been easy targets for men who run fast and throw stones well. As the throwing stick, the bow and arrow and eventually the gun came into play, duck hunting took on new dimensions. Nets and traps have also been used, along with a very sophisticated form of lure developed by the original inhabitants of the New World, the decoy.

Today, duck hunting, with often very expensive shotguns as weapons mandated by law, can take on near-religious intensity. It is taboo to shoot a "sitting duck." They are hunted during their seasonal long-distance migrations to their wintering grounds. And it has become, in some places at least, a ritual of manhood. There are clubs to belong to, special clothing to wear and preferred dogs to own. The weather is usually appalling, and if you don't suffer from the cold and wet, you just don't get it. In other parts of the world where duck hunting is essential, not a "sport," they are hunted as they always have been—in any way possible. The flesh of many species is highly regarded.

Man generally has set up housekeeping as near to water as possible for all the obvious reasons. As beach or bank dwellers, early men would have been able to catch ducks and herd them in convenient pens. It has always been easier to pick a duck from a captive flock than to hunt it.

Ducks may have been kept and possibly domesticated as far back as Mesopotamia. It is difficult to determine if the figurines that suggest this are of ducks or geese. The Egyptians, apparently, did not domesticate the duck, although they did hunt it. That is also true as far as we can tell of Greece. The Romans kept ducks in enclosures called *nessotrophia*. However, these pens could have been used to hold wild or domestic ducks, and the distinctions here are not clearly established. The Germans may have had domestic ducks and the Chinese certainly did. It is impossible to set dates or precise locales, but in China, at least, the domestic ducks so beloved now appear to have very ancient lineage.

As far as we know, all domestic ducks held today are descendants of the mallard *(Anas platyrhynchos)* with the exception of the Muscovy, which is the descendant of the wild Muscovy or "scovy" *(Cairina moschata)*. The former has a natural range from Alaska to Mexico, North Africa to India as well as China and Borneo. The Muscovy ranges from Mexico to Argentina. But why domestication was limited to two species when at least a hundred species were hunted is another mystery.

Just about all the ducks raised as domestic fowl in the United States today are fast-growing white Pekins, a Chinese breed first imported into North America in 1873. Fourteen specimens were brought in to launch the duck industry. They have been developed here to the point where they are slaughtered at under two months and are therefore efficient grain converters. Although now a substantial-enough industry in the United States, ducks are far, far behind chickens and even turkeys in numbers and dollar value. They are much more commonly eaten in parts of Europe and in Asia. They are often seen as a farmyard bird, a highly regarded incidental food animal. They are friendly and even-tempered creatures, although they can be protective of their young. Why the most famous duck in the world—Donald—is so irascible is not clear.

The Goose

There are at least twenty-eight species of geese in the family Anatidae. They come from all over the world, all continents except Antarctica and a vast number of islands, some of them very remote. There are other species where the distinction between the vernacular names *duck* and *goose* are not as clear as most people think.

Geese have been kept by man since at least the New Stone Age, the Neolithic. The most commonly kept species was the greylag *(Anser anser)*, whose range is as enormous now as it surely was then. It breeds where habitat is still available over northern and central Europe all the way east to Manchuria and Mongolia. As a powerful, long-distance migrant, the greylag was known seasonally on Crete, to the Egyptians and many other cultures as well. It was probably domesticated within its breeding range, in southern Europe more to the east than the west. But we don't know when greylags ceased being simply easily taken captives and became truly domesticated.

The Greeks kept geese but may not have used them as food, although that would be strange if true. They make excellent guardians and are aggressively territorial, desirable characteristics then as now and certainly admired by the Romans. The militaristic Romans also liked them for their feathers, which could be used in decorative ways, but especially because they were excellent in the manufacture of arrows. The Romans also cherished them as food and reckoned their livers a great delicacy. That part, at least, has changed very little.

Goose fat appears in many ancient pharmacopoeias under the name of *lard* or *goose lard*. By Pliny's time, the greylag had already evolved into a snow-white bird, particularly those imported into Rome from Germania. The white goose was much preferred over darker birds from other parts of Europe.

Along the Nile, the greylag was kept in captivity with the related white-fronted goose *(Anser albifrons)*. Geese of these two species, and probably others as well, were kept as pets, for food, for their feathers and their abilities as "watchdogs." They were also specified as sacrificial animals in a number of rites.

The Chinese domesticated yet another species, now sometimes known as *Cygnopsis cygnoides*, or *Anser cygnoides*, which is also its wild counterpart. The most popular domestic goose breeds in the United States today

are the Toulouse, the Embden, the African and Chinese. The greylag is now a specialty bird kept in pairs as pets. The Toulouse comes from southern France and is a domestic version of the greylag. It is the largest domestic breed and the gander can weigh an impressive twenty-six pounds. The Embden was one of the earliest domestic geese seen in the New World. It was also developed from the greylag in Hanover, but it is known that it came here from Bremen and was once known here as the Bremen. It was preceded in the United States by an old English breed that became known as the Pilgrim goose. That was a greylag derivative, too.

The African goose probably was developed in India, using a mixture of Chinese breeds and again incorporating greylag stock. The snow-white Chinese goose is the breed most commonly seen on farms in the United States today and it was evolved in China. The Chinese swan-goose is distinctive. It has a very pronounced knob on its head. The Canada goose, so beloved of waterfowl hunters, is as easy to manage as our domestic breeds but is not as attractive a food animal as the greylag descendants that have been developed. Their long-distance migratory flights over North America in the familiar V-formations or skeins are one of nature's premier spectacles.

Geese are remarkably easy to tame, and from there to domesticate. When taken as eggs (and not eaten in that form) or as chicks from their ground or shallow water floating nests, they will immediately imprint and follow anyone who is there at hand. They can be shooed or herded by people with or without dogs. They apparently "enjoy" or at least take an interest in the activities of people and naturally keep close to human habitations. Even wild geese today will land near domestic geese they spot from the air, and some of them will take up with the domestic flock.

Geese are excellent pets except for two characteristics. They are naturally bullies and will lord it over any person or dog that does not first lord it over them. Children have to be taught how to "bully" geese with voice and gesture (nothing more is required) if they are to avoid being victims. That is all easily managed, but the second characteristic is not, at least not with freely wandering geese. These large birds eat a great deal of both feed and grass and they process their food with amazing speed. A back porch can become a veritable minefield in fifteen minutes when geese come to peck at the windows. Unpenned yard geese are somehow pleasing as pets, talkative and interactive any time they have a chance, but unfortunately they are absolutely filthy. Still, they are amusing and we thoroughly enjoy our pet flock. All it takes is a hose.

TWENTY-TWO

The Pigeon, the Falcon and Other Birds:
Special Niches

The Ubiquitous Rock Dove

There are an estimated 310 species of birds in the family Columbidae, the pigeons and doves of the world, terms that are generally used interchangeably. The family's distribution is worldwide. Only one species has been domesticated, however, and is today found almost everywhere man has settled except in the high Arctic and on some islands. This most common of the world's birds is the rock dove or rock pigeon, *Columba domestica*.

The original range of the pigeon was large: the Faroe Islands, Shetland and Orkney islands, Ireland and Scotland south to the Mediterranean, across Africa north of the Equator, western Asia, Arabia, India and Sri Lanka and just possibly east to Mongolia and China. Today, those areas still know their familiar pigeon, but now, because of man, the rest of the world shares it with them. Where domestic versions of the rock dove do not dwell, ferals do by the millions. The three groups, wild, feral and domestic, are able to interbreed, and the result is a pulsating blanket of rock dove genes that fairly covers the world. It is one of the most populous birds on the planet and clearly one of the most adaptable.

Feral pigeons are the descendants of domestic "dovecote" pigeons that have been lost, temporarily strayed or been abandoned and have bred themselves back into wild populations, or simply bred up populations on their own. Almost inevitably, the ferals are descended from domestic flying breeds like homing and racing pigeons, and not from the fancy strutting breeds often referred to as "monstrous" by ornithologists. The feral birds differ from true wild rock doves by having proportionally narrower bodies, longer tails, broader bills and larger ceres at the base of their bills. For most people, they are indistinguishable.

As wild or feral birds, pigeons seem naturally to "hang around" human habitation. That has always been the case when man lived within the original bird's range. Men and women were probably keeping pigeons, or at least feeding relatively tame wild pigeons, by the time of the New Stone Age. The species is not as easily "spooked" as most wild birds, and the simple practice of scattering almost any kind of seeds will bring them in. They are ridiculously easy to trap.

It is not known when they were domesticated. The bone evidence is not very rewarding and it is virtually impossible to determine, in by far the greatest number of cases, whether we are looking at the bones of wild pigeons that were hunted or trapped or birds at least on the way to domestication.

From about 5000 to 4500 B.C., pigeons were kept in Mesopotamia. The Minoans had them and so did the Hebrews. Towers were built for pigeons to nest in and that practice is still seen today. The Romans built towers or *columbaria,* too. Pigeons were considered a delicacy and they were eaten in huge numbers. It is not clear whether earlier societies ate their pigeons regularly or whether the birds were kept at hand for religious purposes. The pigeon has long been a convenient, inexpensive bird for sacrificial ceremonies. But I suspect that when people kept pigeons for any purpose, some managed to get eaten.

The homing pigeon's remarkable skill was known at least as far back as the Roman occupation of Egypt, and the military used them as a general practice to transport urgent messages and news. Nero used them in the first century and both sides used them during the Crusades. They were, in fact, used in large numbers up through World War I.

Today, pigeons are marketed as squab and are something of a delicacy. Millions of birds are kept by hobbyists either in fancy breeds and varieties for show or as athletes for cross-country racing.

The wild or feral pigeon is for most people the first bird they see or at least notice. They live easily as feathered pariahs picking up what man drops or leaves behind in his agriculture or on town and city streets. They are such commonplace birds that many people fail to appreciate how beauti-

ful they can be and what wonderful acrobats they are when airborne. Whether hunted, trapped, eaten, raised, shown, raced or sacrificed, they have long been utilized by man. As a domestic bird, they have been developed into a remarkable variety of shapes, colors, styles and sizes. Scores of exotic pigeon species other than *Columba domestica* are kept by fanciers as well, but they cannot be said to be domesticated. Some may be altered somewhat by the aviculturists' zeal, but it is doubtful that they will become truly domestic birds in the ways demonstrated by the rock dove.

The Falcon

A large but unknown number of birds of prey have been utilized by man in the hunting sport known as falconry. I have been unable to locate a census or catalog showing the many species actually used around the world, but they have included falcons, hobbies, kestrels, eagles, even owls, and certainly hawks of many kinds.

The preferred species is unquestionably the peregrine falcon, *Falco peregrinus*. Its natural distribution is cosmopolitan or worldwide, and trained birds have been carried almost everywhere man has gone by enthusiasts and fanciers. With its 80-mile-an-hour level flight and 250-mile-an-hour dive or stoop, the peregrine has earned the name and reputation of royal falcon.

Peregrine falcons generally have been unavailable to the average man. Today, they are protected and a black market exists in which trained birds can bring as much as $35,000 to $40,000. In other areas and in other times, it was a crime, often a very serious one, for anyone but royalty or at least the nobility to own one. Falconry was distinctly a gentleman's sport.

The Egyptians were using the falcon as a symbol in their preoccupation with death and the cult of the dead before 3000 B.C. They may have been flying their birds as well, but that has not been proven. The Assyrians did fly their birds from the evidence at hand, but apparently the Greeks did not. Nor did the Romans, which is strange. How the militaristic art and glory of setting a falcon loose on prey escaped the lovers of the arena and its lethal games is a mystery. By the Middle Ages, the sport of falconry was a ritual, and no royal court would be without its staff of falconers any more than it would be without its musicians, armorers or masters of the horse. Many portraits exist of kings, queens and gentlefolk with their beloved falcons on their arms. The bird was a badge, its use a passion.

For all that, no bird of prey, neither the peregrine falcon nor any of its many substitutes, can be considered a domestic animal. Utilized, certainly, but not altered by selective breeding. That would make sense because the endearing characteristics in this case are the elemental savagery and wild skill of the airborne hunter. Nothing man could have done would have improved on these splendidly honed killers. The demands of survival perfected the falconer's bird, not the eyes and tastes of man.

The Ostrich

There is a small group of rather large birds known as ratites, a name that comes from the Latin word for raft, indicating flatness. The reference is to their sternum or keel bone, to which a bird's flight muscles are attached.

These birds have lost the power of flight, and thus the need for either the muscles of flight or their anchor.

The ratites are by far the largest birds left on earth, and although small in comparison with the extinct giants like the moa of New Zealand (eleven to twelve feet tall) or Madagascar's elephant bird, which had leg bones as heavy as a modern ox, they are big. The largest of all is the three-hundred-pound ostrich of African semiarid savannas and steppes. Others include the rheas of South America, two species, the three cassowaries of Australia, New Guinea and nearby islands and the emu of Australia.

Ostriches have been "kept" for millennia. They were hunted and raised for their flesh, the feathers of the cocks and for the mammoth eggs the hens produced in large numbers. It is generally believed that the first jewelry was made from small circular chips of ostrich egg shell strung on a leather cord. It is a material that is durable and far easier to work than stone. Eggs were traded sometimes for food and often as works of art, painted, gilded and otherwise adorned.

The French in Algeria began farming ostriches in the middle 1800s, and there are reports of earlier attempts on Sicily and elsewhere. The art of raising these giant birds has probably reached its highest state in South Africa, and it has become something of a speculation or fad in the United States in recent years. Emus are also being raised in captivity in the United States in the hope, no doubt, that giant birds in the backyard will have wide

appeal. Absurdly high prices are being asked, but there is a problem with the scheme. These giants are singularly dangerous. A kick from an ostrich can hospitalize an adult or kill a child. I have seen a hen in Kenya, infuriated by the approach of a van to its nest (a mere shallow depression in the dirt), attack the vehicle. The first kick tore out the van's left taillight assembly and severely dented the tailgate. A second kick, achieved while chasing the van at thirty miles an hour down a dirt road did major damage to the right rear fender. Not a wise backyard bird.

It is doubtful that the ostrich in captivity is significantly different from the wild bird that has been hunted for tens of thousands of years. The ostrich is perhaps best described as an intensely utilized or exploited bird but not a domesticated one. As for the emu, it is probably best considered a relatively minor utilization, and the history of that exploitation will probably be short-lived.

The idea, incidentally, that the ostrich buries its head in the sand to avoid confronting reality is fun but fiction. With very large eyes and long, swivelling necks, ostriches are extremely alert to everything going on around them.

The Cormorant

Japanese and Chinese lake and river fishermen have long used cormorants to catch fish for them. Charles I of England employed a Mr. Wood as his "master of the cormorants," and Louis XIII of France also kept these sleek diving birds. There are thirty-one species of cormorants worldwide, all members of the family Phalacrocoracidae. Those used in the exotic fishing exercise have probably belonged to two or three species or subspecies, the common Chinese cormorant, *Phalacrocorax carbo sinensis,* from India and China, and Temminck's cormorant, *P. capillatus,* from Japan and Korea. The European cormorant, *P. carbo,* is the third. Actually this last species is found all over the world.

Are cormorants domesticated birds? Some scholars believe so. Cormorant eggs are placed under domestic fowl to hatch. But if the eggs are taken from the nests of wild birds, the form of incubator used would not alter the biology of the hatchlings. Some cormorants display irregular pale patches, but wild birds do as well. It is an open question. I do not know specifically of significant differences between wild and captive birds that would qualify the species for the designation "domesticated."

There are nearly nine thousand species of birds in the world and, as hunted animals, several thousand of them at least have helped feed man. However, fewer than ten species have been truly domesticated and come to have economic significance. The chicken, surely, is the most significant of all. With eight to ten billion being held at any one time, they are a major source of protein. Their eggs are also of enormous importance. As for the few other species, beyond the turkey, the duck and the goose, their economic importance has been marginal and local.

There is a trade-off that is forced upon any animal to which we take a fancy, and it is certainly true for birds we use for food. For all the benefits they provide us, we provide few, if any, benefits for them. Their lives are not longer or more comfortable because of man. Indeed, just the opposite is true. Man is wholly egocentric in his view of life and living things. He takes, but does not give in return. If domestication is viewed as one of his greatest achievements, one could argue that it is also the ultimate form of predation.

TWENTY-THREE

Companion Birds: Connections to the Wild

· There are a number of bird species that have been domesticated, or nearly so, yet have no real economic importance except to fanciers who breed them and sell the young. The pet industry markets birdseed, cuttlebone, cages, toys, perches, dishes, cage gravel and paper, voice training tapes, scores of books and home-care products. But for all of that, the principal value of companion birds is psychological, not economic. In this regard, they are very like their traditional enemy, the house cat.

The Canary

It is commonly believed that canaries are birds found only in the Canary Islands, which are located off the northwest coast of Africa. In fact, various species of canaries, members of the family Fringillidae, are found from the highlands of Ethiopia to the southern tip of Africa. The family to which they belong is huge and includes, among other familiar birds, the finches, goldfinches, bullfinches, cardinals, siskins, sparrows, seedeaters, buntings, longspurs, juncos, grassquits, towhees, grosbeaks and tanagers.

The bird that was domesticated, however, did come originally from the Canary Islands. It is *Serinus canaria* and is also found in the Azores off the Portuguese coast and on Madeira, the island off Morocco, between the Canary and Azore groups. When the canary was first kept in captivity is probably no longer possible to determine. The islands were claimed by the Portuguese in 1341, but awarded to Castile by the pope three years later. Spain eventually conquered all of the archipelago late in the fifteenth century. It is quite likely that they found the canary already the companion of the aboriginal Guanche. That is suggested by the speed with which they began exporting male birds to a growing European market.

The story is widely accepted that a Spanish ship carrying a cargo of canaries foundered off Elba, which belonged then as now to Italy. It is said that the birds escaped onto the island, established a feral population that the Italians harvested as a means of entering into the small but profitable canary trade. England was eventually a player in the trade, but Germany became preeminent, especially in the Harz Mountains in central Germany between the Elbe and Weser rivers. Canaries as cage birds are now found around the world. And because some have inevitably escaped and some have been "liberated," there are also pockets of feral birds in areas with a suitable climate.

The canary was singled out for captivity because of the male's territorial song. It is particularly pleasing and has lent itself to selective breeding. Canaries have been bred for singing ability as well as shape, feather style, posture and color. The original wild bird is small and relatively drab, olive green with yellow (in the male), gray and brownish stripes.

There are many stories of canaries being bred to other related species to gain color and feather quality, but how much is fact and how much fiction has never been sorted out. The competition to produce the best singers and the most beautiful birds has been so intense since the sixteenth century that it is likely that smokescreen stories of how choice varieties were developed have always been used to guard trade secrets. It is enough, perhaps, to say that the canary, usually bright yellow and the most beloved singer of all cage birds, is domestic and has as its ancestor the drab little canary of the Canary Islands.

Other Companions

Aviculturists have kept literally hundreds of species of birds in captivity and have managed to breed a large number of them. Everything from flamingos and exotic waterfowl to toucans, pheasants and nightingales have adorned the homes and gardens of bird fanciers around the world.

The large and fascinating family Psittacidae, with well over 320 species, has offered companion bird enthusiasts the lories, lorikeets, cockatoos, corellas, cockatiels, parrots, rosellas, lovebirds, parakeets, macaws, conures, parrotlets, caiques and Amazons. Many species, like the cockatiel from Australia *(Nymphicus hollandicus)*, the budgerigar or parakeet *(Melopsittacus undulatus)*, also from Australia, and the lovebirds *(Agapornis,* 9 spp.) from Africa, have been bred for so many hundreds of their generations that some must be considered domestic animals. Many others have been kept but not significantly altered. In the process of domestication, years or numbers of birds in captivity do not count. The shaping of a species by man, using selective breeding to replace natural selection, does. Most cage birds are wild captives; of the hundreds kept, only a few have been truly turned into domestic animals. It would take a case-by-case, species-by-species examination to determine which birds are wild, which are on the road to domestication and which have actually reached that goal.

Bird fanciers buy their pets from pet dealers and give little thought to where they may have come from or what the real cost in terms of lost lives and suffering may have been if they were wild-caught. But, in the future, it will become more and more necessary for cage bird enthusiasts and their suppliers to rely on captive breeding for their stock. The days of

raiding the wild places and hoping enough of the captives will survive both capture and transport to make the venture economically viable are drawing to a close. It is none too soon. Far too many species and too many habitats are seriously endangered to allow old practices to continue. Ports of entry everywhere in this world that handle live cargo report whole shipments of birds dead en route to their destinations. The cruelty has been unimaginable, and today the trade has been slowed to the point where smugglers are at work trying to milk the last dollar out of wild stock. The shipping mortality they realize is, if anything, worse than the records show for former "legitimate" dealers. The exotic pet business in general has always had an air of banditry about it, but is now being forced to an end.

What the unavailability of wild stock will do to the domestication status of popular species is difficult to say. In the past, easy access to wild-caught birds kept significant breeding efforts to a minimum except in the case of a few select species. That may change. And whether it means that more species will be domesticated is an open question. But the ground rules for obtaining man's companion birds must change out of dire necessity.

TWENTY-FOUR

Fish, the Silkworm and the Bee:
Finery and Food

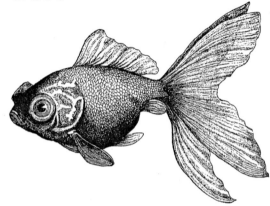

Fish First

Given the facts that fishponds are holes in the ground and that fragile fish bones usually don't offer paleontologists a lot of information, our knowledge of early pisciculture has to be less than comprehensive. And where a fish appears in artwork, it is more than a little difficult to identify the subject as wild-caught, pond-raised or actually domesticated. Even so, fish have long played a significant role in human nutrition. The intricate art of fly-fishing and the cranking machinery of deep-sea trolling are modern developments. Long before those methods of capture evolved, men used their bare hands and pieces of bark to shovel fish out of shrinking water holes as the sun sucked them dry, killing off entire fish populations of what had only weeks before been running rivers and streams.

Paddling along astride logs or wading waist deep in water, man learned early on how to drive fish into weirs and traps, where they could be scooped up in baskets at his leisure. From there, he obviously went on to manage water flow in restricted areas. From that, surely came ditches, ponds and other water impoundments that were used at first to contain fish and ultimately to breed some species for the table. It was an inevitable chain of events.

We know the Sumerians had fishponds or containments roughly forty-five hundred years ago. Artificial ponds were used by the Mesopotamians, Egyptians and Assyrians. The science of pisciculture came to blossom in Rome, possibly taught to the Romans by the Sicilians. The Egyptians apparently maintained a highly esteemed food fish that is still being harvested in captive ponds today, the tilapia.

The Chinese may well have been the first true fish culturists, a practice that goes back at least three thousand years. Their first fish was probably the carp, *Cyprinus carpio*. The carp family, Cyprinidae, is the largest of all fish families. This "rough," hardy fish is found over much of Europe and penetrates deep into Asia. It can tolerate far more silting than most other fish and it can be fed garbage, literally, and still produce a lot of good-quality flesh. It is possible that the carp was domesticated independently in Europe, perhaps in monasteries, and that the domestic carp was not an import from China as often stated.

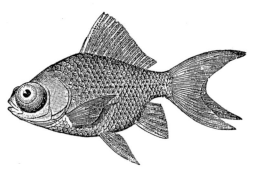

Domesticated carp are distinctive and some varieties barely resemble their wild ancestors. The wild fish are normally gray, quite dark in color, while domestic carp are red or white or patterned and mottled. The scales are often quite different, and some domestic carp have been bred to have no scales at all.

The Japanese took up the practice of carp culture from the Chinese and developed it into a science that they then celebrated in their art, ceramics, fabrics, graphics and sculpture. The Japanese have further developed a carplike fish, the koi (*Cyprinus* sp.), into an art form. Koi are not raised as a food fish but as pets, a hobby and a sophisticated decoration in the pools and ponds of Japanese parks and gardens. Koi are an element in the pursuit of inner peace and tranquillity. They are to fish what bonsai trees are to silviculture. A big difference, however, is recognition. Koi recognize people who come pondside to feed them and literally rise to the occasion. There can be a sense of interaction that does not come from trees and plants no matter how lovingly tended. Domestic koi come in a number of colors, notably red, white, silver, black, yellow and gold. A beautifully patterned, prizewinning koi can be valued at well over $10,000 and is highly sought after even at that price.

The Romans highly esteemed a moray eel, *Muraena muraena* (also given as *M. helena*). These fish can be quite fierce and do bite, but they were still raised in large numbers for the table and even as pets. (Stories of Roman aristocrats feeding slaves to their pet eels are probably not true.) In pools or impoundments called *piscinae* or *vivaria* (specifically *salae* or *maritimae*, seawater pools, as opposed to *dulces*, fresh or sweet-water pools), the mottled Roman eels were kept and harvested and are thought to have been domesticated. It is not clear exactly what makes a captive-bred moray eel a domestic animal unless it is the fact that the ancestors of the fish have been in captivity for millennia.

There is no question in the case of the goldfish *(Carassius auratus)*, a descendant of a common, rough carp. The highly selective breeding of goldfish in China began around A.D. 1000, during the Sung dynasty. By the 1500s, the hobby was firmly established in Japan as well, where examples of the now-domesticated fish had been imported as pets for the aristocracy. They were much admired. By 1611, there were fairly regular shipments of goldfish to Europe, and by 1876, they were being sold in the United States.

The goldfish is one of the most highly domesticated of all animals. It has been developed into forms as widely diverse in appearance as the dog breeds. Its genes, obviously, are very easy to manipulate. Highly diverse

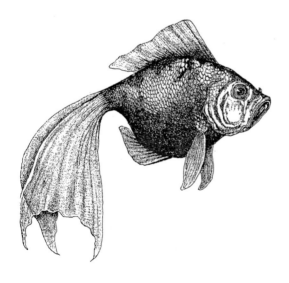

goldfish are raised today in Japan, particularly in the prefectures of Nara, Aichi and Tokyo. At one time, in Nara, the hobby was reserved for the samurai class. Today, the hobby and the business of raising goldfish are universal.

Most of these types of goldfish could not possibly survive in the wild. The United States, along with Japan and China, has developed a large number of these races or varieties. Some of them are truly spectacular, others true monstrosities. A number of varieties have their eye sockets outside their skulls, while others have long, lacy tails that all but cripple the fish. Some have even been bred to be blind, actually lacking eyes, although it is not clear exactly why. Standards of beauty are not always easy to comprehend. The incredible color variations include the basic red/gold along with blue, black, white, silver, brown, chocolate, purple, pearl, calico and mottled or otherwise patterned. There are scores of varieties, over thirty types from China alone with protruding eyes, and twenty more distinguished by the lack of a dorsal fin.

The paradise fish *(Macropus viridi-auratus)* has been bred by the Chinese for centuries. But it is not known whether these usually red rice-paddy fish of no economical value are altered wild stock or simply feral stock from long ago. The fish are much admired by the Chinese and are a small decorative pleasure that can be maintained without cost in the water impoundments required for cultivating rice.

Scores of freshwater and saltwater species are maintained by aquarists today. There is not even an accurate count of the number of species, much less the varieties that have been developed. Many species are bred in such vast numbers in captivity today that importation is no longer economically sensible. Often a collector will ship in to wholesalers a heretofore unknown species from a stretch of reef or a lake in a remote area that has never been "collected" before. For a time, the species is widely sought after, but if it proves difficult to breed, the original stock will die off. It may be years before that fish is again offered for sale.

In some areas, collectors have depleted wild stock so badly or done so much habitat damage that the rarer species are unlikely to appear again for sale in the foreseeable future, if ever. An assessment of the actual damage done by fish collectors needs to be undertaken. It is to the benefit of wild stock to see that domestic species evolve. The very fact of domestication always means that captive breeding has been going on for some extended period of time. In this case, the economic realities of the situation mean that domestication—captive breeding—results in reduced pressure on wild stocks and their habitats.

As for the measure of domestication, as it is with cage birds, it would have to be a species-by-species determination. It is difficult, however, to think of fish like the guppy *(Poecilia reticulata)* or the discus *(Symphysodon* sp.) as anything but domestic, although the latter has only been known to science since 1840 and has only been an available aquarium fish since 1933. So many color varieties have been developed and, in guppies, so many tail and fin styles, as well as colors and markings, that they can only be seen as domestic animals.

Going down the list of even the most common species from reef and pond held by hobbyists today, one finds bettas, cichlids in great variety, mollies, various catfish, small eels, oscars, tetras, reef fish and hundreds of others. The inevitable conclusion is that if all of the species that have been selectively bred into desired colors and forms fit the criteria we established for domestication and are thereby properly on the roster of domestic animals, man has domesticated more species of fish than of mammals and birds combined.

Unexpected Domestic Animals: Silkworms, Bees and Others

The word *unexpected* is used advisedly because most people don't think of invertebrates as domesticated animals or, for that matter, as animals at all. They are animals, certainly, and a number have been genetically controlled by man long enough to warrant domestic status.

Silk is a secretion from the mouth of a moth caterpillar that solidifies once it makes contact with air. The secretion forms into a fiber that the caterpillar uses to form a cocoon. A single cocoon may contain as many as two kilometers of the silk strand. Over five thousand years ago, the Chinese learned how to unwind the mile or more of silk from each cocoon and spin it into fiber that could be woven into a highly desirable fabric. According to the many legends about silk and its origins, that would have been during the reign of the emperor Fu-Shi, around 3000 B.C.

For thousands of years, the secrets of silk origin and production were jealously guarded by the Chinese. Before silk became a commodity in demand outside China, the exchange of information between the East and the West was minimal. Eventually, however, the secrets of silk got out, perhaps in an early case of industrial espionage, and China opened its door to trade. The so-called silk road to Europe was initially five thousand kilometers long. It started in Xi'an in Shaanxi Province and crossed bleak Central Asia to the Mediterranean cities of Antioch and Tyre and thence to Rome. Mediterranean craft awaited the caravans and carried the silk to ports leading upriver and overland into the heart of Europe. The market for silk penetrated Spain and from there crossed the Atlantic to Latin America, then north into North America. The French Huguenots took up the art of fiber production or sericulture and are still at it—as are the originating Chinese. Other silk-producing centers grew up along the trade routes.

Domestication came into the world of silk production out of necessity. The caterpillars that established the industry and still produce most of the best-quality silk eat white mulberry leaves as their natural diet. Fiber production would thus depend on the leafing season of white mulberry trees had masters of the trade not developed synthetic foods that allow production to go on all year round. These artificially fed producers of silk fiber are known as test-tube caterpillars.

Silkworms

Silkworms (silk moth caterpillars) are cooperative little beasts in that they are not prone to wander far as long as food is available to satisfy their brief gluttonous appetites. They can be raised on simple trays on equally simple racks. In the millennia of silk history, artisans have evolved a domestic animal that even in the moth phase of its life won't "wander." The moths evolved in domestication have lost the ability to fly. Since so many individual animals are required for the commercial production of silk, millions upon millions of them, control of the insect labor force is essential. The need for caterpillar and moth police to keep the "workers" from escaping would make the production of silk far less attractive as an industry.

The moth used initially by the Chinese was undoubtedly *Bombyx mori.* In the Himalayas, there is a related moth, *Bombyx huttoni*, that also produces a commercially valuable silk thread in its caterpillar stage. The two have been experimentally cross-bred. It is possible that some of the other domestic *Bombyx* moths are descended from *B. huttoni*. In all, about a dozen species of moths produce usable silk fiber. They all belong to three families, Bombycidae, Saturniidae and Lasiocampidae. The single species from the last listed family is the only one not from the Indo-Chinese region.

Silk known as coa vestris was produced by the Mediterranean silk moth or cos moth before the time of Christ and could have been an invention independent of the Chinese accomplishment. Different moths were used in India, Korea and Japan. The caterpillars in these cases feed on oak leaves and do not depend on the white mulberry tree.

Silk may not be viewed by some as a linchpin of modern culture, and therefore the domestication of the silk moths may be considered to be of minor significance. That falls far short of reality. Putting aside the role silk production and trade played in societies and economies as diverse as those in China, Japan, Persia, Greece, France and England, much more was, in fact, involved.

The silk road was a trade route of enormous importance. Much more than the distribution of pretty silk fabrics for use by the aristocracy was facilitated. Exotic dog breeds and other wild and domestic animals, recipes, spices, oils, flavorings, healing potions, incense, other fabrics besides silk, furs, gunpowder, fireworks, gems, art forms, saddlery, military equi-page, artifacts in precious and base metals, human genes—all traveled with the boats and caravans that distributed silk and sent fortunes spiraling back to China.

But the most important commodity to travel those routes had no material being. The international caravan's most princely trade goods were ideas. The East and the West were joined together economically and, insofar as it has ever happened, culturally by strands of silk. For a very long time, silk fabric was the only evidence the West had that the East was even there and, if it was there, that it mattered. In terms of cultural as opposed to simply economic exchange, silk, for what it is, for the messages it has carried and for the world of ideas it drew behind it as it unwound around the world, has been a major player in the history of the development of man. Silk and therefore the domestication of silkworms undeniably have been highlights in the story of man and the animals he has brought totally under his control.

The Honeybee

The honeybee *(Apis mellifera)* has been an animal of great importance to man since at least the Old Stone Age. The original relationship was as usual hunting/gathering, only it wasn't the bee man hunted and gathered but the things bees made. From cave art, we know that man pursued the hazardous business of hive-robbing from very early days. This entailed scaling trees, cliffs and cave walls and risking stings that were painful and even fatal if received in large numbers. A man high on a cliff attacked by hundreds of furious bees was a man in imminent danger of dying.

Three things were needed for successful hive raids. Generally, a rope or line of some kind for scaling the heights or attaching oneself to a tree while scooping out the honey and wax, a container for carrying the treasure away and the control of fire. Early man used the same substance for stunning and controling bees that is in use today—smoke. Smoldering grass and leaves in some kind of container would give a Stone Age honey-hunter as much of an edge over the bees' organized defense as a commercial honey producer has today.

The next step—hollowing out logs and building inviting hive sites —was apparently something that was done well before the time of dynastic Egypt. Honey was the only natural sweetener available to man in reasonable quantities over much of the world. Eventually, sugar cane and beets and a variety of cultivated fruits would supply man with sugars, but they came much later. Hive sites were established close enough to the ground to preclude the necessity of long climbs and the risk of being attacked while aloft. Nevertheless, it was still a kind of hunting. The bees that were invited in were ignored insofar as their well-being was concerned. Colonies were destroyed in the collection process, but it didn't matter; there were plenty more where they came from. Before the advent of pesticides and mass habitat destruction, there was no shortage of these tenacious, highly organized insects.

Man had to have followed the activities of honeybees closely and eventually the role of the queen was understood. By taking queens from hives when the defenses were the least fierce and using them to establish new hives, man was on the road to another domestication. Ease of keeping was one goal, rate of production of the honeycombs was another. In time, man was able to flavor his honey by locating his hives near flowers of choice. The honey he harvested was the most important single part of the endeavor, but he had many uses for the comb itself. He could eat it, use it in balms and unguents and medications and make candles of it. It was also used to make writing tablets.

Propolis is a kind of resin bees collect from trees and use as a cement and a sealant, helping to secure the integrity of the hive's inner structure. Also called bee glue, it is an architectural material of considerable importance. It was collected with the comb and used in medications and, probably early in man's association with bees, for attaching stone points to arrows and spears.

Eventually, in dozens of cultures, people stopped simply raiding hives and started propagating bees and taking care to drive them away with smoke at harvesttime without actually harming them. The use of honey was so widespread and the evolution of beekeeping such an inevitable process that it was unlikely to have had a single place of origin. Well before the time of Christ, there were traditions of bee culture in Egypt, Syria, Palestine, over much of the Middle East, Crete, Greece and Rome. When or how it developed in Africa and distant areas of Asia is beyond reckoning.

Apis mellifera is not native to the New World. The species being used in Brazil in the 1950s were imports from temperate Europe and were not doing well holding their own against wild tropical bees. Warwick Kerr, a geneticist in Brazil, imported some queens from an aggressive African strain of *Apis,* and thus began the saga of the so-called killer bee. Kerr's plan was that the mild-mannered European *Apis* when coupled with the aggressive African strain would provide Brazilian beekeepers with a tough, hardy, high-producing bee that would be easy to manage. That was not quite the way it worked. The Africanized bees of Brazil are ferociously territorial. When their hive is disturbed, they come boiling out in a furious cloud of stinging insects.

Inevitably, swarms of Africanized bees were lost and became feral. By 1956, there were colonies fanning out of the Amazon Basin heading north and south. By 1975, they were in French Guiana; by 1976, in Venezuela. They reached Colombia by 1980, Panama by 1983, and Costa Rica in the same year. They were in south Texas in 1990 and Louisiana in 1992. It is projected that they will be in North Carolina by 1997. How far north of that they move will depend upon their ability to adjust to harsher climates.

Contrary to the fictional representations of these ferocious creatures, the sting of the Africanized honeybee is no worse than that of any other form of *Apis mellifera.* Unless a person is allergic, one or two stings are of little moment. The real danger lies in the number of stings a person receives when attacked by killer bees. In the jungles of Panama, I was attacked and stung twenty-seven times in about ten seconds by killer bees. Only because I ran and distanced myself from the hive was I able to avoid further insult. I was fortunate; I had no systemic reaction. People or animals who stop and roll or swat at the bees can be stung so many times that they are overwhelmed by the foreign proteins in bee venom and the body's reaction to it. There is little consolation in the knowledge that bees die after using their stingers. But beekeepers can eventually, if necessary, restructure the personality of the Africanized bee and regain the relatively easygoing European strains they have been using for centuries.

Beekeeping is an art, and although industrialized man has other, perhaps easier sources for his sugars, honey is still an enormously popular natural food coveted around the world. The study of these highly evolved social insects is endlessly fascinating. "Busy as a bee" falls far short of describing what goes on in and near a hive. The use of bees as pollinators probably has an even greater dollar value than the products of the hive.

Beyond the Bee

A number of other insects have been utilized by man. Cochineal insects of the family Dactylopiidae are pests that attack the prickly pear cactus. And as that cactus has been spread around the world, the cochineals, natives of Mexico, have moved with it. Pests though they may be, they are also the source of a carmine dye used by man in a number of ways. The cochineals, however, cannot be considered domesticated, merely utilized.

Various shellac-scale insects have also been collected and used by man. Mealworms, actually the darkling beetle *(Tenebrio molitor)*, a cosmopolitan pest of stored cereals, are raised by the billions to feed a wide variety of captive animals kept in laboratories and as pets. And a number of other insects are collected, held, sometimes raised in captivity and utilized in agriculture. Ladybugs (Coccinellidae) are collected by the millions and shipped to gardeners to prey upon aphids, a major pest of rose growers. Praying mantis egg cases (ootheca) are harvested and also sold to gardeners as a natural means of pest control. Parasitic wasps are similarly used against a variety of pest species. The list is a long one. A growing hobby is the captive butterfly garden and suppliers in the United States, Japan and Europe raise and sell the beautiful insects to fanciers.

None of these insects can be considered domesticated. But as more and more biological pest control techniques are developed, bioengineering of the control organisms is inevitable. In some pest species, males are now being sterilized by irradiation and then released into wild populations to disrupt breeding success rates. Scores of species will soon be involved in both bioengineering and biocontrol of noxious organisms. It is clearly an idea whose time has come. Whether these manipulated insects should be considered domesticated has no ready answer yet.

The relationship of this kind of manipulation to the domestications of the past presents a fascinating quandary. It appears now as if man knows what he is doing and is bound to benefit from the increasingly sophisticated technologies of domestication, whether they are used to produce a fatter or leaner pig, a plumper chicken or a pest-controlling insect. In that case perhaps, after all, we might eventually come to settle on that single fact, the benefits to man, as the measure of true domestication. Unfortunately, man is not now, has never been and is unlikely to become omniscient. It is possible that some "benefit" man has extracted from the animal kingdom in the domestication process will have an unforeseen consequence and harm man and/or his environment. The surprise factor has always played a major role in the domestication process, and there is no reason to think it will not continue to do so. We should be careful in the future, very careful indeed.

TWENTY-FIVE

Past Failures and Future Hopes

The Plans That Went Awry

We can assume that an unknown number of animals were available for domestication over the millennia, but either the animals themselves or the people involved were not up to the task. Perhaps the time was not right, or success with other species capable of fulfilling the same needs went faster and easier and these other efforts were abandoned. Domestication has always been a case of the right animal in the right place at the right time, with the right people waiting to capitalize on their presence. But always the need was there, and prior association.

By no means can we assume that any domestication started on square one and marched unerringly along a straight line until success was realized. Almost certainly attempts were made again and again to domesticate the horse, the aurochs, the ass and the camel before these tasks were accomplished. It must have been the same with every domestication in turn. At some point in each case, someone was more successful than anyone had been before and a new domestication cranked slowly into gear. It was a long process of trial and error.

The Zebra

Dorcas MacClintock, in her book *A Natural History of Zebras* gives a brief history of efforts to domesticate that animal. When we consider the visual treat that zebras provide and a few other factors—man's overall success with and dependence on equids, his unquenchable desire to own beautiful horses and their kin, and the ready availability of huge numbers of zebras in Africa—it is really amazing that this domestication was never accomplished.

The three species of zebras living in the wild do not appear to interbreed. In the Northern Frontier District of Kenya near the Samburu River, I have noted mixed herds innumerable times, the common or Burchell's zebra *(Equus burchelli)* moving easily along with groups of Grévy's zebra *(E. grevyi)*, each obviously discrete in its reproductive practices. In southern Africa, mountain zebra *(E. zebra)*, the rarest of the surviving zebras, also move with the plains zebras without interbreeding.

In captivity, however, they can be interbred, although the offspring are generally infertile. As MacClintock recounts, all three zebra species have been bred to horses. In a sanctuary called Askania-Nova in southern Russia, a Chapman zebra stallion was bred to a horse again and again. The zebra apparently preferred this mare to other zebras, although he did eventually kill her. Zebra stallions can be like that. The Chapman is a variety of the common or Burchell's zebra.

Raymond Hook of Nanyuki, Kenya, regularly crossed a Grévy's zebra stallion with a horse and produced docile, surefooted zebroids. They were common enough as pack animals on the nearby slopes of Mount Kenya for there to be signs restricting passage in some areas for "Horses, Donkeys and Zebroids." I saw such signs at the fourteen-thousand-foot level on the mountain in the 1970s. Horse- and donkey-zebra crosses have been known by a number of names: zebrula, zebrule, zebret and zebryde. The Hagenbecks, wild animal dealers in Germany, were involved in breeding experiments using ponies and zebras.

In the 1700s, French naturalist François LeVaillant caught, broke and rode zebras under saddle without difficulty, according to his account. Lord Lugard in the 1800s examined the value of the disease-resistant zebra as a beast of burden in Africa. Up near Archer's Post, Kenya, in the 1920s, a rancher by the name of Rattray was breaking and driving the large and powerful (and stunningly handsome) Grévy's zebra with, according to him, ease and success.

In the 1890s, in South Africa, Boers were breaking the now extinct quagga *(E. quagga)* and using them to a limited degree. The same species was broken to harness on Mauritius, or at least imported and used there. Mr. Sheriff Parkins had a pair in harness in London early in the 1800s. The London Zoo had a quagga it used to pull a wagon in the 1800s. There is also a considerable body of literature on the suitability of one zebra or another for domestication, and a review of the literature and of old photographs reveals the animals were utilized over and over again.

The banker Walter Rothschild had three zebras trained to harness, and they were a common sight in London. Naturalist Sir Richard Lyddeker wrote about their potential value. There were zebra farms late in the 1800s southeast of Mount Kilimanjaro in Tanzania (then Tanganyika) and near Lake Naivasha, just sixty-five miles outside of Nairobi in Kenya. The animals were sold for around $10.

American naturalist/taxidermist Carl Akeley wrote that the taming of zebras was never much more than a personal entertainment because they don't have the stamina of horses. The observation was shortsighted. Stamina is a prime quality that husbandmen breed for in working animals. It was usually not found in the original package.

Still, there are no domestic zebras today. It is believed that man first emerged in Africa, so it can be said that he has been exposed to zebras, many more species than we have now, for all of his history there. He has had incredible equine success stories, but zebras are not on the list. They can be driven, they can be ridden, they can be eaten (the meat is highly palatable), and they are resistant to indigenous African diseases (a very attractive characteristic). They are so good at defending themselves against predators like hyenas that they have been turned out and used as guards for horses. They are fertile and extremely tough and hardy and they are handsome enough to attract attention and be status symbols. Yet they have not been domesticated. Why?

Before there were captive and then domestic horses and asses (donkeys), when zebras could have been most useful, the indigenous peoples of Africa had not developed the skills or traditions of domestication. For whatever else happened south of the Sahara, the people remained without stock of any kind. When people there did have a tradition for domestication —either coming as settlers from more advanced areas where animals were used, or as indigenous people upon whose cultures domestic animals had been superimposed by explorers and landsteaders—the zebra was no longer needed. The right animal was in the right place but at the wrong time, given the cultural emphases of the people with whom they shared the land.

Other Failures

Although we do not know their stories nearly as well as we know some of the efforts to domesticate zebras, there were numerous other failed attempts. Hyenas, specifically the striped hyena *(Hyaena striata)*, were kept as pets in Egypt, albeit probably tricky ones, and as food animals. Fallow deer, both the common *(Dama dama)* and the Mesopotamian *(D. mesopotamica)*, in the Middle East and the dorcas gazelle *(Gazella dorcas)* and the mountain gazelle *(G. gazella)* in the same region were under man's management for a time. Addax and oryx were also probably tried, as were the small goats called ibex. Red deer *(Cervus elaphus)* were at least herded, as well as hunted in Europe.

There were other abandoned domestication attempts, but the list would simply get more and more difficult to substantiate with evidence of bone and art. It is almost impossible to tell when man was manipulating wild herds and when he was actually keeping them captive. The captive herds, of course, surrendered up the new species that we now call our own. The managed wild herds gave us nothing enduring except vague history.

Still, the known history of animals that evolved in the care of man is a long and eventful one. From natural selection came man-controlled selective breeding, and we are now just emerging into the startling, blinding light of what may prove to be the ultimate scientific accomplishment of man. Or it may be simply step one, the threshold of an unimaginable future. It holds the ultimate destiny of domestication, the beginning of a new beginning.

Bioengineering

In 1953, at Oxford University, scientists Francis Crick and James Watson discovered the intricate structure of an organic chemical called deoxyribonucleic acid. This substance, now known as DNA, contains the genetic code by which living matter re-creates itself in kind. In the worlds of organic chemistry, biology and molecular science, here at last was the key. An Austrian monk, Gregor Mendel, had demonstrated the existence of

genes and chromosomes late in the 1800s and outlined their role in reproduction and selective breeding but could not demonstrate how the process
worked. Crick and Watson did, and for assuming their place in the contin-
uum of science, they were awarded the Nobel Prize in Medicine. Overlooked was an Englishwoman, an X-ray crystallographer, the equally
brilliant and obsessed Rosalind Franklin. She was to die from cancer before
the oversight was revealed. She, too, had helped uncover the double helix
structure of the key.

DNA and the subsequently defined RNA not only carry the messages of all that living creatures are, but they can also be manipulated,
altered, subjected to surgery and implantation. Thus, the messages they
carry are changed, and the organisms they govern are themselves altered in
sometimes subtle and sometimes significant ways. Proteins ordered into
being by the DNA itself become the instruments by which the genetic code
is changed. Acting as scalpels, those proteins can be used to excise error,
faulty genes, and replace them with normal healthy ones. Conversely and
unfortunately, they also have the ability to remove that which is healthy and
good and make unimaginable changes for the worse. There is no way for
the chemical instruments to know if they are being manipulated by malign
intent or ignorance. They reflect, ultimately, the manipulator's view of how
things ought to be. Their use is subjective and susceptible to errors in
judgment. The potential for better or worse is without limit and no form
of life is exempt.

In 1976, scientists working at MIT in Cambridge, Massachusetts,
announced they had actually synthesized a gene of their own design and
that it had become functional in a living cell, where they had inserted it.
Now genes are routinely opened and altered. Chromosomes are opened
with equal ease and genes are inserted. A gene may have a small element
within its impossibly small mass that signals its host organism to produce a
certain substance or react in a certain way. And as fast as those elemental
information networks are located and identified, they become susceptible
to human interference.

On Plum Island, off the tip of New York's Long Island, there stands
the remote and forbidding U.S. Department of Agriculture's maximum
security disease laboratory. On this island, scientists identified a critical gene
within the virus that causes foot-and-mouth disease. It is the gene that
signals the virus to produce the protein that causes the infected animal to
become deathly ill. They removed that gene from the virus and implanted
it in the almost infinitely larger E. coli bacteria. The same gene keeps giving
the same signal, but the protein as produced by the bacteria is not toxic. All
it does is alert the animal into which it has been implanted to produce

antibodies. It cannot impart disease. That is one small example of what is being done.

As tempting as it may be for a bioengineer—for that is what this new science is known as, the engineering of life—to meddle with existing life forms, great restraint has so far been shown. And although the tools of this science have been designed and built, and the techniques developed, as far as we know, experiments for which we are wholly unprepared have not been done—yet.

Clearly, there is great potential in this new science—both for harm and for good. Almost without a doubt, bioengineering and the manipulation of reproductive physiology will play dominant roles in any new domestications man undertakes and in the further evolution of the ones we already have. With artificial insemination, sperm and zygote storage and both inter- and intraspecific embryo transfer already old hat, the rate of reproduction of the most highly desirable species and specimens is fully under control. And now that we are on the threshold of being able to determine with ever-greater precision what characteristics the animals in our care will inherit, there would appear to be a wholly open-ended future. If we are wrong in how we choose to apply and utilize this new science, it will be the greatest mistake man has ever made.

An Afterword

As man evolved through the ages, he needed help to reach his potential, and along the way, he created new ecological niches into which the animals that could help him also evolved. When they, in turn, achieved a perfect fit, they became what we call domesticated. And now that we have achieved at least a part of our potential, we can take our domesticated partners along with us into an undreamed-of future.

It has indeed been a partnership. We have made the journey together. Domesticated animals would not even exist without us (that, by definition, is what domestication means), and we clearly would not be what we are without them. Does that suggest predestination, fate, inevitability? Or that man has been able to meet his needs with ever-increasing intelligence and ingenuity?

No species that we have dealt with in the wild or as a domesticated animal is as intelligent as we are. I don't think that there is any serious argument with that. In terms of intelligence, we are at the top. But that is probably a temporary title. Either we are going to evolve into something even more intelligent than we presently are or we are going to be replaced with something quite different. And we have generally reckoned intelligence to be the one and only yardstick of worth. Anything less intelligent than we are—and that is everything, as we see it—deserves less, so gets less. We have assumed they need less. I suggest we have been wrong on all counts. All animals, wild and domestic, have natural requirements, but we have persistently ignored them and given them what we wanted, when we wanted to, in the amounts that satisfied our needs, not theirs. It has been according to our definitions of need and worth that we have evolved the animals in our care. And we have treated wild animals and their natural habitats just as selfishly.

But there is inherent vice in that yardstick. Our present farming and husbandry practices are the epitome of cruelty. Killing animals in order to eat them is the least of it. It is the way we treat these animals from birth until they must die that is most abhorrent. Animals need natural foods, not chemical concoctions; they need space; they are frequently social and require room to interact. Animals need consideration in transport and, yes, in dying. We have the technology and we have the room. What we don't have are care and compassion. They must go into the creation of the environments in which our domestic animals live, or at some point in the not very distant future, we will fail to take the curve and we will trash ourselves. We control the physical, the chemical and the ethical environment in which both we and all other animals live. It is foolish to think that we can stand apart from those realities. We are the makers of our own bed and we share it with many other forms of life.

We would now do well to recognize our obligation to the dogs, cats, horses, pigs, chickens and cows and all of the other creatures in our domestic pantheon. We should be able to acknowledge their worth and give them their due. As a first step toward becoming truly caring and compassionate beings, we might also acknowledge the natural needs of all other species and award them what they need, not because of their lack of intelligence relative to our own, but because it is clearly the right thing for us to do and the best way to ensure our own survival. There would be no better way to demonstrate that we are as intelligent as we like to think we are. And if we cannot do that, or will not, perhaps our reliance on intelligence for self-image has been a smoke screen. There is a difference, after all, between being clever and manipulative and really brilliant.

Glossary

The following terms appear in this book and are used according to the definitions provided below.

ANTLER(S) Frequently a pair of large and heavy growths from the head of a member of the deer family (Cervidae). Unlike horns (see), antlers do not have a bony core and are shed and replaced every year. Males or males and females may have antlers depending on species.

ARTIODACTYLA The still very large mammalian order that includes all even-toed hoofed animals, swine, hippopotamuses, camels, deer, buffalo, bison, antelope, sheep, goat, cattle. See also Perissodactyla.

BREED Variously defined but used here to define a variety within a domestic species achieved by man through selective breeding. Originally serendipitous, now intended and scientifically accomplished.

BRONZE AGE The human cultural period between the Neolithic (see) and the Iron Age. For Europe, usually given as the eighth century B.C.

BROWSE To feed on leaves, twigs and shoots generally above the ground, as opposed to graze (see).

CLASS The taxonomic classification ranking between phylum and order. Frequently a very large grouping such as Insecta, containing millions of species.

Domestic, Domesticated   A plant or animal species taken from the wild state and placed under the genetic control of man. Selective breeding has replaced natural selection in all such species (see).

Family   A taxonomic classification ranking above a genus (see) and below an order (see). A sometimes large grouping such as Canidae, which contains all the canines, or Mustelidae, which contains all the weasels and their kin.

Feral   An individual plant or animal or a species of either that was once truly domesticated but is now again living in a wild condition.

Genus   A taxonomic category ranking above a species (see) and below a family (see). The "first name" in the scientific designation of a species.

Graze   To feed on grasses and low-growing herbage at ground level. (See also *browse*.)

Hinney   The offspring of a female donkey and a male horse. See also *mule*.

Horn(s)   Usually a pair of growths from the head of a herbivore other than members of the deer family (Cervidae). Horns grow up from a bony core and, with the single exception of the American pronghorn, are never shed.

Hybrid   The offspring of genetically dissimilar parents, i.e., of different varieties, races or species (see). Hybrids are often but not always sterile or mules (see).

Imprint   In the sense used in this book, imprint refers to the phenomenon of a young, newly born, or newly hatched animal accepting an adult animal of its own or another species as a parent and/or protector and/or role model.

Mesolithic   The Middle Stone Age. Variously 12,000 to 15,000 years ago (at the end of the Paleolithic [see]) until the beginning of the Neolithic (see) about 10,000 years ago in the Middle East, later elsewhere. A cultural period usually defined by the use of the bow and arrow and cutting tools.

Mule   A hybrid that is sterile and cannot reproduce itself. Also the offspring of a female horse (mare) and a male donkey (jack).

Neolithic   The New Stone Age. The cultural period following the Mesolithic (see) about 10,000 years ago in the Middle East but later elsewhere. A period marked by the widespread development of animal domestication and the beginnings of agriculture.

ORDER The taxonomic classification ranking above family (see), below class (see). Often a significantly large grouping that may include a fairly broad group such as Anseriformes (in the class Aves) that includes all screamers, ducks, geese, and swans.

PALEOLITHIC The Old Stone Age. The cultural period beginning an estimated 750,000 to 1,000,000 years ago and lasting until the beginning of the Mesolithic (see), variously given as 12,000 to 15,000 years ago.

PERISSODACTYLA The mammalian order including all odd-toed hoofed animals—equines, tapirs, and rhinoceroses. Once a very much larger group than it is today. See also Artiodactyla.

SOCIALIZED see Tame.

SPECIES The fundamental category of animal and plant classification. It is generally used to describe organisms that can breed and reproduce but as such is vague and ill defined since hybrids (see) occur.

TAME Socialized; conditioned and/or trained to live in the company, i.e., under the control of, man.

TAXONOMY The scientific discipline classifying living organisms and designating names denoting relationships.

WILD A plant or animal, whether described as an individual or a species, living in its original, natural condition, reproducing by natural selection and not by selective breeding, i.e., undomesticated.

Bibliography

Alderson, Lawrence. *The Chance to Survive,* 1989.

American Rabbit Breeders Assoc. *Standard of Perfection,* 1981.

Anderson, Sydney and J. Knox Jones, Jr., eds. *Recent Mammals of the World: A Synopsis of Families,* 1967.

Atz, James W. *Aquarium Fishes,* 1971.

Axelrod, Herbert R. *Breeding Aquarium Fishes,* 1971.

Axelrod, Herbert R. and Leonard P. Schultz. *Handbook of Tropical Aquarium Fishes,* 1983.

Axelrod, Herbert and William Vorderwinkler. *Encyclopedia of Tropical Fishes,* 1974.

Bates, Henry J. and Robert I. Busenbark. *Parrots and Related Birds,* 1969.

———. *Finches and Soft-Billed Birds,* 1970.

Bell, Robert E. *Dictionary of Classical Mythology,* 1982.

Bennet, Bob. *The T.F.H. Book of Pet Rabbits,* 1982.

Bixby, Donald E., et al. *Taking Stock: The North American Livestock Census,* 1994.

Blond, Georges. *The Elephants,* 1961.

Bokonyi, S. *History of Domestic Mammals in Central and Eastern Europe,* 1974.

Bowes, Anne Labastille. *Birds of the Mayas,* 1964.

Braider, Donald. *The Life, History and Magic of the Horse,* 1973.

Brereton, J. M. *The Horse in War,* 1976.

Briggs, Hilton M. *Modern Breeds of Livestock,* 1958.

Budiansky, Stephen. *The Covenant of the Wild: Why Animals Chose Domestication,* 1992.

Bulliet, Richard W. *The Camel and the Wheel,* 1975.

Burenhult, Goran, general ed. *People of the Stone Age,* 1993.

Burland, Cottie. *North American Indian Mythology,* 1965.

Burland, Cottie, et al. *Mythology of the Americas,* 1970.

Campbell, Joseph. *The Way of the Animal Powers.* vol. 1, *Historical Atlas of the World, Mythology,* 1983.

Carrington, Richard. *Elephants: A Short Account of Their Natural History Evolution and Influence on Mankind,* 1959.

Cartmill, Matt. *A View to a Death in the Morning,* 1993.

Christie, Anthony. *Chinese Mythology,* 1968.

Clark, G. and S. Piggott. *Prehistoric Societies,* 1965.

Clark, James L. *The Great Arc of the Wild Sheep,* 1964.

Clements, James F. *Birds of the World: A Checklist,* 1978.

Clutton-Brock, Juliet. *Domesticated Animals: From Early Times,* 1981.

———. *A Natural History of Domesticated Animals,* 1987.

———. *Horse Power: A History of the Horse and the Donkey in Human Societies,* 1992.

Conrad, Jack. *The Horn and the Sword: The History of the Bull as a Symbol of Power and Fertility,* 1957.

Corbet, G. B. and J. E. Hill. *A World List of Mammalian Species,* 1980.

Crane, Eva. *The Archaeology of Beekeeping,* 1983.

Dale-Green, Patricia. *Cult of the Cat,* 1963.

Dasmann, Raymond F. *African Game Ranching,* 1964.

Davidson, H. R. Ellis. *Scandinavian Mythology,* 1969.

Davis, P. D. C. and A. A. Dent. *Animals That Changed the World,* 1968.

De Grahl, W. *The Parrot Family,* 1984.

Delacour, Jean. *The Pheasants of the World,* 1965.

———. *Wild Pigeons and Doves,* 1980.

Dembeck, Hermann. *Animals and Man: An Informal History of the Animal as Prey, as Servant, as Companion,* 1965.

Desmond, Adrian and James Moore. *Darwin, the Life of a Tormented Evolutionist,* 1991.

Dorson, Richard M. *Folk-Tales Told Around the World,* 1975.

Edmonson, Munro. *The Book of Counsel: The Popol Vuh of the Quiche Maya of Guatemala,* 1971.

Edwards, Elwyn Hartley, general ed. *Horse and Pony Breeds,* 1989.

Ehrman, Lee and Peter A. Parsons. *Behavior Genetics and Evolution,* 1981.

Elward, Margaret. *Encyclopedia of Guinea Pigs,* 1980.

Epstein, H. *Domestic Animals of China,* 1971.

———. *The Origin of the Domestic Animals of Africa,* vols. 1 and 2, 1971.

———. *Domestic Animals in Nepal,* 1977.

Escobar, Rigoberto Calle. *Animal Breeding and Production of American Camelids*, 1984.

Evans, J. Warren and Alexander Hollaender, eds. *Genetic Engineering of Animals: An Agricultural Perspective*, 1986.

Ewers, John C. *The Horse in Blackfoot Indian Culture*, 1955.

Feltwell, John. *The Story of Silk*, 1990.

Flamholtz, Cathy J. *A Celebration of Rare Breeds*, 1986.

Fox, Susan. *Rats*, 1983.

Fraser, Allan. *The Bull*, 1972.

Fritzsce, Helga. *Bantams*, 1985.

Gamble, Clive. *Timewalkers: The Prehistory of Global Colonization*, 1994.

Garrett, Laurie. *The Coming Plague*, 1994.

Goddall, Daphne Machin, *Horses of the World*, 1965.

Goodwin, Derek. *Pigeons and Doves of the World*, 1970.

Gos, Michael W. *Doves*, 1981.

Gray, John. *Near Eastern Mythology: Mesopotamia, Syria, Palestine*, 1969.

Gregory, Diana. *Dairy Goats*, 1976.

Grzimek, Bernhard. *Grzimek's Animal Life Encyclopedia*, 13 vols., 1975.

Guirand, Felix, ed. *Larousse Encyclopedia of Mythology*, 1959.

Haines, Francis. *Appaloosa: The Spotted Horse in Art and History*, 1972.

Hall, Stephen J. G. and Juliet Clutton-Brock. *Two Hundred Years of British Farm Livestock*, 1989.

Hams, Fred. *Old Poultry Breeds*, 1978.

Hedgepeth, William. *The Hog Book*, 1978.

Henderson, G. N. and Leslie S. Smith. *The International Encyclopedia of Cats*, 1973.

Hirschhorn, Howard. *All About Mice*, 1974.

———. *All About Rabbits*, 1974.

Hyams, Edward. *Animals in the Service of Man*, 1972.

Innes, William T. *Exotic Aquarium Fishes*, 1966.

Isaac, Erich. *Geography of Domestication*, 1970.

Jeffrey, Fred P. *Bantam Chickens*, 1974.

Johanson, Donald, et al. *Ancestors: In Search of Human Origins*, 1994.

Johnsgard, Paul A. *Grouse and Quails of North America*, 1973.

Jones, Steve, et al. *The Cambridge Encyclopedia of Human Evolution*, 1992.

Keeling, C. H. (Rev. Mario Migliorini). *Guinea Pigs*, 1971.

Klingender, Francis. *Animals in Art and Thought, to the End of the Middle Ages*, 1971.

Kozloff, Arielle P. *Animals in Ancient Art*, 1981.

Kuper, Adam. *The Chosen Primate: Human Nature and Cultural Diversity*, 1994.

Leeds, Anthony. *Man, Culture, and Animals: The Role of Animals in Human Ecological Adjustments*, 1965.

Lorenz, Konrad Z. *Man Meets Dog*, 1954.

Low, Rosemary. *Lories and Lorikeets*, 1977.

MacClintock, Dorcas. *A Natural History of Zebras,* 1976.

Mason, I. L. *A World Dictionary of Livestock Breeds: Types and Varieties,* 1969.

Matsui, Yoshiichi. *Goldfish Guide,* 1981.

Matthews, L. Harrison. *The Life of Mammals,* 2 vols., 1969.

Mazonowicz, Douglas. *Voices from the Stone Age: A Search for Cave and Canyon Art,* 1974.

McGrew, T. F. and George E. Howard. *The Perfected Poultry of America,* 1907.

Mellin, Jeanne. *The Morgan Horse,* 1961.

Mery, Fernand. *The Cat,* 1967.

Mills, Dick, ed. *The Aquarium Encyclopedia,* 1983.

Mills, Frank C. and Helen L. Hall. *History of American Jacks and Mules,* 1975.

Nowak, Ronald M. and John L. Paradiso. *Walker's Mammals of the World,* 4th ed., 2 vols., 1983.

Ostrow, Marshall E. *Bettas,* 1980.

Ostrow, M. *The T.F.H. Book of Gerbils,* 1981.

Parker, Rob. *The Sheep Book,* 1983.

Parrinder, Geoffrey. *African Mythology,* 1967.

Patten, John W. *The Light Horse Breeds,* 1960.

Paysan, Klaus. *Guide to Aquarium Fishes,* 1975.

Poignant, Roslyn. *Oceanic Mythology,* 1967.

Pond, Grace, ed. *The Complete Cat Encyclopedia,* 1972.

Pond, Grace and Muriel Calder. *The Longhaired Cat,* 1974.

Pond, Grace, Ivor Raleigh, and Richard H. Gebhardt, eds. *A Standard Guide to Cat Breeds,* 1979.

Radtke, Georg A. *Encyclopedia of Budgerigars,* 1979.

Reed, A. W. *Myths and Legends of Australia,* 1973.

Rice, Elmer C. *The National Standard Squab Book,* 1923.

Ritter, William. *The T.F.H. Book of Guinea Pigs,* 1982.

Roberts, Mervin F. *The T.F.H. Book of Hamsters,* 1981.

———. *Zebra Finches,* 1981.

———. *Starting Right with Rabbits,* 1983.

Roberts, Sonia. *Bird-keeping and Birdcages: A History,* 1972.

Rogers, Cyril. *Parakeet Guide,* 1970.

———. *Parrot Guide,* 1981.

Rouse, John E. *Cattle of Africa and Asia,* 1970.

———. *Cattle of Europe, South America, Australia and New Zealand,* 1970.

———. *Cattle of North America,* 1973.

———. *The Criollo, Spanish Cattle in the Americas,* 1977.

Rowland, Beryl. *Animals with Human Faces: A Guide to Animal Symbolism,* 1974.

Ryden, Hope. *America's Last Wild Horses,* 1990.

Shaler, Nathaniel Southgate. *Domesticated Animals: Their Relation to Man and to His Advancement in Civilization,* 1907.

Sikes, Sylvia K. *The Natural History of the African Elephant,* 1971.

Silva, Tony and Barbara Kotlar. *Discus,* 1980.

Sims, John A. and Leslie E. Johnson. *Animals in the American Economy,* 1972.

Singh, Harbans. *Domestic Animals,* 1966.

Spencer, Robert F. *The North Alaskan Eskimo: A Study in Ecology and Society,* 1959.

Spiegel, Marjorie. *The Dreaded Comparison: Human and Animal Slavery,* 1988.

Stefferud, Alfred. *Birds in Our Lives,* 1966.

Stringer, Christopher and Clive Gamble. *In Search of the Neanderthals,* 1993.

Sweet, Orville K. *Birth of a Breed: The History of Polled Herefords—America's First Beef Breed,* 1975.

Tannahill, Reay. *Food in History,* 1973.

Tener, J. S. *Muskoxen in Canada: A Biological and Taxonomic Review,* 1965.

Texas Crop and Livestock Reporting Service. *Texas Sheep and Goat Industry,* 1968.

Towne, Charles Wayland and Edward Norris Wentworth. *Pigs from Cave to Cornbelt,* 1950.

Toynbee, J. M. C. *Animals in Roman Life and Art,* 1973.

Ucko, Peter J. and G. W. Dimbleby, eds. *The Domestication and Exploitation of Plants and Animals,* 1969.

Voelker, William. *The Natural History of Living Mammals,* 1986.

Voss, J. *Color Patterns of African Cichlids,* 1980.

Vriends, Matthew M. *Encyclopedia of Softbilled Birds,* 1980.

———. *Handbook of Canaries,* 1980.

———. *The Complete Cockatiel,* 1983.

———. *Pet Birds,* 1984.

Wayre, Philip. *A Guide to the Pheasants of the World,* 1969.

Weil, Martin. *Mynahs,* 1981.

Wellstead, Graham. *Ferrets and Ferreting,* 1982.

White, K. D. *Roman Farming,* 1970.

Whitlock, Ralph. *Rare Breeds,* 1980.

Wilmore, Sylvia Bruce. *Swans of the World,* 1974.

Winsted, Wendy. *Ferrets,* 1981.

Winston, Mark L. *Killer Bees,* 1992.

Wolfgang, Harriet. *Short Haired Cats,* 1963.

Young, J. Z. *The Life of Mammals,* 1957.

Zeuner, Frederich E. *A History of Domesticated Animals,* 1963.

Index

About the Author

ROGER A. CARAS is the eighteenth president of the ASPCA, the oldest humane organization in the Western Hemisphere. Prior to taking on the leadership of the "A," he was ABC's Special Correspondent for Animals and the Environment for seventeen years (and was the only reporter in national broadcast journalism to be awarded this title). The author of over sixty books on pets and wildlife, he has also written thousands of articles for publications ranging from *The New York Times Sunday Magazine* to *Ladies' Home Journal* and *The National Observer.* He lives on a farm in Maryland.